The Future of Post-Human Unconsciousness

The Future of Post-Human Unconsciousness: A Preface to a New Theory of Anomalous Experience

By

Peter Baofu

Cambridge Scholars Publishing

The Future of Post-Human Unconsciousness: A Preface to a New Theory of Anomalous Experience, by Peter Baofu

This book first published 2008 by

Cambridge Scholars Publishing

15 Angerton Gardens, Newcastle, NE5 2JA, UK

British Library Cataloguing in Publication Data
A catalogue record for this book is available from the British Library

ISBN (10): 1-84718-614-9, ISBN (13): 9781847186140

To Those in the World of Unfolding Unconsciousness

BOOKS ALSO BY PETER BAOFU

• *The Future of Information Architecture* (2008) •

• *The Rise of Authoritarian Liberal Democracy* (2007) •

• *The Future of Aesthetic Experience* (2007) •

• *The Future of Complexity* (2007) •

• *Beyond the World of Titans, and the Remaking of World Order* (2007) •

• *Beyond Nature and Nurture* (2006) •

• *Beyond Civilization to Post-Civilization* (2006) •

• *The Future of Post-Human Space-Time* (2006) •

• *Beyond Capitalism to Post-Capitalism* (2005) •

• Volume 1: *Beyond Democracy to Post-Democracy* (2004) •

• Volume 2: *Beyond Democracy to Post-Democracy* (2004) •

• *The Future of Post-Human Consciousness* (2004) •

• *The Future of Capitalism and Democracy* (2002) •

• Volume 1: *The Future of Human Civilization* (2000) •

• Volume 2: *The Future of Human Civilization* (2000) •

CONTENTS

Part One: Introduction

Part Two: The Mind

Part Three: Nature

Part Four: Culture

Part Five: Society

Part Six: Conclusion

TABLES

Category III: Visions on History

Category IV: Visions on Methodology

Category V: Visions on the Mind

Category VIII. Visions on Society (Socio-Political)

Category IX. Visions on Society (Socio-Economic)

FOREWORD

It was probably inevitable that the curiosity of futurist Peter Baofu would lead him to address the subject of unconsciousness. It's a fascinating area with a bevy of adherents and detractors who have expressed strong opinions with a notable lack of sufficient evidences on both sides.

Dr. Baofu brings a new approach to this controversy. By first examining the tenets of three strongly held viewpoints in a rigorous way and then exploring the nature of the controversy from original perspectives, he takes the reader on a trip that turns out to be uniquely satisfying as it brings the reader closer to the unknown.

For readers who share a high level of curiosity about life and human nature, this book raises yet another challenge on a topic of intellectual intrigue.

Sylvan Von Burg
School of Business
George Washington University

ACKNOWLEDGMENTS

Like all previous books of mine, this one is written to challenge conventinal wisdom, be it in the past and present.

It therefore receives no external funding nor aid from any formal organization or institution, as is true for all my previous books, which are all politically incorrect.

The only reward is that amazing feeling of proposing something new about reality, in a way that no one else in history has done before.

There is one person, however, that I want to acknowledge, namely, Sylvan von Burg at George Washington University School of Business, for my appreciation of his foreword in this book.

In any event, I bear the sole responsibility for all ideas presented herein.

ABBREVIATIONS

ALD = Peter Baofu. 2007. *The Rise of Authoritarian Liberal Democracy: A Preface to a New Theory of Comparative Political Systems*. Cambridge, England: Cambridge Scholars Publishing, Ltd.

BCIV = Peter Baofu. 2006. *Beyond Civilization to Post-Civilization: Conceiving a Better Model of Life Settlement to Supersede Civilization.* NY: Peter Lang Publishing, Inc.

BCPC = Peter Baofu. 2005. *Beyond Capitalism to Post-Capitalism: Conceiving a Better Model of Wealth Acquisition to Supersede Capitalism*. NY: The Edwin Mellen Press.

BDPD1 = Peter Baofu. 2004. Volume 1. *Beyond Democracy to Post-Democracy: Conceiving a Better Model of Governance to Supersede Democracy*. NY: The Edwin Mellen Press.

BDPD2 = Peter Baofu. 2004. Volume 2. *Beyond Democracy to Post-Democracy: Conceiving a Better Model of Governance to Supersede Democracy*. NY: The Edwin Mellen Press.

BNN = Peter Baofu. 2006. *Beyond Nature and Nurture: Conceivng a Better Way to Understand Genes and Memes.* Cambridge, England: Cambridge Scholars Publishing, Ltd.

BWT = Peter Baofu. 2007. *Beyond the World of Titans, and the Renaking of World Order: A Preface to a New Logic of Empire-Building.* Cambridge, England: Cambridge Scholars Publishing, Ltd.

FAE = Peter Baofu. 2007. *The Future of Aesthetic Experience: Conceiving a Better Way to Understand Beauty, Ugliness and the Rest*. Cambridge, England: Cambridge Scholars Publishing, Ltd.

FC = Peter Baofu. 2007. *The Future of Complexity: Conceiving a Better Way to Understand Order and Chaos.* London, United Kingdom: World Scientific Publishing Co.

FCD = Peter Baofu. 2002. *The Future of Capitalism and Democracy.* MD: The University Press of America.

FHC1 = Peter Baofu. 2000. Volume 1. *The Future of Human Civilization.* NY: The Edwin Mellen Press.

FHC2 = Peter Baofu. 2000. Volume 2. *The Future of Human Civilization.* NY: The Edwin Mellen Press.

FIA = Peter Baofu. 2008. *The Future of Information Architecture: Conceiving a Better Way to Understand Taxonomy, Network, and Intelligence.* Oxford, England: Chandos Publishing (Oxford) Limited.

FPHC = Peter Baofu. 2004. *The Future of Post-Human Consciousness.* NY: The Edwin Mellen Press.

FPHST = Peter Baofu. 2006. *The Future of Post-Human Space-Time: Conceivng a Better Way to Understand Space and Time.* New York: Peter Lang Publishing, Inc.

FPHU = Peter Baofu. 2008. *The Future of Post-Human Unconsciousness: A Preface to a New Theory of Anomalous Experience.* Cambridge, England: Cambridge Scholars Publishing, Ltd.

• PART ONE •

Introduction

CHAPTER 1
INTRODUCTION—THE MYSTERY OF UNCONSCIOUSNESS

> [M]ost professionsl scientists do not have the time and motivation to review the scientific accuracy of [paranormal] explanations, since parapsychology by definition, does not deal with phenomena that are observable, which are exclusively what science deals with....Psi phenomena...are yet not conclusively proven to exist. The only reasonable view would be to not permanently rule out the existence of any paranormal events.
>
> —Aparthib Zaman (2003)

The Inscrutable Unconscious Mind

Why should anomalous experience, in a general sense, be proven to exist, before they can be taken seriously?

Contrary to the conventional wisdom held by many scholars in human history hitherto existing, the imaginative exploration of anomalous phenomena, even should all of them be merely the fabricated products of psychological con artists, would still have tremendous implications for the future of intelligent life, both on earth and in deep space unto multiverses.

For the critics, this is a bold (or even outrageous) claim, for sure. So, a good question to ask is, Why should the conventional wisdom on anomalous experience be challenged in this way?

The Varieties of Anomalous Experience

To start, the words "anomalous experience" (in a general sense) can refer to a lot of different experiences not normally encountered in daily routines.

In 2000, for instance, the American Psychological Association published a report titled "Varieties of Anomalous Experience," in which "anomalous experiences" are defined as "strange, extraordinary, and unexplained experiences and encounters with the unknown." (F. MacHovec 2002)

Consequently, this definition covers different unusual experiences under a rather broad heading, ranging from near-death experiences through religious miracles to psychic encounters. (S. Begley 2001; F. MacHovec 2002)

The Categories of Anomalous Experience

With this broad heading in mind—anomalous experience can therefore have many different types.

For the convenience of scholarly analysis, let me propose the following three categories of anomalous experience (as summarized in *Table 1.1*), solely for illustration, as a way to start the conversation on the very nature of anomalous experience for this book.

For instance, the first category, which is so often cited in the literature, refers to "psychic" experiences.

Good examples include "telepathy" (viz., reading the minds of others), "telekinesis" (viz., moving things without contact), extraordinary senses (e.g., "clair-sentience" in feeling, "clair-voyance" in seeing, "clair-audience" in hearing, "clair-austance" in tasting, "clair-alience" in smelling, and "clair-cognizance" in knowing), and whatnot. (WK 2007m & 2007n; MWD 2007)

The second category is more "transcendental" in focus, mostly for some (not all) forms of mystical and spiritual (or at times religious) experiences. In other words, not all mystical and spiritual (or even religious) experiences are necessarily about anomalous experience, but some of them are.

Some good examples are "reincarnation" (viz., the rebirth of a soul), "miracle," "past-life experience" (viz., "experience…or impression…of oneself …in a previous time or life"), "healing experience" (viz., "shamanic and…alternative therapies"), "mystical experience" (viz., "religious conversion or belief"), and so on. (MWD 2007a; F. MacHovec 2002; S. Begley 2001; J. Kennedy 1995a)

And the third category includes the rest (that is, the "miscellaneous" types).

This last category can come in all shapes and sizes, and good examples include "haunting" (viz., the appearance of a ghost), "mediumship" (viz., communicating with the dead), "near-death experience," "synesthesia" (viz., "a 'curious' perception of sensed imagery or 'qualities of one modality' that are 'transferred to another modality' such as a food or beverage taste"), "out-of-body experience" (viz., one's perception of "being outside of the body"), "alien abduction experience," and the like. (MWD 2007b; F. MacHovec 2002; S. Begley 2001; J. Kennedy 1995a)

Four Qualifications

This classification should be taken with caution, and four qualifications are needed.

Firstly, the types in the categories are not exhaustive, but solely illustrative. For instance, the phenomenon of subliminal messages (as will be discussed in Chapter Five) can be included in the heading of anomalous experience, although it also involves the subconscious level, not just the unconscious one.

Secondly, nor are the categories independent of each other, since some types may overlap with others in a different category. For instance, "haunting" can be classified, for some scholars, under the category of "spiritual" anomalous experience.

Thirdly, some types can be divided instead into special sub-types. As an illustration, for some scholars, "precognition" (viz., knowing the future) can be treated as a special case of "clair-cognizance" (or even "clair-voyance")—just as "presentiment" (viz., feeling the future) can be regarded as a special case of "clair-sentience" (or even "clair-voyance"). (WK 2007n)

And fourthly, some types may involve different other types simultaneously. For instane, "telepathy" can use multiple extraordinary senses at the same time.

Two Confusions

With these four qualifcations in mind—two clarifications should also be added at the outset, to avoid any further confusion in regard to the terms used in the literature on anomalous experience.

Consider two common confusions about terms on anomalous experience below—for illustration.

Firstly, there is a confusion between what is "miraculous" and what is "paranormal," which are similar in one way but differ from each other in another way.

For instance, "[b]oth miracles and paranormal phenomena relate to incidents whose existence cannot be verified objectively," so "their existence only relies on testimony and anecdotes." (A. Zaman 2003)

But their similarity ends here, since "[m]iracles (also known as supernatural) are those incidents that violate or contradict known laws of nature (physics, biology, logic). Paranormal phenomena are those incidents that do not violate known laws of nature but are nevertheless inexplainable by the known laws." (A. Zaman 2003)

And secondly, another confusion involves terms like "transendental" and "paranormal." (J. Kennedy 1995a)

The two are not the same, since transcendental experiences are more "mystical" and "spiritual" in nature, whereas paranormal experiences concerns, for instance, "psychic" experiences (e.g., telepathy, clairvoyance), "out-of-body experiences," "healing miracles," "mediumships," "apparitions" (or hauntings), or else.

In this sense, the second category (the "spiritual" one) and the third category (the "miscellaneous" one) can sometimes be merged into a larger category called "paranormal," depending on how the "miscellaneous" types are classified.

Unconsciousness and Anomalous Experience

This broad heading of anomalous experience (and its four qualifications as well as two clarifications) aside—it should be clearly stressed, at the outset, that anomalous experience should *not* be equated with unconscious experience.

Of course, the illusive idea of unconsciousness (or broadly speaking, the unconscious mind) requires a careful analysis, for sure, which, however, falls into the jurisdiction of the next chapter (that is, Chapter Two on unconsciousness and the mind) and the rest of the book.

Here, it suffices to simply point out that anomalous experience has conscious, subconscious, and unconscious dimensions.

But this is not to say that unconscious experience necessarily implies anomalous experience, since they are not the same. After all, why should different forms of cognition, emotion, and behavior at the unconscious level (as shown in *Tables 2.8-2.12*) have necessarily anything to do with anomalous experience, for instance?

Yet, with this caveat in mind—anomalous experience, under certain conditions, is closely related to the conscious, subconscious, and unconscious layers of the mind.

For instance, in relation to the conscious dimension—an individual can be quite conscious of an anomalous experience that he claims to personally encounter, so he is quite aware, even if subjectively, of its existence at the time.

In relation to the subconscious dimension—the individual may sometimes be only partially aware of the anomalous experience at the time (e.g., the situation concerning subliminal messages, which will be discussed, especially in *Sec.5.3*).

In relation to the unconscious dimension—the problem here is that the individual in question may not exactly know how the anomalous experience comes about, or why it happens in the way that it does.

And this constitutes the unconscious dimension of anomalous experience, which has remained the most controversial (among the three dimensions of anomalous experience) in the scientific community.

This book thus focuses on this very delicate relationship between the nature of the unconscious mind and the most controversial aspects of anomalous experience so understood.

As to the layer of the conscious mind (in relation to its subconscious and unconscious counterparts), I already explicitly dealt with the issue in one of my previous books, namely, *The Future of Post-Human Consciousness* (or *FPHC*) and, to some extent, *Beyond Capitalism to Post-Capitalism* (or *BCPC*).

In this sense, this book, *The Future of Post-Human Unconsciousness* (*FPHU*), is a logical sequence to *FPHC* (and to some extent, *BCPC*), since the former (*FPHU*) focuses more on the nature of the unconscious mind (and, to some extent, its subconscious and conscious counterparts), whereas the latter (*PFHC* and, to some extent, *BCPC*) concern more the analysis of the conscious mind (and its relation to the subconscious and unconscious counterparts, to an extent).

The Theoretical Debate

With this distinction between the unconscious mind and anomalous experience (and their interactive relationship) in mind—there are, of course, numeorus theoretical approaches in the literature on anomalous experience.

But an introduction of three major theoretical approaches hereafter is deemed sufficient to illustrate this unsettling state of the theoretical debate on anomalous experience, with the fourth to be my original contribution to the literature (as shown in *Table 6.1*).

(a) Firstly, a major theoretical approach to the study of anomalous experience can be understood, in the absence of better terms, as the *skeptical argument*.

The skeptics argue, with psychic claims as an illustration, that, since "there is no scientific evidence supporting such abilities," it is thus "apparent [that] psychic phenomena are nothing more than intentional trickery or self delusion." (WK 2007)

For instance, the skeptic James Randi once went so far as to offer "a $1 million prize to any individual who can, under controlled circumstances, demonstrate any paranormal or supernatural ability. As of yet no one has passed the preliminary challenge." (WK 2007) And thus, anomalous experience, for the skeptics, is not believable.

And Jonathan P. Dowling once even wrote that "[a]rticles dealing with parapsychology should not be published in *PRA* [viz., *Physical Review A*]—period."

But the skeptic argument is not convincing to those who claim to have personally experienced it. Besides, to believe or not can be a matter of faith, and the requirement of conclusive evidences may not be relevant to the believers.

(b) Secondly, an alernative theoretical approach is less extreme than the skeptical argument, so it can be called, in the absence of better terms, *the agnostic argument.*

An agnostic, unlike a skeptic, does not think that anomalous experience can simply be dismissed on the basis of the lack of some conclusive evidences concerning its general existence. Instead, so they think, one should be more open-minded to the possibility of its existence.

Henry Stapp (1995), for one, argued that one "cannot rationally rule out the possibility" of anomalous experience, "when they can be accounted for by plausible physical models," even if not conclusively proven. (J. Beichler 1998)

Another good illustration of the agnostic argument is the one by Aparthib Zaman (2003) in the quotation at the beginning of this chapter, in that, since "Psi phenomena…are yet not conclusively proven to exist….[t]he only reasonable view would be to not permanently rule out the existence of any paranormal events."

But for the believers, although the agnostic argument is welcome, it remains too weak.

(c) Thirdly, another theoretical approach is undoubtedly most supportive of the existence of anomalous experience, when contrasted with those of the skeptics and the agnostics, so it can be labeled, in the absence of better terms, as *the anomalous argument*.

Unlike the skeptics and agnostics, those who defend the anomalous argument genuinely think that anomalous experience really exists, especially for those who experience it, although those who never do are unfortunate to not encounter something which, for the defenders, is one of the most amazing experiences for intelligent life on earth.

There is no lack of people who claim to have encountered anomalous experience in human history.

For instance, a good illustration concerns those who claims to possess psychic powers: "Early examples of individuals thought by some to have psychic powers include the Oracle of Apollo at Delphi who was thought to provide prophecies from Apollo himself as well as Nostradamus, a French apothecary who is thought by some to have had the ability to predict the future. During the 19th century belief in psychics became more common and many notable individuals gained notoriety including Daniel Dunglas Home. Psychics are also very popular in science fiction today and many works of fiction include individuals with psychic abilities, including *The Dead Zone* by Stephen King as well as Jean Grey from the Marvel and DC comic book universes. Today, belief in psychic phenomena is widespread amongst the general public. A 2005 Gallup poll concluded that 41% of Americans believe in extra-sensory perception." (WK 2007)

But then, the problem with the anomalous believers is what the skeptics and the agnostics have persistently pointed out, in that there is no conclusive proof of the existence of anomalous experience.

(d) Lastly, unlike the previous three theoretical approaches is my *unfolding argument*, in the absence of better terms.

My unfolding argument goes beyond the previous three approaches so far mentioned and learns from each of them, without, however, favoring one over the others (or even trying to integrate them in a harmonious whole, since they are not very compatible)—and in the process adds something new to the literature.

This constitutes my theoretical contribution to the debate, as summarized in the next section.

The Unfolding Theory of Anomalous Experience

My *unfolding argument* can be more formally called *the unfolding theory of anomalous experience*, in the context of anomalous experience and its relation to the dimension of unconsciousness.

Yet, since the most important feature of the theory concerns what I originally call, in the absence of better words, *the unfolding unconsciousness*, the theory can be more precisely called instead as *the theory of unfolding unconsciousness*.

This theory of mine contains six major theses, namely, (a) the openness-hiddenness principle, (b) the expansion-contraction principle, (c) the symmetry-asymmetry principle, (d) the progression-regression principle, (e) the explicability-inexplicability principle, and (f) the post-human mastery—to be elaborated in the rest of the book and summarized in Chapter Six (the concluding chapter) and *Table 6.2*.

Theory and Meta-Theory

But my theory, just like any other theory, presupposes a meta-theory (i.e., ontology and methodology), either explicitly spelt out or implicitly assumed.

More explicitly, my theory appeals to two distinctive (original) meta-theories of mine, which were already worked out in my previous books, namely, (a) existential dialectics and (b) sophisticated methodological holism.

A summary of (a) and (b) will be provided in the next two sections, respectively, for the convenience of the reader—as it is something that I also did in my previous books, *often verbatim*.

The Logic of Existential Dialectics

The ontology of existential dialectics can be summarized in this section—to be repeated, *often verbatim* (with only a few updated revisions), from my previous works—as this is something that I regularly do as an introduction to some background information for the convenience of the reader.

After all, this book, like all others of mine, is in conversation with all previous ones of mine, for the final aim to converge all of them into a larger grand project on the future of intelligent life, both here on earth and there in deep space unto multiverses.

The summary can be organized in relation to (a) the conception of existential dialectics (or its ontics), (b) the syntax of existential dialectics (or its ontomethodology and ontologic), (c) the semantics of existential dialectics (or its ontosemantics), and (d) the pragmatics of existential dialectics (or its ontopragmatics), respectively hereafter—again *often verbatim*.

This means that, for those readers who had read some of my previous books, the summary below is really nothing new (*almost verbatim*, with only some minor revisions) and can be skipped.

But for those who have never read them, it is a good review of my previous works.

The Conception of Existential Dialectics (or Its Ontics)

This ontology was originally designated as "existential dialectics" in *Beyond Capitalism to Post-Capitalism* (herein abbreviated as *BCPC*), although it was also analyzed in other books of mine like the 2 volumes of *The Future of Human Civilization* (*FHC*), *The Future of Capitalism and Democracy* (*FCD*), *The Future of Post-Human Consciousness* (*FPHC*), and the 2 volumes of *Beyond Democracy to Post-Democracy* (*BDPD*).

Lest any confusion occurs, it is important to stress at the outset that the word 'existential' in "existential dialectics" has nothing to do with Existentialism, which I rebuked in *FHC*, *FCD*, and also *FPHC*. Instead, the word merely refers to the existence of intelligent life (both primitive and advanced) in a broad sense.

Some Basic Concepts

The conception of existential dialectics (or its ontics) makes use of different concepts (like "sets," "elements," "relations," "operations," "functions," "truth values," "axioms," "postulates," and "principles"—as shown in *Table 6.7*), which are important for the understanding of any logic of ontology.

That clarified—existential dialectics, as a language of ontology, can be analyzed in different ways that a language, as an analogy, is often analyzed, namely, in relation to phonology ("the study of patterns of a language's sounds"), phonetics ("the study of the physical aspects of sounds of human language"), morphonology ("the study of the internal structure of words"), syntax ("the study of how words combine to form grammatical sentences"), semantics ("the study of the meaning of words [lexical semantics] and fixed word combinations [phraseology]"), and pragmatics ("the study of how utterances are used…literally, figuratively, or otherwise…in communicative acts"). (WK 2007)

But since my theory of existential dialectics makes use of the English language for communication here, it does not propose a new way to make the patterns of a language's sounds (as in phonology), to study the physical aspects of sounds (as in phonetics), or even to strive for a new organization of the internal structure of words for the English language (as in morphonology).

For this reason, the language of existential dialectics to be analyzed hereafter is not concerned with the phonological, phonetic, and morphonological aspects of the English language. Instead, the analysis will explore the syntax, semantics, and pragmatics of existential dialectics as a language of ontology to improve our understanding of reality.

The Ontic Dispute

But first, there is an ontic dispute to be addressed.

To start, the conception of existential dialectics is not without controversy, since there is what I want to call *the ontic dispute*, on how to understand the very nature of ontology.

Traditionally, scholars in the field use to study the conception of ontology in terms of its entities (e.g., material objects, abstract numbers), properties (e.g., duration, plurality), and relationships (e.g., causation).

This is a good starting point, but it suffers from different problems. Consider three examples of bias below, which are quite common in the literature, and the recent version (of treating concepts and principles in ontology on the basis of "plurality," "dynamism," "duration," "interaction," "life," and "consciousness," and "volition") by Reginald Firehammer (2005) only constitutes a recent addition to this old (impoverishing) tradition.

Firstly, the classification of entities, properties, and relationships is too material-centric, in often favoring the existence of material entities over non-material ones.

Secondly, the classification is too anthropo-centric, in often favoring the factor of human agency in depicting reality.

And lastly, the classification is too confused among the three categories relating to each other, in often lumping them together without due consideration of their intricated interrelationships (both in relation to each and in relation to all).

A good alternative is precisely what I want to offer in this debate, that is, a new classification of ontological entities, properties, and their relationships in terms of *method*, *structure*, *process*, *agency*, and *outcome* instead.

In relation to method, it concerns how ontology is to be studied.

In relation to structure, it concerns what the general patterns of entities, properties, and relationships are.

In relation to process, it concerns how these general patterns change over time.

In relation to agency, it concerns how agency affects any change of these general patterns over time.

And in relation to outcome, it concerns what the output of this change over time is.

The Syntax of Existential Dialectics (or Its Ontomethodology and Ontologic)

The syntax of existential dialectics, analogously speaking, refers here to the structure of an ontology which can be studied by way of combining ideas into complex relationships like ontological principles to depict reality in the world—and can be analyzed in six sub-sections, namely, (a) the selection criteria, (b) three qualifications on classification, (c) ontomethodology, (d) ontologic, (e) the principles as family resemblances, and (f) the principles of existential dialectics, respectively hereafter.

The Selection Criteria

To start, not any pair of relationship can be chosen as an ontological principle in existential dialectics; otherwise, there could be billions of them under the sky.

Four illustrations below suffice to clarify this point.

(a) Firstly, an ontological principle cannot *overlap* with other principles, in that it is too closely related with other ones.

Of course, one cannot totally rule out any relationship between two entities, especially in a complex world of everything being linked to everything else—but the comparison here is relative, not absolute.

In this sense, the flexibility-inflexibility pair cannot be an ontological principle, since it has something closely in common with other ones (like the simpleness-complicatedness principle, for instance).

As an illustration, something which is flexible in interpretation is more likely to allow multiple viewpoints and thus makes the overall picture more complicated than otherwise (simple).

(b) Secondly, an ontological principle cannot be *redundant* in relation to other principles, in that it somehow duplicates other principles.

In this sense, for instance, the directness-indirectness pair cannot be an ontological principle, because it somehow duplicates other ontological principles (like the preciseness-vagueness principle, for instance).

As an illustration, something which is direct means to be right to the point and does not need to go to an unnecessarily long loop—so it is less vague, in being clearer about the thing in quesiton.

(c) Thirdly, an ontological principle cannot be *derived* from other ones—as if it is a child-parent relationship.

In this sense, the convenience-inconvenience pair cannot be an ontological principle, because it can be derived from other ones (like the slowness-quickness principle, for instance).

For instance, something which is convenient already implies that it can be obtained quickly (rather than slowly)—all things considered.

(d) Fourthly, an ontological principle cannot be *trivial* (or *parochial*)—as if it is only one component competing with other ones for inclusion in a set.

In this sense, the consistency-inconsistency pair cannot be an ontological principle, because its validity is limited (or parochial), as it can be easily challenged and replaced by opposing major (not minor) theories (e.g., the correspondence theory of truth, the pragmatic theory of truth, the semantic theory of truth, and whatnot), not just in accordance to the consistency theory of truth (for consistency).

In this sense, the consistency argument is only one among different opposing arguments in relation to the logic of what constitutes "truth."

Although these examples are not exhaustive, they illustrative the selectiveness of any ontological principle to be existentially dialectic.

Three Qualifications on Classification

Lest any misunderstanding carelessly occurs, three qualifications on classification should be made here.

(a) Firstly, the total number of ontological principles is unknown, to be discovered later, as our knowledge of the world becomes more advanced.

Consequently, the principles as introduced in my books are not exhaustive, with new ones being added, whenever more of them are discovered in later research.

At least, future generations can pick up where I leave off and continue the discovery.

In this sense, my work should be treated as a pioneering effort for the development of a systematic, comprehensive analysis of a new general ontology for the future of knowledge.

(b) Secondly, each ontological principle is generic, with some other comparable ontological pairs to be put in the same family (like a *family resemblance*).

Ludwig Wittgenstein (1953) once suggested the idea of "family resemblance" in explaining different games classified under the same family called *games*. Why should, for instance, playing football and chess as playing "games," when it is well understood that football is not the same as chess? The answer is that, although each game is different and has different rules, many of them share, more or less, some commonalites (e.g., scoring as necessary for winning).

And this is so, even though some games share more than some others in any given selection of critieria, and no two games are exactly identical. So, his point here is that there is no essential core which is common to all games, and the best that one can look for is some characteristics which are common to many (but not all) games. (A. Biletzki 2006)

By analogy—in the previous section on selection criteria, the flexibility-inflexibility pair can be put in the family resemblance of the simpleness-complicatedness principle. Likewise, the directness-indirectness pair can be put in the family resemblance of the preciseness-vagueness principle.

In this sense, which specific pair in a family should be used to designate the name of the family is a bit arbitrary.

And (c) thirdly, the principles are not mutually exclusive and can be reclassified in a different way. For instance, the preciseness-vagueness principle is classified under the category of "structure" but can be reclassified under the category of "method," although in so doing, it has a different meaning in the context of method. The same logic applies to the sameness-difference principle under the category of "outcome," which can be reclassified under the category of "structure," although in so doing, once more, it has a different meaning in the context of structure.

These qualifications are important to remember.

Ontomethodology

With these selection criteria and qualifications in mind—the syntax of existential dialectics can be divided into two main smaller sections for analysis, since they are related to each other in the context of some fundamental principles, that is, (a) ontomethodology and (b) ontologic, to be addressed hereafter respectively.

In the context of ontomethodology, some ontological principles are proposed here in relation to the nature of methodology, which however is tied up with the general issue of ontology in the context of knowledge.

In this sense, ontomethodology (in the context of these ontological principles) are related with ontologic in general (in the context of ontological principles in general).

Three good instances of ontological principles involving ontomethodology include the predictability-unpredictability principle, the explicability-inexplicability principle, and the partiality-totality principle, which will be introduced in conjunction with ontological principles in the ontologic of existential dialectics in general hereafter.

Ontologic

With this clarification of the interrelationship between ontomethodology and ontologic in mind—the first three principles in the ontological logic of existential dialectics were introduced in *BCPC*. And more principles were later added to the logic in my subsequent books (like *FC*, *FAE*, and others).

More specifically, in *BCPC*, I proposed three principles (based on previous works of mine, not just something out of the blue) for the ontological logic, namely, (a) the regression-progression principle on the direction of history, (b) the symmetry-asymmetry principle on the relationships among existents, and (c) the change-constancy principle on the alteration of things—or in a more elegant term, the dynamics of space-time (in *FC*).

In *The Future of Complexity* (*FC*), I added three more principles, on top of the three aforementioned, namely, (d) the partiality-totality principle on the relationships between parts and whole, (e) the order-chaos principle on the pattern of things, and (f) the predictability-unpredictability principle on the occurrence of things—as part of the ontological logic of existential dialectics.

In *The Future of Aesthetic Experience* (or simply *FAE*), another principle is added, namely, (g) the evolution-transformation principle (on the multiple kinds of agency).

Also in *FAE*, I then reclassified the 7 principles into four categories, namely, (i) in relation to method, for the partiality-totality principle and the predictability-unpredictability principle, (ii) in relation to process, for the change-constancy principle and the order-chaos principle, (iii) in relation to agency, for the symmetry-asymmetry principle and the evolution-transformation principle, and (iv) in relation to outcome, for the regression-progression principle.

In *The Rise of Authoritarian Liberal Democracy* (*ALD*), I added two more principles, namely, (h) the softness-hardness principle on the force of agency (which is to be classified in the category about agency) and (i) the same-difference principle about the metamorposis of change (which is to be classified in the category about outcome).

In *The Future of Information Architecture* (*FIA*), I introduce three additional principles, that is, (j) the simpleness-complicadness principle on the interconnection among things, (k) the preciseness-vagueness principle on the refinement of things, and (l) the slowness-quickness principle on the speed of change—with the first two in relation to structure and the third in relation to process.

And in *The Future of Post-Human Unconsciousness* (*FPHU*), I added three more principles, that is, (m) the openness-hidden principle on the detection of things, in relation to structure, (n) the explicability-inexplicability principle on the underlying mechanisms of things, in relation to method, and (o) the expansion-contraction principle on the growth of things, in relation to process.

With this update, there are fifteen principles so far in existential dialectics, that is, three principles for the category in relation to method (viz., the partiality-totality principle, the predictability-unpredictability principle, and the explicability-inexplicability principle), three principles for the category in relation to structure (viz., the simpleness-complicatedness principle, the preciseness-vagueness principle, and the openness-hiddenness principle), four principles for the category in relation to process (viz., the change-constancy principle, the slowness-quickness principle, the order-chaos principle, and the expansion-contraction principle), three principles for the category in relation to agency (viz., the symmetry-asymmetry principle, the evolution-transformation principle, and the softness-hardness principle), and two principles for the category in relation to outcome (viz., the regression-progression principle and the same-difference principle).

There are thus fifteen principles in existential dialectics—so far (as summarized in *Table 6.8*).

The Principles as Family Resemblances

These principles, as this should be clarified at the outset, should be treated as a kind of "family resemblance" (as already mentioned earlier), in that each ontological principle is identified by a name, which, however, can take different variations in different ontological pairs.

For illustration, in the context of method, the partiality-totality principle can take the different form like individualisticness-holisticness—just as the explicability-inexplicability principle can take the different form like underlyingness-regularness.

A more comprehensive listing of this family resemblance for all other principles is shown in *Table 6.8* on the syntax of existential dialectics.

The Dialectic Constraints Imposed by the Principles

The principles, as they constitute the syntax of existential dialectics, are dialectic in character, such that, when they are applied, they impose dialectic constraints on how reality is to be understood.

Consider, say, the symmetry-asymmetry principle as an illustration here, in order to summarize two main characters of the dialectic constraints in question (as summarized in *Table 6.9*).

Firstly, to be dialectic here is to go beyond the narrow dichotomies (and, for that matter, any rigid multi-dimensional classificatory scheme), be they about "self" vs. "world," "freedom" vs. "unfreedom," "barbarity" vs. "civilization," "individuality" vs. "communality," and so on.

One way to do so (to go beyond) is to consider them all in terms of co-existence (without favoring one over the rest). For instance, my theory of "post-civilization" (to be summarized later in the section on the pragmatics of existential dialectics) is to go beyond barbarity and civilization in terms of understanding barbarity and civilization as being co-existent.

And the same logic can be said in relation to my theories of "post-democracy," "post-capitalsm," and others (also to be introduced later in the section on the pragmatics of existential dialectics), in regard to freedom vs. unfreedom, equality vs. inequality, communality vs. individuality, spirituality vs. materiality, and so on.

But to consider them all (in the dichotomies—and, for that matter, in any rigid multi-dimensional classifactory schme) as co-existent is not the same as to imply that the opposing categories in any classificatory scheme are all equal, since, in accordance to the symmetry-asymmetry principle (as an illustration here), if they are equal in terms of being considered as co-existent, they are asymmetric in terms of being unequal in dialectic interaction (e.g., X can be more dominant than Y in case A, or Y is more dominant than X in case B).

For this reason, there are different versions of "post-democracy" and "post-capitalism" in my theories. As an illustration, in version I of the theory of post-democracy, freedom is more dominant than equality, whereas in version II of the theory of post-democracy, equality is more so than freedom.

But this "X more than Y" has to be understood in the context of dialectic logic (not in symbolic logic, as conventionally understood), in that both "X" and

"Y" are important in post-democracy (in the context of dialectic logic), but in an asymmetry way. By contrast, in symbolic logic, it often favors one over the other—be it in regard to privileging freedom over equality in Fascism, favoring freedom relatively more than equality in Liberal Democracy, or favoring equality relatively more than freedom in Socialist Democracy. In regard to the latter two cases (about Liberal Democracy and Socialist Democracy), the difference between dialectic logic and symbolic logic can be one in degree, not in kind—in this sense, albeit not in other senses.

The same reasoning can be said about the relatonships between individuality and communality, between spirituality and materiality, and between formal legalism and informal legalism in the different versions of my theory of "post-capitalism."

Secondly, to be dialectic is to go beyond the narrow dichotomies (and, for that matter, any rigid multi-dimensional classificatory scheme) in another way, this time, in a transcendent way, that is, in exploring other possibilities or even other issues not considered within the narrow confines of narrow dichotomies (and, for that matter, any rigid multi-dimensional classificatory scheme).

As an analogy, in this second meaning, to go beyond the narrow dichotomy of "black" vs. "white" is not just to choose both "black" and "white" (as in the first meaning) but also to explore other options (e.g., "green," "purple," "blue," etc.—and, alternatively, "shade," "line," "curve," etc.).

By the same reasoning, to go beyond "democracy" is to transcend democracy (as in version III of my theory of "post-democracy") and to explore other possibilties of lifeforms (e.g., "floating consciousness," "hyper-spatial consciousness," etc., to live beyond the narrow obsession with freedom and equality).

This dialectic character of the principles in existential dialectics has important implications for the pragmatics of existential dialectics (as will be clear shortly, in the section on the pragmatics of existential dialectics).

The Semantics of Existential Dialectics (or Its Ontosemantics)

The syntax of existential dialectics so understood in terms of ontological principles only gives us the structure of ontology in the world, in an abstract (general) sense. These principles by themselves do not tell us the specific meanings in a given context.

In order to grasp the specific meanings of the principles in a given context, it is necessary to study the semantics of existential dialectics (as summarized in *Table 6.10*).

For this reason, I have often gone in great lengths in my previous books on different subjects to explain the specific meanings of the principles when applied in different contexts.

Consider two examples below for illustration, which are not exhaustive.

In *FPHST*, for instance, I used the first three principles (i.e., the change-constancy principle, the regression-progression principle, and the symmetry-asymmetry principle) to propose "the perspectival theory of space-time," for a better way to understand space and time—especially, though not exclusively, in relation to future post-human history (as summarized in *Table 3.1*, *Table 3.2*, *Table 3.3*, and *Table 3.4*). In so doing, I had to introduce concepts and theories specific to the field of physics and other related fields (e.g., "absolute space" and "absolute time" in "classical mechanics" and "relative space-time" in "the theory of relativity").

And in *BNN*, I also exploited the three principles to propose the "transcendent" approach to the study of genes and memes as a new way to understand the interaction between nature and nurture. In so doing, I had to explore concepts and theories in the world of evolutionary biology (e.g., "mutation," "variation," "adaptation," "selection," and "inheritance" in evolutionary theory) and neural biology (e.g., "chromosome," "gene," "DNA," "RNA," "protein," "neuron," "neural network," and "behavior").

The Pragmatics of Existential Dialectics (or Its Ontopragmatics)

Even the semantics of existential dialectics is not enough to understand reality, since semantics by itself does not tell us the nature of intentionality in relation to the matrix of power formations and human interests when existential dialectics as an ontology is applied.

For this reason, the pragmatics of existential dialectics needs to be studied too, in special relation to the inclusion of power formation and human interests in the application of the principles of existential dialectics (as summarized in *Table 6.11*).

It is thus no wonder that all my previous books have shown in different ways how and why these ontological principles and their theoretical applications can reveal the future world to come in a way that humans have never known, in a totally different battleground for competing human (and later post-human) interests by myriad groups fighting for their own versions of hegemony.

Perhaps a summary of my previous works in relation to existential dialectics and their contributions to my new theories as proposed over the years is deemed revealing here, for the further understanding of the pragmatics of existential dialectics (in close relation to the semantics of existential dialectics too).

That stressed—the following summary in the next four sub-sections is something that I often do in my previous books too, as a way to introduce the intellectual background of my ideas. So, for those reader who had read my previous works, the following sub-sections serve as a reminder, as they are repeated hereafter *often verbatim* (with only some minor changes, with the rest kept intact).

The Two-Way Street Connecting Theory and Meta-Theory

However, lest misunderstanding occurs, it is more important to remember that the pragmatics of existential dialectics is not a one-way street (that is, using the ontological principles for theoretical insights in praxis) but a two-way one, namely, (a) from meta-theory to theory, and (b) from theory to meta-theory.

(a) On one side of the street, the ontological principles can inspire some theoretical insights in praxis, that is, in relation to some specific fields.

(b) On the other (opposing) side of the street, however, the study of a subject matter in the specific fields in turn reveals some more hitherto unknown ontological principles to be discovered and identified. For this reason, three new principles were added in *FC*, one in *FAE*, two in *ALD*, three in *FIA*, and three in *FPHU*, on top of the original three in *BCPC*—after some research on the specific subject matters.

Both theory and meta-theory enrich each other in all my works over the years.

The Theoretical Application of Existential Dialectics

For instance, at the beginning, in *FHC*, two examples of the theoretical application of existential dialectics are to reveal no freedom without unfreedom (as shown in *Table 6.12*) and no equality without inequality (as shown in *Table 6.13*), especially in relation to the seven dimensions of life existence first worked out in *FHC* (i.e., the technological, the everyday, the true, the holy, the sublime/beautiful, the good, and the just).

In Ch.10 of *FCD*, the relationship between these two examples of the theoretical application of existential dialectics was extended further, so as to provide some new visions to understand the future forms of political and economic systems.

In regard to politics, my vision of a path-breaking political system in future times concerns the different forms of "post-democracy" to supersede democracy unto the post-human age. My vision of post-democracy was called "the theory of post-democracy" (as summarized in *Table 5.2*, *Table 5.3*, and *Table 5.4*), whereas *Table 5.5* explains the distinctions among democracy, non-democracy, and post-democracy. And *Table 5.6* stresses the multiple causes of the emergence of post-democracy, while *Table 5.7* clarifies some possible misunderstandings in regard to post-capitalism and post-democracy.

In regard to economics, I also offered another vision, this time to understand the future forms of economic systems, that is, the different forms of "post-capitalism" to supersede capitalism unto the post-human age. My vision of post-capitalism was referred to (in *FCD*, *BDPD* and *BCPC*) as "the theory of post-capitalism" (as summarized in *Table 5.8*, *Table 5.9*, *Table 5.10*, *Table 5.11*, and *Table 5.12*). And *Table 5.13* clarifies the differences among capitalism, non-capitalism, and post-capitalism, whereas *Table 5.14* shows multiple causes of the emergence of post-capitalism.

This vision on "post-capitalism" constitutes the third theoretical application of existential dialectics, this time, in that there is no wealth without poverty (or the wealth/poverty dialectics).

More importantly, these existential constraints hold true for the age of pre-modernity, modernity, post-modernity, and, in the future, what I originally suggested in *FHC* as "after-postmodernity"—as shown in *Table 1.2*, *Table 1.3*, *Table 1.4*, and *Table 1.5*.

This is all the more so, in the "post-human" age at some distant point of "after-postmodernity," long after human extinction, to be eventually superseded by post-humans of various forms. Some good candidates of the post-human lifeforms include, for instance, thinking robots, thinking machines, cyborgs, genetically altered superior beings, floating consciousness, and hyper-spatial consciousness. This post-human vision of mine was first originally worked out in *FHC* and further elaborated in both *FCD* and *FPHC*, for instance.

In the end, a most fundamental question about intelligent life now has an answer, in that, if asked, "What is the future of human civilization?"—my answer in *FCD* (89) is thus: "As addressed in Ch.7 of *FHC*, a later epoch of the age of after-postmodernity (that is, at some point further away from after-postmodernity) will begin, as what I called the 'post-human' history (with the term 'post-human' originally used in my doctoral dissertation at M.I.T., which was finished in November 1995, under the title *After Postmodernity*, still available at M.I.T. library, and was later revised and published as *FHC*). The post-human history will be such that humans are nothing in the end, other than what culture, society, and nature (with some luck) have shaped them into, to be eventually superseded by post-humans (e.g., cyborgs, thinking machines, genetically altered superior beings, and others), if humans are not destroyed long before then."

A conclusion which is shocking indeed for many contemporaries is none other than that "[t]he post-human history will therefore mark the end of human history as we know it and, for that matter, the end of human dominance and, practically speaking, the end of humans as well. The entire history of human civilization, from its beginning to the end, can be summarized by four words, linked by three arrows (as already discussed in *FHC*)":

Pre-Modernity → Modernity → Post-Modernity →
After-Postmodernity

In *BDPD*, this thesis of mine was specifically called "the theory of the evolution from pre-modernity to after-postmodernity," at the historical level.

Therefore, "[t]he end of humanity in the coming human extinction is the beginning of post-humanity. To say an untimely farewell to humanity is to foretell the future welcome of post-humanity." (P. Baofu 2002: 89) This thesis of mine was known in *BDPD* as "the theory of post-humanity," at the systemic level.

In Ch.9 of *FCD* (367-8), I further showed "that civilizational history will continue into the following cyclical progression of expansion, before it is to be superseded (solely as a high probability, since humans might be destroyed sooner either by themselves or in a gigantic natural calamity) by posthumans at some distant point in after-postmodernity (which I already discussed in *FHC*)" unto multiverses (different constellations of universes):

Local → Regional → Global → Solar → Galactic →
Clustery… → Multiversal

In *BDPD*, this thesis of mine was referred to as "the theory of the cyclical progression of system integration and fragmentation," at the systemic level.

In *BWT*, a different version of this thesis is "the theory of cyclical progression of empire-building," at multiple levels (e.g., institutional, structural, systemic, and others), in providing a better way to understand the logic of empire-building on earth and beyond.

In *BNN*, I further worked out "the theory of contrastive advantages" (which was originally proposed in *FCD* and summarized in *Table 2.13*), to show the nature-nurture interactions of multiple levels in action (e.g., the biological, the psychological, the structural, the systemic, the cultural, and others) for humans and post-humans on earth and beyond, to the extent that different groups, be they on the basis of race, gender, ethnicity, class, age, or else, are not equal, on average, and have never been, nor will they be.

In fact, even greater transformations are yet to come in the post-human age. For instance, even the existence of human consciousness will be superseded one day too, with "floating consciousness" (as first proposed in *FCD*) and "hyper-spatial consciousness" (as first proposed in *FPHC*) as a climax of evolution in consciousness, after the future extinction of human consciousness:

———

Primordial consciousness → Human consciousness →
Post-human consciousness (with floating consciousness and hyper-spatial consciousness as a climax in the evolution of consciousness)

———

In *BDPD*, these latest theses of mine were called "the theory of floating consciousness" and "the theory of hyper-spatial consciousness," both at the cosmological and psychological levels (as summarized in *Table 2.15* and *Table 2.14*).

In *FPHC*, the nature of consciousness was further detailedly analyzed, especially in relation to the conceptual dimensions of consciousness (as shown in *Table 2.1*), the theoretical levels of consciousness (as shown in *Table 2.2*), the thematic issues of consciousness (as shown in *Table 2.3*), the different dimensions of human existence (viz., having-ness, belonging-ness, and being-ness) in relation to consciousness (as shown in *Table 2.4*, *Table 2.5*, *Table 2.6*, and *Table 2.7*).

In *BCPC*, the nature of consciousness was explored further in relation to cognition, emotion, and behavior, which can be in consciousness and other mental states (e.g., subconsciousness and unconsciousness), in the context of existential dialectics, as shown in *Table 2.8*, *Table 2.9*, *Table 2.10*, *Table 2.11*, and *Table 2.12*.

But this is not the end of the matter yet. In *FPHU*, even the unconsious mind will undergo tremendous change, to the rise of what I originally called "unfolding unconsciousess" in relation to anomalous experience, as a climax of evolution in unconsciousness, in conjunction with the conscious mind (both human now and post-human later), especially at the psychological level:

———

Primordial unconsciousness → Human unconsciousness →
Post-human unconsciousness (with unfolding unconsciousness as a climax in the evolution of unconsciousness)

———

In *FPHU*, this thesis of mine is called "the theory of unfolding unconsciousness" in a small sense, or "the unfolding theory of anomalous experience," in a larger one, as shown in *Table 2.16*, *Table 2.17*, and *Table 6.2*.

The Further Use of Existential Dialectics

Even more interestingly, in *BDPD* and later in *BCIV*, I further revealed a theoretical refinement of existential dialectics, this time, in arguing that there is no civilization without barbarity, with human civilization to be eventually superseded by what I originally analyzed as "post-human post-civilization" (which should not be confused with "post-human civilization"), in the context of the freedom/unfreedom and equality/inequality dialectics.

In the final analysis, civilization cannot live without barbarity and has to learn to co-exist with it in ever new ways. Preposteorus as this may seem to many contemporaries—it is no more imperative to preserve civilization than necessary to destroy barbarity, and the ideal of civilization is essentially bankrupt, to be eventually superseded by "post-civilization" (as summarized in *Tables 4.1-4.9*).

Yet, this requires some understanding of my analysis of the trinity of modernity and other ages. For instance, in both *FCD* and *FPHC*, I worked out the structure of "post-human civilization" in terms of the trinity of after-postmodernity (i.e., "free-spirited after-postmodernity," "post-capitalist after-postmodernity," and "hegemonic after-postmodernity").

Both conceptually and theoretically, the trinity of after-postmodernity is a sequential extension to the trinity of modernity (i.e., "free-spirited modernity," "capitalist modernity,"and "hegemonic modernity") and the trinity of postmodernity (i.e., "free-spirited postmodernity," "capitalist postmodernity," and "hegemonic postmodernity") as first proposed in *FHC*.

And the trinity of pre-modernity (i.e., "pre-free-spirited pre-modernity," "pre-capitalist pre-modernity" and "hegemonic pre-modernity") was later conceived in *BCIV* to complete the historical set from pre-modernity to after-postmodernity.

In *BDPD*, this thesis about the trinity of pre-modernity, modernity, postmodernity, and after-postmodernity was collectively known as "the theory of the trinity of modernity to its after-postmodern counterpart," at the cultural level (as summarized in *Table 1.2*, *Table 1.3*, *Table 1.4*, and *Table 1.5*).

At the structural level, all these trinities are subject to the existential constraints (e.g., the freedom/unfreedom and equality/inequality dialectics in the context of "the cyclical progression of hegemony"), be the historical epoch in pre-modernity, modernity, postmodernity, or after-postmodernity in future times. Each of the historical epochs has its ever new ways of coming to terms with the ever new (different) mixtures of freedom/unfreedom and equality/inequality.

This is importantly so, not because, as is falsely assumed in conventional wisdom, one certain way is superior (or better) than another in terms of achieving more freedom and less unfreedom, or more equality with less inequality.

On the contrary, indeed, in each of the historical epochs, each increase of unfreedom greets each freedom achieved, just as each increase of inequality welcomes each equality achieved, albeit in ever new (different) ways. In *BDPD*, this thesis of mine was labeled as "the theory of the cyclical progression of hegemony," at the structural level, though it was first analyzed in *FCD*.

In *BDPD*, more theoretical applications of existential dialectics were further examined, in relation to five main features, in the context of the duality of oppression, namely, (a) that each freedom/equality achieved is also each unfreedom/inequality created, (b) that the subsequent oppressiveness is dualistic, both by the Same against the Others and itself and by the Others against the Same and themselves, (c) that both oppression and self-oppression can be achieved by way of downgrading differences (between the Same and the Others) and of accentuating them, (d) that the relationships are relatively asymmetric among them but relatively symmetric within them, even when the Same can be relatively asymmetric towards itself in self-oppression, and the Others can be likewise towards themselves, and (e) that symmetry and asymmetry change over time, with ever new players, new causes, and new forms, be the locality here on Earth or in deep space unto multiverses—as summarized in *Table.6.12*, *Table 6.13*, *Table 6.14*, and *Table 6.15*.

The same logic also holds both in relation to wealth and poverty (as addressed in *BCPC* and summarized in *Table 6.16* on the wealth/poverty dialectics) and in relation to civilization and barbarity (as addressed in *BCIV* and summarized in *Table 6.17* on the civilization/barbarity dialectics).

In *BDPD*, this thesis on existential dialectics was labeled as "the theory of existential dialectics,".

Direct and Indirect Applications of Existential Dialectics

A different way to appreciate the usefulness of existential dialectics is by way of the analysis of its (a) direct and (b) indirect applications.

(a) In direct applications, on the one hand, the logic of existential dialectics can shed some theoretical insights on diverse phenomena in the world, and good instances are the usage of the principles of existential dialectics for the theoretical insights on the freedom/unfreedom dialectics, the equality/inequality dialectics, and the wealth/poverty dialectics (as introduced above).

My books like *FPHST*, *BNN*, *FAE*, *FC*, *FIA*, and *FPHU* also use the principles to reveal some theoretical insights on the perspectives of space and time (as in *FPHST*), of nature and nurture (as in *BNN*), of beauty and ugliness (as in *FAE*), of order and chaos (as in *FC*), of taxonomy and network (as in *FIA*), and of the unconscious mind (as in *FPHU*).

(b) In indirect applications, on the other hand, the theoretical insights can further be used to reveal other phenomena directly from them (viz., the theoretical insights) and therefore indirectly from the principles themselves.

A good illustration is of course the use of the theoretical insights on the freedom/unfreedom and equality/inequality dialectics for the understanding of the civilization/barbarity dialectics.

This distinction between direct and indirect applications may sound a bit academic, since even in indirect applications, the phenomena under study can still be directly related back to the principles themselves.

In the previous example, as an illustration, the civilization/barbarity dialectics can be directly related to the principles of existential dialectics without the intermediate role of the freedom/unfreedom and equality/inequality dialectics.

Multiple Levels of Application

There is another issue to be clarified, however. In other words, the theoretical insights can be applied to multiple levels of analysis—even though, in a given example, it may refer to one level or a few only.

For instance, in the example concerning the freedom/unfreedom dialectics, it can be used at the structural level (e.g., in relation to the theory of the cyclical progression of hegemony), but it can also be exploited for other levels (e.g., the theory of post-capitalism at the institutional level).

All these levels of application should not be misleadingly construed, as I stress this before, as a one-way street (that is, to use the ontological principles for theoretical application at multiple levels of specific analysis) but a two-way one, in which theoretical insights in praxis, when studied in more specific contexts, can in turn refine the nature of existential dialectics (for example, with the addition of new principles).

Sophisticated Methodological Holism

The summary of my original meta-theory on methodology is provided below, again, to be repeated *often verbatim* from my previous works—as this is something I regularly do to introduce my past works, which are in conversation with this current one.

This original contribution of mine to the study of methodology takes the form of an approach known as "the theory of methodological holism" or "methodological holism" in short, as already worked out in *FPHC* (2004).

I have made good use of this methodological approach of mine for all of my previous works.

Yet, it is imperative to stress at the outset, as I have so emphasized in all my previous books, that my approach of "methodological holism" does not oppose or exclude "methodological individualism" (as some reader may be tempted to assume, as is conventionally understood) but actually includes it.

For this reason (and others too, as summarized in *Table 1.6*), my version of methodological holism is *sophisticated*—not *vulgar* as sometimes used by inapt scholars employing the same term.

The Ontological Constraints

Sophisticated methodological holism is subject to some ontological constraints, and three good examples (although there are more than three) include "the partiality-totality principle," "the predictability-unpredictability principle," and "the explicability-inexplicability principle" in existential dialectics.

The first two were already analyzed in previous books of mine like *FC* and *FAE*, whereas the third one is addressed in *FPHU*.

For now, it suffices to show that sophisticted methodological holism, because of these ontological constraints on methodology, targets two major sins of methodology, namely, what I call, in the absence of better words, (a) *reductionism* and (b) *reverse-reductionism*—both of which come in all shapes and sizes, to be summarized below (and also shown in *Table 1.7*).

Against the Varieties of Reductionism

There are four versions of reductionism to be summarized here, which sophisticated methodological holism rejects, namely, (a1) conceptual, (a2) theoretical, (a3) methodological, and (a4) ontological forms of reductionism.

(a1) In methodological reductionism, a good illustration can be the debate between different versions of qualitative and quantitative methods (as already analyzed in *FC* and also *FHC*).

(a2) In ontological reductionism, an excellent instance involves another debate, this time between emergentism and reductionism in complexity theory (as addressed in *FC*) and also in psychology (as elaborated in *FPHC*, in the context of Being and Belonging).

(a3) In conceptual reductionism, a good case in point concerns myriad dualities like mind vs. body, self vs. world, democracy vs non-democracy, and the like (as already addressed in *FHC*, *FPHC*, and *BDPD*, for instance).

(a4) In theoretical reductionism, an illuminating case study is best exemplified by what I originally called "the foundation fallacy" in *FPHST*, in any attempt to naively understand space-time from the physical perspective as the foundation and, consequently, to dangerously dismiss (or belittle) other perspectives.

In *FAE*, I elaborated further these versions of reductionism in the literature on aesthetics (e.g., form vs. content, representation vs. expression, critics vs. artists, and externalism vs. internalism).

In *FIA*, I revealed other forms of reductionism in the literature on information architecture (e.g., the constructivist argument).

And in *FPHU*, I hereafter show the persistent legacy of reductionism, this time, in the literature on anomalous experience (e.g., the obsession with physics, chemistry, and biology for explaining anomalous experience).

Against the Varieties of Reverse-Reductionism

The other side of the same coin is of course the reverse version of reductionism, which is what I want to call, in the absence of better words, *reverse-reductionism*. My sophisticated version of methodological holism targets against the varieties of reverse-reductionism (just as it also rejects the ones of reductionism).

Perhaps nothing expresses better the popularity of reverse-reductionim than the "anything-goes" mentality in postmodernism of our time, as shown in the following four versions.

(b1) In conceptual reverse-reductionism, any concept of "art" (e.g., fine art, applied art, outsider art, junk art) is welcome in postmodernism (as already analyzed in Ch.4 of *FHC*—and also in *FAE*).

(b2) In theoretical reverse-reductionism, a variety of art and literary theories co-exist. Take the case of literature, as there are now Literary Structuralism, Marxist Literary Criticism, New Criticism, Phenomenology, Hermeneutics, Language-Game Literary Criticism, Feminist Literary Criticism, Reception Theory, Reader Response Criticism, Poststructuralism, Semiotics, Pyschoanalytic Literary Criticism, just to cite some well-known ones, with no one being said to be better than any others (as detailedly analyzed in Ch.4 of *FHC*). (S. Raman 1997) In *BNN*, I even introduced "the compromise fallacy" as another good illustration of theoretical reverse-reductionism, in misleadingly treating both genetic and environmental approaches as equally valid.

(b3) In methodological reverse-reductionism, multiple methodologies are deemed as acceptable in postmodernism (e.g., doing art without praxis, doing art with praxis, and doing art by sublation), as analyzed in Ch.4 of *FHC*.

(b4) In ontological reverse-reductionism, no privileged ontology is allowed, and the door is open practically for anything in postmodernism (e.g., the equal status of the ontology of Being vs. that of Becoming, as already addressed in Ch.4 of *FHC*—and also in *FPHC*).

In *FAE*, I also introduced another version of reverse-reductionism, that is, "the pluralist fallacy," in the context of understanding aesthetic experience, for instance.

These dual dangers against reverse-reductionism (in this sub-section) and reductionism (in the previous sub-section) are something that sophisticated methodological holism rejects.

The Holistic Organization of an Inquiry

With these dual dangers against reductionism and reverse-reductionism in mind—sophisticated methodological holism suggests that an inquiry of any given phenomenon is more complete, if treated in the context of a comprehensive analysis at all relevant levels, which challengingly encompass all the fields of human knowledge, ranging from the natural sciences through the social sciences to the humanities.

This section is something that I had already stressed in all my previous books and repeat (*often verbatim*) hereafter. But, for those readers who had read my previous books, this serves as a reminder.

With this reminder in mind—there are multiple ways to engage in a holistic inquiry with all relevent levels of analysis. Over the years, I have proposed different ways to fulfill this holistic methodological requirement, as repeated in my previous books.

Hereafter is a summary of four major ways, namely, (i) by discipline, (ii) by domain, (iii) by subject, and (iv) by meta-analysis—all of which fulfill the holistic requirement of sophisticated methodological holism on a given issue.

(i) In a holistic organization by discipline, a good illustration is the multiple levels of analysis, namely, (i1) the micro-physical, (i2) the chemical, (i3) the biological, (i4) the psychological, (i5) the organizational, (i6) the institutional, (i7) the structural, (i8) the systemic, (i9) the cultural, (i10) the macro-physical (cosmological), and (i11) other relevant levels, which are either a combination of all these levels or the practical applications with a combination of them. This holistic organization is used in *FCD* and *BCPC*, for instance.

(ii) In a holistic organization by domain, some good candidates include the classification of different perspectives of analysis in relation to (ii1) nature, (ii2) the mind, (ii3) society, and (ii4) culture, as already worked out in *BCIV*, *FPHST*, *FC*, *FAE*, and *FPHU*.

In this re-classification, culture in (ii4) is the same as culture in (i9). Society in (ii3) includes the organizational in (i5), the institutional in (i6), the structural in (i7), and the systemic in (i8). The mind (ii3) has more to do with the chemical in (i2), the biological in (i3), and the psychological in (i4), although it can overlap with (i1), (ii3) and (ii4), for instance. And nature in (ii1) refers to the micro-physical in (i1) and the macro-physical (cosmological) in (i10), although it can also overlap with (i2), (i3) and (i4).

(iii) In a holistic organization by subject, some excellent examples concern the analysis of consciousness in *FPHC* (i.e., on Having, Belonging, and Being), of civilization in *FHC* (i.e., the True, the Holy, the Everyday, the Technological, the Beautiful/Sublime, the Good, and the Just), of international politics in *BWT* (i.e., Hyper-Empires, Meso-Empires, and Micro-Empires), of nature and nurture in *BNN* (i.e., genes and memes), and of taxonomy and network in *FIA*—by incorporating all the relevent levels of analysis as cited above in each.

(iv) In a holistic organization by meta-analysis, two good cases in point involve the works on post-capitalism in *BCPC* and on authoritarian liberal democracy in *ALD*, with the classification of analysis in theory and meta-theory.

The essential point to remember here, as I thus stress in all my previous books, is that the multiple levels of analysis can be reorganized in many different ways, insofar as none of the levels (if relevant to an inquiry in question) is ignored or dismissed, to avoid the danger of reductionism (and for that matter, the one of reverse-reductionism, in the opposite direction).

Three Clarifications

Three clarifications are needed here, however, to avoid hasty misunderstanding.

Firstly, the entities in each classification are not mutually exclusive. For instance, in the holisitc organization by domain, nature in (ii1) can also be linked to the chemical in (i2), the biological in (i3), and the systemic in (i8). And the mind (ii3) can alternatively be related to the micro-physical in (i1) and the chemical in (i2), for example.

Secondly, there is also the important factor of luck (or uncertainty in conventional usage), but it is already implied or allowed in each of the organizations of an inquiry—especially in relation to the predictability-unpredictability principle in existential dialectics (as will be elaborated in Chapter Three).

And lastly, the comparison in a classification is not absolute, but relative, as there are often some shades of gray, not exactly black or white (figuratively speaking).

Some further clarifications and qualifications of sophisticated methodological holism are shown in *Table 1.5*.

Chapter Outline

With this summary of my two unique meta-theories (on methodology and ontology, *almost verbatim* from my previous works) in mind—this book is then organized in six main parts, namely, (a) Part I on the introduction of this book, (b) Part II on anomalous experience and the mind, (c) Part III on anomalous experience and nature, (d) Part IV on anomalous experience and culture, (e) Part V on anomalous experience and society, and (f) Part VI on the conclusion of this book.

In other words, the book is organized in six chapters, starting with the introductory chapter, Chapter One titled "Introduction—The Mystery of Unconsciousness," which introduces the phenomenon of anomalous experience in relation to unconsciousness, together with the theoretical debate in the literature, my unfolding theory of anomalous experience, methodological holism, and existential dialectics.

Chapter Two titled "Unconsciousness and the Mind" examines anomalous experience in relation to unconsciousness from the perspectives of biology and psychology, with a critical assessment of each.

Chapter Three titled "Unconsciousness and Nature" explores anomalous experience in relation to unconsciousness from the perspectives of chemistry, micro-physics, and macro-physics (cosmology), with an evaluation of the weaknesses and strengths of each.

Chapter Four titled "Unconsciousness and Culture" studies anomalous experience in relation to unconsciousness from the perspectives of morality, religion, aesthetics, and epistemology, with a constructive critique of each of them.

Chapter Five titled "Unconsciousness and Society" looks into anomalous experience in relation to unconsciousness from the perspectives of social organizations, social institutions, social structure, and social systems, with a deconstructive analysis of each.

The last chapter titled "Conclusion: The Future of Unconsciousness" finally summarizes the analysis in the book with the six theses in my unfolding theory of anomalous experience, namely, (a) the first thesis on the openness-hiddenness principle, (b) the second thesis on the expansion-contraction principle, (c) the third thesis on the symmetry-asymmetry principle, (d) the fourth thesis on the regression-progression principle, (e) the fifth thesis on the explicability-inexplicability principle, and (f) the sixth thesis on the post-human mastery.

In the end, the future direction of the unconscious mind, in special relation to anomalous experience, will mark a tremendous milestone for intelligent life, something that humans in their entire history so far can only dream or fantasize about, or, in more than occasional cases, have to resort to fraudulent claims to sustain their credibility.

Three Clarifications for Thought

But there is one more business to do, before a formal analysis of the nature of anomalous experience is to begin.

This has to do with three further clarifications for thought, in order to avoid any potential misunderstanding by the reader, that is, in relation to (a) the conversation with my previous books, (b) the number of case studies and examples, (c) the use of neologisms.

These three clarifications for thought are something that I also regularly repeat in my previous books too, so these points are repeated hereafter, *often verbatim*—albeit in a different context this time, that is, in relation to anomalous experience.

In Conversation with My Previous Books

Firstly, my unfolding theory of anomalous experience (or my theory of unfolding unconsciousness in short) is constructed on the theoretical foundation of my previous books (i.e., *FHC*, *FCD*, *FPHC*, *BDPD*, *BCPC*, *BCIV*, *FPHST*, *BNN*, *BWT*, *FC*, *ALD*, and *FIA*—as explicated in "The List of Abbreviations," on page xix).

Although a summary of my previous books is provided whenever necessary, as shown in the two sections above (*often verbatim*) and in different tables at the end of some chapters, I still expect the reader to read my previous books directly for more details.

Case Studies and Examples

Secondly, the case studies and examples in the chapters on anomalous experience are not exhaustive but solely illustrative. Nor are they necessarily mutually exclusive, as they can be reclassified in a different way. And exceptions are allowed.

One is tempted to assume, however, that, since the case studies and their examples are not exhaustive, more case studies and examples are needed. But the problem here is that just adding more of them does not necessarily change much of the conclusions to be drawn and may even lead to redundancy.

After all, the case studies and examples used in this book are chosen with care and deemed sufficient for the purpose at hand, even though they are solely illustrative.

The Use of Neologisms

And thirdly, I use different neologisms in my books, mostly to introduce my original concepts and theories, and good instances include those here or elsewhere in my previous books (e.g., "the unfolding theory of anomalous experience," "unfolding unconsciousness," "the openness-hiddenness principle," "the expansion-contraction principle," "post-democracy," "hyper-spatial consciousness," "post-capitalism," and whatnot). Needless to say, they are used here solely for our current intellectual convenience, as they will be renamed differently in different ways in future history.

As I thus wrote in *FCD* (508-9), "all these terms 'post-capitalism,' 'post-democracy'...and other ones as introduced in...[the] project (e.g.,...'posthuman elitists,' and 'posthuman counter-elitists,' just to cite a few of them) are more for our current intellectual convenience than to the liking of future humans and post-humans, who will surely invent more tasteful neologisms to call their own eras, entities, and everything else, for that matter. But the didactic point here is to use the terms to foretell what the future might be like, not that its eras and entities must be called so exactly and permanently. After all, William Shakespeare (1995: Act II, Scene II, Line 47) well said long ago: 'What is in a name? That which we call a rose by any other name would smell as sweet.'"

As I had also stressed time and again before, each of the neologisms can be re-written as a different "X," only to be re-named differently by the powers that be in different eras of future history.

With these clarifications for thought in mind—I now proceed to Chapter Two on unconsciousness and the mind in the context of anomalous experience.

Table 1.1. The Varieties of Anomalous Experience

- **Psychic Types**
  - —Ex: "telepathy" (viz., reading the minds of others)
  - —Ex: "telekinesis" (viz., moving things without contact)
  - —Ex: extraordinary senses
    - Ex: "clair-sentience" (in feeling)
    - Ex: "clair-voyance" (in seeing)
    - Ex: "clair-audience" (in hearing)
    - Ex: "clair-austance" (in tasting)
    - Ex: "clair-alience" (in smelling)
    - Ex: "clair-cognizance" (in knowing)

- **Transcendental Types**
  - —Ex: "reincarnation" (viz., the rebirth of a soul)
  - —Ex: "miracle"
  - —Ex: "past-life experience" (viz., "experience… or impression…of oneself … in a previous time or life")
  - —Ex: "healing experience" (viz., "shamanic and…alternative therapies")
  - —Ex: "mystical experience" (viz., "religious conversion or belief")

- **Miscellaneous Types**
  - —Ex: "haunting" (viz., the appearance of a ghost)
  - —Ex: "mediumship" (viz., communicating with the dead)
  - —Ex: "near-death experience"
  - —Ex: "synesthesia" (viz., "a 'curious' perception of sensed imagery or 'qualities of one modality' that are 'transferred to another modality' such as a food or beverage taste")
  - —Ex: "out-of-body experience" (viz., one's perception of "being outside of the body")
  - —Ex: "alien abduction experience"

Notes: I introduced these categories to start the conversation on anomalous experience in this book. The examples in the categories are solely illustrative (not exhaustive), and the comparison is relative (not absolute), nor are they necessarily mutually exclusive. And some can be easily re-classified elsewhere. As generalities, they allow exceptions.

Source: From Ch.1 of *FPHU*, based on the data from various sources like WK (2007m & 2007n), MWD (2007, 2007a & 2007b), F. MacHovec (2002), S. Begley (2001), and J. Kennedy (1995a)

Table 1.2. The Trinity of Pre-Modernity

- **Pre-Free-Spirited Pre-Modernity (Pre-Modernism) and Its Internal Split**
  —Competing worldviews and values both within and between linear centric (e.g., Islamic, Christian, Judaic, Imperial Roman) and cyclical-centric (e.g., Confucian, Taoist, Hindu, and Buddhist) orientations
  —Compare modernism with pre-modernism here in relation to the seven dimensions of human existence like the true and the holy (e.g., different versions of epistemic dogmas and religious superstitions), the everyday and the technological (e.g.,different versions of non-technophilism and non-consumerism), the beautiful/sublime (e.g., different versions of aesthetic non-autonomy), and the good and the just (e.g., different versions of moral particularism).

- **Pre-Capitalist Pre-Modernity (Pre-Modernization) and Its Own Discontents**
  —Competing versions of societal arrangements (e.g., feudalism, monarchism, and the holy order)

- **Hegemonic Pre-Modernity and Its Countervailing Forces**
  —Different power centers and their enemies (e.g., the Roman Empire and the "barbarian hordes," the "Holy Crusades" and the Muslims, the Middle Kingdom and the invading tribes, different social castes in India, and warring Greek city-states)

Notes: The examples in each category are solely illustrative (not exhaustive) nor necessarily mutually exclusive, and the comparison is relative (not absolute). As generalities, they allow exceptions. Also, it does not matter what the "base" era is in the analysis of any trinity. And in the present context, the "base" era is modernity (for instance, with its "free-spirited modernity" and the other two parts). So, for pre-modernity, the trinity takes the form of, say, "pre-free-spirited pre-modernity," together with the other two parts.
Sources: From Ch.2 of *BCIV* and also the 2 volumes of *FHC*

Table 1.3. The Trinity of Modernity
(Part I)

- **Free-Spirited Modernity (Modernism) and Its Internal Split**
  —*On the True and the Holy*
    - The freedom from the dogmas of the past to the better understanding of, and union with, the world and self (Ch.3 of *FHC*)
    - Alternative discourses: about the true (e.g., anti-science discourses) and the holy (non-mainstream theologies) (Ch.3 of *FHC*)

  —*On the Technological and the Everyday*
    - The freedom from life harshness to the higher technophilic, consumeristic lifeform (Ch.2 of *FHC*)
    - Alternative discourses: about the everyday (e.g., transcendental mindsets) and the technological (e.g., Arcadianism) (Ch.2 of *FHC*)

  —*On the Good and the Just*
    - The freedom from the theo-aristocratic tyranny to the moral universality for a just society (Ch.5 of *FHC*)
    - Alternative discourses: about the just (e.g., Communism, Anarchism) and the good (e.g., Nazism/Fascism, and Zarathustrianism) (Chs.5-6 of *FHC*)

  —*On the Beautiful and the Sublime*
    - The freedom from the external distortion of aesthetic pleasure to the boundless infinity of totality in artistic autonomy (Ch.4 of *FHC*)
    - Alternative discourses: about the beautiful/sublime (e.g., kitsch and historical avant-gardism) (Ch.4 of *FHC*)

- **Capitalist Modernity (Modernization) and Its Own Discontents**
  —*During the Industrial Revolution*
    - Ex: Marx on the institution of inequality (Ch.1 of *FHC*)

  —*During the Modern Rational-Instrumental Epoch*
    - Ex: Weber on the politics of soft liberal institutions (Ch.5 of *FHC*)

  —*During the Great Depression*
    - Ex: Keynes on the myth of the free market (Chs.1-3 of *FHC*)

  —*During the Cold War*
    - Ex: Lasch on the narcissistic culture industry (Chs.2-3 of *FHC*)

(continued on next page)

Table 1.3. The Trinity of Modernity
(Part II)

- **Hegemonic Modernity and Its Countervailing Forces**
  —*The Legacies of Colonialism and Imperialism*
    - Ex: European colonization of most of the modern world (Ch.1 of *FHC*)
  —*The Struggle for Decolonialization*
    - Ex: The countervailing forces of resentment, rechantment, and regionalism (Chs.1 & 6 of *FHC*)

Notes: The examples in each category are solely illustrative (not exhaustive) nor necessarily mutually exclusive, and the comparison is relative (not absolute). As generalities, they allow exceptions.
Sources: From the 2 volumes of *FHC*—and also from *FCD*

Table 1.4. The Trinity of Postmodernity

- **Free-Spirited Postmodernity (Postmodernism) and Its Internal Split**

  —*On the True and the Holy*
  - Postmodern performative turn for knowing and its enemies (Ch.3 of *FHC*)
  - Postmodern comparative theology and its opponents (Ch.3 of *FHC*)

  —*On the Technological and the Everyday*
  - Postmodern corporate technological mindset and its adversaries (Ch.2 of *FHC*)
  - Postmodern postmaterialism and its critics (Ch.2 of *FHC*)

  —*On the Good and the Just*
  - Postmodern politics of difference and its foes (Ch.5 of *FHC*)

  —*On the Beautiful and the Sublime*
  - Postmodern deconstruction and its dissenters (Ch.4 of *FHC*)

- **Capitalist Postmodernity (Postmodernization) and Its Own Discontents**

  —*During the Post-Cold War and Beyond*
  - Ex: post-Fordism and its shortcomings (Ch.6 of *FHC*; Chs.6-7 of *FCD*)

- **Hegemonic Postmodernity and Its Countervailing Forces**

  —*The Debate on the Global Village*
  - Ex: uni-civilizationalism vs. multi-civilizationalism (Ch.6 of *FHC*)

  —*The Resistance Movement*
  - Ex: rechantment and the politics of civilizational claims (e.g., Islamic, Confucian and other ethos in relation to the Same) (Ch.6 of *FHC*; Ch.10 of *FCD*)
  - Ex: resentment and the politics of resurgence (e.g., the rising Chinese superpower, the growing EU, and other players in relation to the U.S. and her allies) (Ch.6 of *FHC*; Ch.8 of *FCD*)
  - Ex: regionalism and the politics of inequality (e.g., trans- or inter- national blocs, the North-South divide, NGO's) (Ch.6 of *FHC*; Ch.5 of *FCD*)

Notes: The examples in each category are solely illustrative (not exhaustive) nor necessarily mutually exclusive, and the comparison is relative (not absolute). As generalities, they allow exceptions.
Sources: From *FCD* and the 2 volumes of *FHC*

Table 1.5. The Trinity of After-Postmodernity

- **Free-Spirited After-Postmodernity (After-Postmodernism) and Its Internal Split**
  —The discourse of naked contingency (Ch.10 of *FCD*; Ch.4 of *FPHC*)

- **Post-Capitalist After-Postmodernity (After-Postmodernization) and Its Own Discontents**
  —Different versions of post-capitalism and post-democracy, and their enemies (Ch.10 of *FCD*; Chs.3-4 of *FPHC*)

- **Hegemonic After-Postmodernity and Its Countervailing Forces**
  —The Cyclical Progression of Hegemony in Multiverses (Chs.9-10 of *FCD*; Ch.4 of *FPHC*)

Notes: The examples in each category are solely illustrative (not exhaustive) nor necessarily mutually exclusive, and the comparison is relative (not absolute). As generalities, they allow exceptions.
Sources: From *FCD* and also *FHC*

Table 1.6. Sophisticated Methodological Holism (Part I)

• "My methodological holism implies the partiality-totality principle in the ontology of existential dialectics (see the table on the partiality-totality principle for summary), which is against the varieties of (a) reductionism and (b) reverse-reductionism, in relation to (i) concept, (ii) theory, (iii) methodology, and (iv) ontology." (*FC*)

• "[M]y methodological holism here is not opposed to methodological individualism but includes it (and, for that matter, other methodologies too)…." (*FPHC*) For this reason (and others too, as summarized hereafter), my version of methodological holism is sophisticated—not vulgar as sometimes used by inapt scholars using the same term. (*FC*)

• "[M]y methodological holism does not democratically presume that all levels are equally valid, as all levels are not created equal. In other words, in relation to issue X, level A may be more relevant than level B, but in relation to Y, level B can be more relevant than level A instead." (*FPHC*) One excellent example of this vulgar democratic presumption is what I called in *BNN* "the compromise fallacy." (*FC*)

• My methodological holism does not presume that a lower level of analysis is more important than a higher level, solely because the former serves as the foundation for the latter—and vice versa, for that matter. One excellent example of this reductionistic presumption is what I called in *FPHST* "the foundation fallacy." (*FPHST, FC*)

• "[M]y methodological holism does not make any a-priori postulation that there must be a definite (and, for that matter, indefinite) number of levels" in any analysis. (*FPHC*) Nor does it dogmatically require that there must be a certain combination of levels of analysis in a given inquiry. (*FC*)

(continued on next page)

Table 1.6. Sophisticated Methodological Holism (Part II)

• "[M]ethodological holism, in my usage, does not assume that all levels…can necessarily be integrated, since methodological holism is not aimed to search for the holy grail of 'an integral theory…' (as is the case for Wilber). In other words, it allows that sometimes some levels may experience irreducible gaps between them, to be understood, at best, as empirical correlations, not as causal relations…." (*FPHC*)

• "[D]ifferent levels may overlap and even interact with each other in a given context (but sometimes may not), and the fact that I even proposed different ways of re-classifying the levels (whenever needed) in *FDC* reinforces this point….The dual danger here is either forcefully making different levels interact when they are just different (or, metaphorically speaking, apples and oranges) or inappropriately ignoring their interactions when some situations instead require them." (*FPHC*)

• "[T]o understand different levels from their own (unique) perspectives (as required by my methodological holism) is not the same as trying to reduce them to a preferred level in the process of learning from other levels. This second kind of multidisciplinary work is not genuine and does no justice to the unique complexities and merits inherent at each level." (*FPHC*)

• "[My] methodological holism walks a fine line between the artificial classification (separation) of levels and the simultaneous incorporation of them, if only for the sake of human scholarly endeavor. It should be reminded that nature does not impose upon itself the academic classification of the levels of analysis as humans have. The enterprise of classification is therefore anthropocentric." (*FPHC*)

(continued on next page)

Table 1.6. Sophisticated Methodological Holism (Part III)

• "[M]y methodological holism advocates neither epistemic subjectivism nor epistemic non-subjectivism (e.g., realism, idealism, and historicism), neither epistemic relativism (e.g., subjectivism, historicism) nor epistemic absolutism (e.g., realism, positivism), neither epistemic reductionism nor epistemic emergencism, and neither epistemic objectivism (e.g., realism, idealism) nor epistemic historicism....Neither does methodological holism, in my usage, accept the false meta-conceptual dichotomy between nominalism and realism....These false dichotomies...are to be transcended. In other words, methodological holism does not fully accept epistemic realism, positivism (a form of epistemic idealism), historicism, subjectivism, and reductionism in epistemology and philosophy of science but learns from the strengths and weaknesses of all of the opposing approaches without siding with any of them...." (*FPHC*)

• "Sophisticated methodological holism is subject to the constraints as imposed by the syntax of existential dialectics (e.g., the partiality-totality principle and the predictability-unpredictability principle). Even in predictability, outcomes are subject to uncertainty, the degree of which varies from case to case." (*FC*)

Sources: A summary of *Sec.1.2* in *FPHC*—and also from *BNN*, *FPHST*, *ALD*, and *FC*. See the books for more detail.

Table 1.7. On Reductionism and Reverse-Reductionism (Part I)

• **The Partiality-Totality Principle**

—The partiality-totality principle in the ontology of existential dialectics targets against the varieties of reductionism and reverse-reductionism (as already worked out in my previous books).

• **Against the Varieties of Reductionism**

—*Methodological Reductionism*

- A good instance concerns the debate between different versions of qualitative and quantitative methods (as already analyzed in *FC* and also *FHC*).

—*Ontological Reductionism*

- An excellent example is the debate between emergentism and reductionism in complexity theory and also in psychology (as elaborated in *FPHC*, in the context of Being and Becoming).

—*Conceptual Reductionism*

- Some illustrative instances involve myriad dualities like mind vs. body, self vs. world, democracy vs. non-democracy, and the like (as already addressed in *FHC*, *FPHC*, and *BDPD*, for instance).

—*Theoretical Reductionism*

- A fascinating case study concerns what I originally called "the foundation fallacy" in *FPHST*, in any attempt to naively understand space-time from the physical perspective as the foundation and, consequently, to dangerously dismiss other perspectives.
- In *FAE*, I elaborated further these versions of reductionism in the literature on aesthetics (e.g., form vs. content, representation vs. expression, critics vs. artists, and externalism vs. internalism).
- In *FIA*, I revealed other forms of reductionism in the literature on information architecture (e.g., the constructivist argument).
- And in *FPHU*, I hereafter show the persistent legacy of reductionism, this time, in the literature on anomalous experience (e.g., the obsession with physics, chemistry, and biology for explaining anomalous experience).

(continued on next page)

Table 1.7. On Reductionism and Reverse-Reductionism (Part II)

- **Against the Varieties of Reverse-Reductionism**
  —*Methodological Reverse-Reductionism*
  - There is the "anything-goes" mentality in postmodernism (e.g., doing art without praxis, doing art with praxis, and doing art by sublation), as analyzed in Ch.4 of *FHC*.

  —*Ontological Reverse-Reductionism*
  - There are likewise no privileged ontology, and the door is open for anything in postmodernism (e.g., the equal status of the ontology of Being vs. that of Becoming, as already addressed in Ch.4 of *FHC*—and also in *FPHC)*.

  —*Conceptual* Reverse-Reductionism
  - Any concept of "art" (e.g., fine art, cave art, outsider art, junk art) is deemed acceptable in postmodernism (as already addressed in Ch.4 of *FHC*).

  —*Theoretical Reverse-Reductionism*
  - There are a plurality of art and literary theories (e.g., New Criticism, Romanticism, Expressionism, Feminist Art Theory) in the postmodern scene, with no one being said to be better than any others (as also addressed in Ch.4 of *FHC*). In *BNN*, I introduced "the compromise fallacy" as another good example of theoretical reverse- reductionism, in misleadingly treating the genetic and environmental approaches as equally valid.

Sources: A summary of my previous books, especially though not exclusively *FHC*, *FCD*, *FPHC*, *BDPD*, *BCPC*, *BNN*, *FPHST*, *BCIV*, *FC*, *FAE*, *ALD*, *FIA*, and *FPHU*

• PART TWO •

The Mind

CHAPTER 2
UNCONSCIOUSNESS AND THE MIND

> [T]he physical nature of our brains limits how we perceive physical reality. Even if our reality is not a construction of our brains, the physical limits of our brains at least bias our perception of reality.
> —Jim Beichler (1998)

The Manipulation of the Mind

The nature of anomalous experience, when examined from the perspective of the mind, especially in the context of both psychology and biology, reveals some fascinating features in the domain of unconsciousness (or broadly speaking, the unconscious mind), which are worthy to be examined hereafter.

The word "unconsciousness," however, should be handled with care at the outset, since it has multiple meanings and can easily become a source of confusion—just as its opposite, "consciousness," has numerous conceptions (which, however, is not to be analyzed in this book, since I already addressed the topic of consciousness in a previous book of mine, titled *The Future of Post-Human Consciousness*, or *FPHC*, to which this book is a logical sequence, so its title *The Future of Post-Human Unconsciousness* is thus suggestive).

For instance, in one simplistic formal definition, "unconsciousness" merely refers to a "loss of consciousness or lack of consciousness," which is "a dramatic alteration of mental state that involves complete or near-complete lack of responsiveness to people and other environmental stimuli. Being in a comatose state or coma is an illustration of unconsciousness. Fainting due to a drop in blood pressure and a decrease of the oxygen supply to the brain is an illustration of a temporary loss of consciousness." (WK 2007a)

Unconsciousness in this sense should not be confused with some "altered states of consciousness" (which can be situated, in different degrees, between total consciousness and total unconsciousness), and good examples include "delirium (when the person is confused and only partially responsive to the environment), normal sleep, hypnosis, and other altered states in which the person responds to stimuli." (WK 2007a)

In another (second) formal definition, "unconsciousness" can be understood in the context of "the psychoanalytic unconscious or cognitive processes (e.g., implicit cognition) that take place outside of awareness." (WK 2007a)

This second definition, unlike the first one, comes closer to the context concerning the delicate relationship between the nature of unconsciousness and the controversial features of anomalous experience (as introduced in *Sec. 1.3*).

Even then, of course, the definitional refinement is still quite broad, since some neuroscientists want to add another (third) formal definition of "unconsciousness" by further narrowing down the study of the unconscious into the domain of "unconcious processes" (say, by way of neuroimaging techniques), instead of the broader "unconscious mind" (say, in terms of its inherent logic). (K. Zipern 2004; WK 2007C)

With this clarification in mind—the analysis of unconsciousness in the context of anomalous experience from the perspective of the mind can be divided into two main sections, namely, (2.2) unconsciousness and psychology and (2.3) unconsciousness and biology, to be discussed hereafter, in that order, and summarized in *Table 6.3*.

Unconsciousness and Psychology

The nature of unconsciousness in relation to anomalous experience can be understood in a distinctive way, when put in the context of psychology.

Two illustrations are in order, namely, in relation to (2.2.1) psychoanalytic theory and (2.2.2) the theory of mind/matter manifestations (which overlaps a bit with the micro-physical level of analysis in Chapter Three)—to be elaborated respectively hereafter.

Psychoanalytic Theory

Sigmund Freud is undoubtedly a major figure in the literature on the nature of unconsciousness in psychoanalysis, even if much of what he said has been subject to serious criticisms of various kinds.

An excellent illustration concerns Freud's idea of the unconscious mind, in that "we are not entirely aware of what we think and often act for reasons that have little to do with our conscious thoughts." (WK 2007b)

Some psychologists like Jacques Van Rillaer argued that "contrary to what most people believe, the unconscious was not discovered by Freud. In 1890, when psychoanalysis was still unheard of, William James, in his monumental treatise on psychology, examined the way Schopenhauer, von Hartmann, Janet,

Binet and others had used the term 'unconscious' and 'subconscious.'" (WK 2007b)

But whether or not Freud is the first to propose the idea of the unconscious mind in the history of psychology is not my concern here.

What is more interesting here, however, concerns the different layers of the human mind, such that some thoughts can occur "below the surface." (WK 2007b)

Dreams and Repression

One good way to access to the unconscious, for Freud (1913), is by way of the study of dreams (in his influential book titled *The Interpretation of Dreams*), or what Freud called the "royal road to the unconscious." (WK 2007b)

A middle layer of the mind can be understood as the "preconscious," as "a layer between conscious and unconscious thought—that which we could access with a little effort." (WK 2007b)

A fascinating feature of the unconscious mind is the mechanism of "repression," in that "people often experience thoughts and feelings that are so painful that they cannot bear them. Such thoughts and feelings—and associated memories—could not...be banished from the mind, but could be banished from consciousness. Thus they come to constitute the unconscious....Moreover,...the process of repression is itself a non-conscious act (in other words, it did not occur through people willing away certain thoughts or feelings). Freud supposed that what people repressed was in part determined by their unconscious. In other words, the unconscious was for Freud both a cause and effect of repression." (WK 2007b)

The study of the unconscious mind has the virtue, so Freud hoped, of "understanding, transforming, and mastering the unconscious, rather than through denying or repressing it," with the ultimate goal of curing (even if not completely) mental illnesses (e.g., neurosis and psychosis). (WK 2007)

Below The Tip of the Mental Iceberg

The relevance of Freud's idea of the unconscious mind can be useful here for the understanding of anomalous experience as a starting point, since Freud figuratively treats the mind as a mental iceberg, on the tip of which the conscious mind (with much of the ego and part of the superego) resides—whereas the unconscious mind lies below the tip of the mental iceberg and consists of a portion of the ego, much of the superego, and all of the id. (EC 2007)

In other words, "[f]or Freud, the unconscious is the storehouse of instinctual desires, needs, and psychic actions"—which can serve as an useful starting point for the study of anomalous experience, be it psychic, transcendental, or else. (WK 2007c)

In this light, part of the dismissive rejection of the existence of anomalous experience by some individuals can be interepreted as an attempt to unconsciously repress socially unacceptable ideas (like the one of anomalous experience, which is not quite accepted in the current scientific community).

Freud, for instance, argued that "the unconscious was a repository for socially unacceptable ideas, wishes or desires, traumatic memories, and painful emotions put out of mind by the mechanism of psychological repression." (WK 2007c)

Thus, in this light, much of the human mind has yet to be fully explored and understood, with the controversial topic of anomalous experience as an excellent example of some alternative states of cognition to be yet thoroughly understood, especially (though not excusively) in the context of the unconscious.

But the reigning scientific ideas of our time are not conducive to the celebration of this controversial topic.

The Shadow of Shallow Scholarship

But Freud's idea of the unconscious mind and its repression has been subject to severe criticisms.

For instance, H. J. Eysenck in *Decline and Fall of the Freudian Empire* (1986) once said that "Freud 'set psychiatry back one hundred years,' consistently mis-diagnosed his patients, [and] fraudulently misrepresented case histories"—and also 'what is true in Freud is not new and what is new in Freud is not true.'" (WK 2007b)

And Mikkel Borch-Jacobsen (2000) was not less lenient in his critique, when he said that "Freud...did not hesitate to build grand theories on...non-existent foundations...he disguised fragments of his self-analysis as 'objective' cases, that he concealed his sources, that he conveniently antedated some of his analyses, that he sometimes attributed to his patients...that he himself made up, that he inflated his therapeutic successes, that he slandered his opponents," and so on. (WK 2007b)

Yet, the idea of the unconscious mind is not dead. After all, some scholars rightfully commented on the Freudian legacy: "Freud has been influential in two related but distinct ways. He simultaneously developed a theory of how the human mind is organized and operates internally, and how human behavior both conditions and results from this particular theoretical understanding." (WK 2007b)

This subtle distinction between the conscious and the unconscious—and their intricated relations—reveals something interesting in the context of an ontological principle in existential dialectics, namely, the openness-hiddenness principle, in that both openness and hiddenness have a major role to play in understanding reality in the world, albeit the analysis of anomalous experience in the context of unconsciousness is used here only as a case study—or better, only as a starting point for the analysis of unconsciousness in relation to anomalous experience.

The Theory of Mind/Matter Manifestations

A related way to understand this linkage between the unconscious mind and anomalous experience concerns the idea of the intangible realm (which overlaps a bit with the micro-physical level of analysis in Chapter Three, as a reminder).

In *The Future of Post-Human Consciousness* (or *FPHC*, in short), I already discussed the importance of the intangible realm to understand anomalous experience: "It is the intangible level, which has been known by different names, for instance, 'quantum holism,' 'implicate order,' 'ontic level,' 'string theory,' and 'vacuum or ZPF physics.' (R.Jahn 2001:451) What is peculiar [here] is that the normal understanding of physical events and processes in the tangible world (all so familiar in our everyday life) does not quite apply to this domain of anomalous experiences. Here, the diffusion of tangible events and processes in everyday world into their intangible counterparts at the micro-physical level (for instance, their information dialogue) remains highly uncertain and far from complete in current understanding." (P. Baofu 2004: 28)

Perhaps an illustration below, in the context of the "modular model of mind/matter manifestations" (or less awkwardly, the theory of mind/matter manifestations) suffices to clarify this point.

The Anomalous and the Intanglible

In an experiment conducted at the Princeton Engineering Anomalies Research laboratory (which was already discussed in *FPHC*), some researchers "proposed a 'Quantum Mechanics of Consciousness' (or more precisely, the 'Modular Model of Mind/Matter Manifestations,' also known as the M5 model) to deal precisely with this anomalous domain. (R.Jahn 2001:448)" (P. Baofu 2004: 29)

In this model, the researchers introduced "a four-part architecture into two domains, the normal and the anomalous. The normal domain includes the interactions between C (consciousness) and T (tangible world), whereas the anomalous one is divided between U (unconsciousness, etc.) and I (intangible world)." (P. Baofu 2004: 29)

In the normal doman, "C includes all the familiar functions of the conscious mind (e.g., perception, cognition, volition) often discussed in the literature of psychology, neuro-physiology, and philosophy of mind. T, for its part, denotes all the events and processes usually discussed in the disciplines of the natural sciences and their technological and medical applications." (P. Baofu 2004: 29)

And in the anomalous domain, "U refers to all mental processes of the unconscious and preconscious, which can be either 'procedural' (e.g., storage of information, autonomic control of physiological functions, instinctive behavior and insight, and preparation for consciousness) or 'dynamic' (e.g., protection from trauma, and experiential overloads)." (P. Baofu 2004: 29)

But the most controversial one certainly concerns the last category, I, which, "not surprisingly, remains the most incomplete, since it is the location where 'the common parameters of substance, energy, and information; space and time; and even mind and matter are undiscriminated....For it is here, at its deepest level, that the common mental and material features surrender their identities to a subliminal indeterminate holism that can be represented only in theoretical abstractions. It is the domain where concept and reality, experience and event, mind and matter become indistinguishable and therefore intrinsically correlated when expressed into the conscious and tangible sectors.' (R.Jahn 2001:451-3)" (P. Baofu 2004: 29-30)

Daunting Shortcomings but Profound Implications

This research at Princeton is not without its shortcomings, however. Consider three instances below.

Firstly, it should be noted that the model classifies the anomalous category in an absolute way, which is a bit differently from the one that I introduced in *Sec.1.3*, in that it does not allow any overlapping of C with the anomalous domain, whereas I allow a part of anomalous experience in C too, while relating it with U and I.

Secondly, its explanation is reductionistic from the perspective of micro-physical analysis, whereas mine here is holistic, incoporating all the domains of knowledge in the social sciences, the humanities, and the natural sciences (as will be clear in the rest of the book).

And thirdly, the model confronts a serious challenge of how to exactly understand the deepest mental layers of the unconcious mind in the intangible realm: "Whether these uncertainties all trace to the quantum uncertainty principle and the essential probabilistic character of quantum wave functions, or whether more systemic sources of dynamical uncertainty, as encountered in the behavior of complex and chaotic systems, are involved is not yet clear."(R.Jahn 2001:454; P. Baofu 2004: 30)

Yet, in spite of these shortcomings, it has profound implications. A good example is none other than some "possible post-hoc applications [which] include the understanding of a broad range of anomalous phenomena like 'clairvoyance, telepathy, precognition, psychic healing, poltergeist phenomena, religious and mystical miracles, and survival of bodily death.' (R.Jahn 2001:456)" (P. Baofu 2004: 30)

Once more, the openness-hiddenness principle is relevant here, in that anomalous experience has both its conscious dimension (which is open to outside view) and its unconscious one, especially (though not exclusively) in relation to the intangible domain here, which is still hidden from outside view.

In addition, another ontological principle, the explicability-inexplicability principle, is useful as well, in that there will remain some uncertainties about the deepest layers of the mind (in the context of anomalous experience) which may well be not clear for a long time to come in any attempt for an adequate explanation, although other aspects will be better explained, however small (as shown in the two case studies above).

Unconsciousness and Biology

There is another perspective, however, this time, in relation to biology, when the issue of anomalous experience in the context of unconsciousness is examined.

Four good case studies can be given here, namely, in the context of (2.3.1) biochemical theory, (2.3.2) neurobiological theory, (2.3.3) biogravitational theory, and (2.3.4) neurophysiological theory, to be analyzed hereafter, in that order.

Biochemical Theory

A good illustration of the relevance of biochemical theory to the study of anomalous experience is by way of the exemplary analysis of "near-death experience" (NDE).

A Research on DMT

One definition of NDE refers "to a broad range of personal experiences associated with impending death, encompassing multiple possible sensations ranging from detachment from the body, feelings of levitation, extreme fear, security, or warmth, the experience of absolute dissolution, and the presence of a light, which some people interpret as their deity or some similar religious concept." (WK 2007d)

With this definition in mind, Dr. Rick Strassman at the University of New Mexico carried out a research on the psychedelic drug Dimethyltryptamine (DMT), whose findings were published in his 2001 book titled *DMT: The Spirit*

Molecule: A Doctor's Revolutionary Research into the Biology of Near-Death and Mystical Experiences.

In this research, "Strassman advanced the theory that a massive release of DMT from the pineal gland prior to death or near-death was the cause of the near-death experience phenomenon. Only two of his test subjects reported NDE-like aural or visual hallucinations, although many reported feeling as though they had entered a state similar to the classical NDE." (WK 2007d)

But what then is the explanation of this slight difference in research outcome?

Strassman's explanation is that it has much to do with "the possible lack of panic involved in the clinical setting and possible dosage differences between those administered and those encountered in actual NDE cases. All subjects in the study were also very experienced users of DMT and/or other psychedelic/entheogenic agents. Some speculators consider that, if subjects without prior knowledge on the effects of DMT had been used during the experiment, it is possible more volunteers would have reported feeling as though they had experienced an NDE." (WK 2007d)

Critique and Response

But the critics are not completely convinced.

For instance, some scientists argue that "neurobiological models often fail to explain NDEs that result from close brushes with death, where the brain does not actually suffer physical trauma, such as a near-miss automobile accident. Such events may however have neurobiological effects caused by stress." (WK 2007d)

This critique, however, led some scientists to come up with a different way to test NDE.

As an illustration, in 2006, Richard Kinseher suggested instead that "the knowledge of the Sensory Autonomic System is applied in the NDE phenomenon. His theory states that the experience of looming death is an extremely strange paradox to a living organism—and therefore it will start the NDE." (WK 2007d)

During the NDE, "the individual becomes capable of 'seeing' the brain performing a scan of the whole episodic memory (even prenatal experiences), in order to find a stored experience which is comparable to the input information of death. All these scanned and retrieved bits of information are permanently evaluated by the actual mind, as it is searching for a coping mechanism out of the potentially fatal situation. Kinseher feels this is the reason why a near-death experience is so unusual." (WK 2007d)

In this sense, "out-of-body experiences, accompanied with NDEs, are an attempt by the brain to create a mental overview of the situation and the surrounding world. The brain then transforms the input from sense organs and stored experience (knowledge) into a dream-like idea about oneself and the surrounding area." (WK 2007d)

While one cannot rule out that "these experiences are hallucinatory, they do have a profound impact on the observer. Many psychologists not necessarily pursuing the paranormal, such as Susan Blackmore, have recognized this. These scientists are not trying to debunk the experience, so much so as searching for biological reasons that cause an NDE." (wk 2007D)

For instance, Prof. Kevin Nelson at the University of Kentucky even followed up with another (comparable) study, published in *Neurology* (2006), the journal of the American Academy of Neurology, and argued that NDE can be a biological experience, since "[p]eople who have had near-death experiences are able to slip into dream sleep more easily than those who have not had one." (R. Highfield 2006)

Biochemical explanation like this, when related to neurobiological one, is even more fascinating in analysis. Consider the case study below.

Neurobiological Theory

Some scholars choose a comparable (though also different) path instead and in the process make use of neurobiological theory for the explanation of anomalous experience.

A good illustration concerns the study of NDE (and other forms of anomalous experience)—but in a way different from the focus on biochemical theory as already discussed above (although the two are also related at the biological level).

Parietal Lobe and the Use of SPECT

Neurobiological theory, unlike biochemical theory, has a different focus, in "discovering, in short, what happens in our brains when we sense that we 'have encountered a reality different from—and, in some crucial sense, higher than—the reality of everyday experience,' as psychologist David Wulff of Wheaton College in Massachusetts puts it." (S. Begley 2001)

A way to conduct neurobiological experiment for the testing of anomalous experience is by way of scanning the brain with the use of SPECT (single photon emission computed tomography).

In *Why God Won't Go Away* (2001), Dr. Andrew Newberg of the University of Pennsylvania and Eugene d'Aquili described their findings on the biology of non-ordinary beliefs with the use of brain-imaging technology.

As an illustration, an experiment participant, Dr. Michael J. Baime, a colleague of Andrew Newberg's at Penn, was asked to sit "onto the floor of a small darkened room, lit only by a few candles and filled with jasmine incense. A string of twine lay beside him. Concentrating on a mental image, he focused and focused, quieting his conscious mind...until something he identifies as his true inner self emerged. It felt 'timeless and infinite,' Baime said afterward, 'a part of everyone and everything in existence.' When he reached the 'peak' of spiritual intensity, he tugged on the twine. Newberg, huddled outside the room and holding the other end, felt the pull and quickly injected a radioactive tracer into an IV line that ran into Baime's left arm. After a few moments, he whisked Baime off to a SPECT (single photon emission computed tomography) machine. By detecting the tracer, it tracks blood flow in the brain. Blood flow correlates with neuronal activity." (S. Begley 2001)

The SPECT images showed something interesting, in that "the prefrontal cortex, seat of attention, lit up: Baime, after all, was focusing deeply. But it was a quieting of activity that stood out. A bundle of neurons in the superior parietal lobe, toward the top and back of the brain, had gone dark. This region, nicknamed the 'orientation association area,' processes information about space and time, and the orientation of the body in space. It determines where the body ends and the rest of the world begins. Specifically, the left orientation area creates the sensation of a physically delimited body; the right orientation area creates the sense of the physical space in which the body exists. (An injury to this area can so cripple your ability to maneuver in physical space that you cannot figure the distance and angles needed to navigate the route to a chair across the room.)" (S. Begley 2001)

What is crucial here is that the "orientation area requires sensory input to do its calculus. 'If you block sensory inputs to this region, as you do during the intense concentration of meditation, you prevent the brain from forming the distinction between self and not-self,' says Newberg. With no information from the senses arriving, the left orientation area cannot find any boundary between the self and the world. As a result, the brain seems to have no choice but...to perceive the self as endless and intimately interwoven with everyone and everything'....The meditators feel that they have touched infinity." (S. Begley 2001)

Another experiment participant, Sister Celeste, a Franciscan nun, encountered similar experience, in that, "when she felt a palpable sense of God's presence and an absorption of her self into his being, her brain displayed changes like those in the Tibetan Buddhist meditators: her orientation area went dark. What Sister Celeste and the other nuns in the study felt, and what the meditators experienced, Newberg emphasizes, 'were neither mistakes nor wishful thinking. They reflect real, biologically based events in the brain.' The fact that spiritual contemplation affects brain activity gives the experience a reality that psychologists and neuroscientists had long denied it, and explains why people experience ineffable, transcendent events as equally real as seeing a wondrous sunset or stubbing their toes." (S. Begley 2001)

The Use and Misuse of Interpretation

But what does SPECT really show in the experiment?

Dr. Newberg himself was quick to caution the public that "[t]he fact that spiritual experiences can be associated with distinct neural activity does not necessarily mean that such experiences are mere neurological illusions. It's no safer to say that spiritual urges and sensations are caused by brain activity than it is to say that the neurological changes through which we experience the pleasure of eating an apple cause the apple to exist." (S. Begley 2001)

So, "[t]he bottom line, he says, is that 'there is no way to determine whether the neurological changes associated with spiritual experience mean that the brain is causing those experiences...or is instead perceiving a spiritual reality.'" (S. Begley 2001)

But then, once more, the openness-hiddenness principle and the explicability-inexplicability in existential dialectics are relevant here, in that certain aspects of reality concerning anomalous experience can be open to view (like the SPECT images) but other parts remain hidden (like the existence of the higher entity)—just as certain parts of reality (like the neurological changes) can be explained, whereas others (like the deeper nature of spiritual reality) remain to be further explored and understood.

Biogravitational Theory

But biochemical theory and neurobiological theory (as introduced in the previous two sub-sections) are only a start. Other scholars have put their hands in different fields.

A good candidate is the use of biogravitational theory for the explanation of anomalous experience. (J. Beichler 1998)

Field-Energy System

For instance, Alexander P. Dubrov (1977) proposed a "field-energy system," which "could be transformed into any type of field or energy, a feature which he developed as the cornerstone of unified field theory of the future. This field was thought to exist in all living beings, but especially in humans. It was called biogravitational because its properties are akin to both living organisms and gravitation. Dubrov suspected the field played a role in such biological processes as cell mitosis as well as physical processes such as gravitational waves. Between these two extremes came biological effects of the whole organism such as 'psi photography and levitation.'" (J. Beichler 1998)

Dubrov then specified the biological and gravitational properties in biogravity, in that "(a) they must act at close or long range; (b) they can be directed and focused; (c) they can be positive or negative (and cause attraction or repulsion, respectively); (d) they can carry information; (e) they are able to convert the energy of the field into matter with weight; (f) a field of such forces can persist in the absence of the source which originally gave rise to them; (g) they can undergo transition into any form of field and energy; and (h) they are closely bound up with change of symmetry groups and with distortion of space at the submolecular level of biological structures." (J. Beichler 1998)

Needless to stress, Dubrov's theory is too hypothetical, to the point that the critics are quick to point out that "biogravitation is a quantity which was invented merely to describe psi and other paranormal phenomena. It is always dangerous to invent hypothetical quantities to explain hypothetical circumstances." (J. Beichler 1998)

W. P. Zinchenko (1978) and others rightly observed that Dubrov's theory "is the product of 'representatives of the exact sciences—engineers, mathematicians and physicists' in the Eastern block countries who entered the field of parapsychology during the late 1960's without any special training in parapsychology. As a biophysicist, Dubrov had some qualifications to develop such a theory, but claims such as levitation are quite beyond the norm in parapsychology." (J. Beichler 1998)

C. Chari (1977) was more specific when he added that "such theories 'seem to be cast in a holistic framework (the anomalous effect shows not in the individual living cells, but in the organism as a whole) and remain obscure for even the limited purposes of experimental testing and replication.' In other words, it is quite unlikely that Dubrov's biogravitational theory can be confirmed." (J. Beichler 1998)

Hyperspace and Psi Phenomena

Yet, this failure does not prevent other scholars from proposing some improved new theories for the explanation of anomalous experience.

Consider, say, the work of Bob Toben (1975) and Alan Wolf.

Toben and Wolf linked the study of anomalous experience with the phenomenon of hyperspace, in that "consciousness is hyperspatial, beyond normal space-time, while normal space-time follows the physical model presented in general relativity. The four-dimensional space-time continuum is itself constructed of a quantum foam which is linked to consciousness via gravity (curvature in a higher dimension) while gravity is the 'master field.'" (J. Beichler 1998)

So, "[v]ibrations of thought patterns in specific harmonics structure all 'matter' and light as we experience it," and "the human mind acts as a 'filter' which focuses our thoughts on specific physical events." (B. Toben 1975; J. Beichler 1998)

In this context, anomalous experience can be explained in terms of biogravity: "Psychokinesis is an effect of consciousness influencing energy/matter fields, while ESP or telepathy occurs when signals travel through 'wormholes' in 'the sea of space.' Living beings generate 'biogravitational' fields which allows them to manipulate space-time curvature to various ends. It is through this manipulation, carried out by consciousness, that other paranormal and psi phenomena are manifested. Therefore, the higher a being's consciousness, the better the being can utilize consciousness to affect psi." (J. Beichler 1998; B. Toben 1975)

Jack Sarfatti, whose visionary physics influenced Toben's work, suggested that "[t]elepathy can be understood as messages traveling through biogravitational wormholes of space-time within a given universe. The wormhole connections constitute only one possibility for a cosmic 'telephone' network. In addition, the 'feeling' or tachyonic model of gravitation that breaks through the wall of light also accounts for telepathic communication. In either case, the strength of telepathic communication should not be affected by distance." (J. Beichler 1998)

Pseudo-Science or Visionary Thought

Like Dubrov's theory—the theories by Sarfatti, Toben, and Wolf raise more questions than answers. Hereafter are four criticisms.

Firstly, they also made use of hypothetical entities for their explanation. For instance, "Sarfatti has…suggested a…method of telepathic communication based on the hypothetical existence of tachyons. Such an uncertainty of explanation…renders this 'theory' as tentative. His explanation of other psi phenomena is no more enlightening." (J. Beichler 1998)

Secondly, "no real quantitative information is given regarding either the biogravitational field [as in the work by Toben and Wolf] or how it is capable of manipulating space-time curvature. The same is true with Sarfatti's explanation of psychokinesis." (J. Beichler 1998)

Thirdly, nor is there any underlying mechanism provided in their explanation. For example, as some critics correctly remarked, "[i]f consciousness controls the biogravitational field and if there is a significant coupling of biogravitation to ordinary gravitation, then there is a direct contribution of consciousness to the quantum potential. No real mechanisms or physical processes have been offered to support this theory." (J. Beichler 1998)

And lastly, they all try to "represent…too many things to too many people." (J. Beichler 1998)

In the case of Toben and Wolf, "[w]hile the theory is all encompassing and broad enough to cover all sorts of paranormal phenomena, it does more to fit all types of claimed phenomena to speculations and theories in modern physics than to explain psi works. It is too general and not specific enough. In one sense, it is necessary to relate Toben's theory to other purely physical theories since any theory of psi must ultimately prove compatible with accepted laws of nature and the theories that express these laws, but in another sense it is bad. While Toben and Wolf's theory seems to be a unified theory of the four fundamental forces (or interactions) of physics, it also appears to be more of a philosophical argument derived from relating seemingly unrelated worldviews and physical theories to each other." (J. Beichler 1998)

And in the case of Sarfatti, his theory "draws analogies to everything from Eddington's fundamental theory to Bohm's holographic universe. These are vastly different theories which have never proven to be compatible. This in itself is not bad, but he draws analogies to these other theories without specifically showing how they interact with each other or relate to Toben's model." (J. Beichler 1998)

All these criticisms notwithstanding—there is something fascinating about this new way of understanding anomalous experience, in that, even for the critics, "it offers important hints and clues for future theorists and demonstrates various ways in which psi could be explained using existing physical theories." (J. Beichler 1998)

In this sense, the ontological principle in existential dialectics, like the openness-hiddenness principle, is rather revealing, in that anomalous reality can be both hidden from view (because of its deeper link with hyperspace in different dimensions of space-time, other than the ordinary four dimensions that we so much get used to) and open to it (because of its conscious dimension for those who personally encounter anomalous reality).

By the same logic, the explicability-inexplicability principle can be relevant here to, in that, while certain reality can be readily explained (through the use of different physical theories already known like the curvature of space in Einstein's theory of relativity), other part are yet to be explained for a long way to come (like the challenges confronting Toben, Wolf, and Sarfatti on biogravity).

Neurophysiological Theory

A different approach, besides the ones afore-discussed (viz., biochemical theory, neurobiological theory, and biogravitational theory) is the use of neurophysiological theory.

Transcendent Experience and Temporal Lobe Epilepsy

A good illustration involves a well-researched subject area concerning the mental illness of "temporal lobe epilepsy" and anomalous experience.

For instance, Clifford Pickover (1999) in his study showed that "temporal lobe epilepsy has often been linked to a variety of transcendent experiences: ecstatic communion with the divine, epiphanies of artistic creation, fearful encounters with alien beings."

To start, temporal lobe epilepsy (or TLE, for short) "is caused by unusual electrical activity in the brain's temporal lobes A significant proportion of people with TLE report that their seizures often bring on extraordinary experiences of transcendent wonder, luminous insight—or, at times, harrowing, uncanny fear." (C. Pickover 1999)

A good instance related to anomalous experience concerns "alien abduction." As Pickover (1999) told us, "TLE researcher Eve LaPlante [1993] has noted that many abductees feel mild, epileptic-like symptoms just before they are 'captured.' Some abductees feel heat on one side of their faces, hear a ringing in their ears, and see flashes of light prior to an abduction. Others report a cessation of sound and feeling, or an overwhelming feeling of apprehension. All of this is typical of certain kinds of epileptic seizures. In fact, LaPlante suggests that the most famous abductee of our time, best-selling author Whitley Strieber, suffers from TLE."

W. Strieber (1987) in the book *Communion* even "described his abduction by 3 1/2 foot aliens with two dark holes for eyes. In his account, Strieber exhibits various symptoms of TLE: *jamais vu* (the feeling of never having been in what should be a familiar place—the opposite of *deja vu*); formication (feeling bugs crawling under the skin); vivid smells, hallucinations, rapid heartbeats, the sensation of rising and falling, and partial amnesia. Magnetic resonance imaging of Strieber's brain has revealed 'occasional punctate foci of high signal intensity' in his left temporoparietal region, which is suggestive of scarring that could lead to TLE." (C. Pickover 1999)

The Search for Explanation

But does this neurophysiological account, if true, explain the problem away, in that anomalous experience may well be the result of certain mental illness in an individual?

Perhaps, a comment by William James long ago can be useful here, in that anomalous experiences "are not less profound simply because they can be induced by mental anomalies." (C. Pickover 1999)

James first stated correctly that, in certain forms of mystical religious experience, "religious leaders have been subject to abnormal psychical visitations. Invariably they have been creatures of exalted emotional sensitivity liable to obsessions and fixed ideas; and frequently they have fallen into trances, heard voices, seen visions, and presented all sorts of peculiarities which are ordinarily classed as pathological." (C. Pickover 1999)

But in the end, his essential point is that "[t]o plead the organic causation of a religious state of mind in refutation of its claim to possess superior spiritual value is quite illogical and arbitrary. [Because if that were the case], none of our thoughts and feelings, not even our scientific doctrines, not even our disbeliefs, could retain any value as revelations of the truth, for every one of them without exception flows from the state of the possessor's body at the time. Saint Paul certainly once had an epileptoid, if not an epileptic, seizure, but there is not a single one of our states of mind, high or low, healthy or morbid, that has not some organic processes as its condition." (C. Pickover 1999)

Michael Persinger was more direct, in pinpointing the source of this mental illness (in relation to anomalous experience) in the form of "altered electrical activity in the brain." (C. Pickover 1999)

In this sense, mystical religious experience "is sometimes our interpretation of altered temporolimbic electrical activity. This is not to demean the mystical experience, because TLE personalities have obviously accomplished great things, whose depth and meaning have radiated far beyond the electric storms of a single cranium." (C. Pickover 1999)

But this is only to reveal, once again, two ontological principles in existential dialectics, namely, the openness-hiddenness principle and the explicability-inexplicability principle in action.

In relation to the openness-hiddenness principle, anomalous experience can be revealed in some way (e.g., the linkage to TLE) but hidden in another way (e.g., the deeper nature of the anomalous experience itself).

And in relation to the explicability-inexplicability principle, some portion of the anomalous experience can be explained in terms of an underlying neurophysiological process (e.g., the altered electrical activity in the brain) but remains mysterious in another way (e.g., a non-reductionistic explanation of the mystical religious experience in question).

The Consumptiveness of the Mind

The mind, when examined from the fields of both psychology and biology, in the context of anomalous experience, especially though not exclusively in relation to the domain of unconsciousness, shows how much its inner nature reveals to outside view in some aspects but remain hidden in others—just as some aspects of its inner nature can be explained, while others await further exploration.

This has deeper implicatons for the understanding of ontological principles in existential dialectics, especially though not exclusively in relation to the openness-hiddenness principle and the explicability-inexplicability principle.

In the meantime, the phenomenon of anomalous experience refuses to go away, and the mind, at least for those who claim to know it first-hand, continues to be consumed by the fascinating aspects of paranormal encounter—even if, for the critics, anomalous experience may well reflect the manipulativeness of the mind, as a form of mental illusions.

But the perspective of the mind is only one dimension to analyze the nature of anomalous experience in the context of unconsciousness. Other ones (like the ones in relation to nature, society, and culture) need to be addressed.

With this in mind, let's now turn to Chapter Three on unconsciousness and nature, in regard to anomalous experience.

Table 2.1. The Conceptual Dimensions of Consciousness (and Other Mental States)

- **On Heredity and Time**
  —Heredity and the Environment
  —The Past and the Present

- **On Layers of Mental States and Abnormality**
  —Consciousness, Unconsciousness, and Preconsciousness
  —Normality and Paranormality

- **On Organicity and Motivation**
  —Mechanicity and Organicity
  —Primary Motivations and Multiple Motivations

- **On Other (Mostly Epistemic) Considerations**
  —Synthesis and Analysis
  —Situation and the Subject
  —Process and Outcome
  —Reasoning and Other Modes of Thinking
  —Meta-Conceptual Nominalism and Realism

Notes:: These examples are solely illustrative (not exhaustive), and some of the items can be reclassified somewhere else. Nor are they always mutually exclusive. Since they are generalities, exceptions are expected.
Sources: From *FPHC*. A re-construction, but with my own contribution, originally from G.Lindzey & C.Hall, *Introduction to Theories of Personality* (NY: John Wiley & Sons, 1985).

Table 2.2. The Theoretical Levels of Consciousness (and Other Mental States) (Part I)

- **At the Micro-Physical Theoretical Level**
  —Quantum-Mechanics
  —Electromagnetism

- **At the Chemical Theoretical Level**
  —Biochemistry

- **At the Biological Theoretical Level**
  —Evolutionary Biology
  —Neuroscience
  —Artificial Intelligence

- **At the Psychological Theoretical Level**
  —Psychodynamic Psychology
    - Psychoanalytical Psychology
    - Analytical Psychology
    - Socially Oriented Psychology

  —Experimental (Behavioral) Psychology
    - Operant Reinforcement Theory
    - Stimulus-Response Theory
    - Social Learning Theory

  —Cognitive (Gestalt) Psychology
    - Humanist Psychology
    - Existential Psychology
    - Field Theory

  —Psychometric Psychology
    - Idiographics
    - Constitutional Psychology

  —Social Psychology
    - Symbolic Interactive Theory
    - Social Exchange Theory

(continued on next page)

Table 2.2. The Theoretical Levels of Consciousness (and Other Mental States) (Part II)

- **At the Organizational Theoretical Level**
  - —Managerial-Bureaucratic Theory
  - —Oligarchic Theory
  - —Network Theory

- **At the Institutional Theoretical Level**
  - —Functionalist Theory
  - —Anomic Theory

- **At the Structural Theoretical Level**
  - —Conflict Theory
    - Marxian Theory
    - Critical Theory
    - Weberian Theory
  - —Games Theory (in Formal Theory)
  - —Feminist Theory
    - Feminist Concerns
    - Feminist Hopes

- **At the Systemic Theoretical Level**
  - —Equilibrium Theory
  - —System Theory
  - —Chaos Theory

- **At the Cosmological Theoretical Level**
  - —Superluminal Model
  - —The Theory of Floating Consciousness

(continued on next page)

Table 2.2. The Theoretical Levels of Consciousness (and Other Mental States) (Part III)

- **At the Cultural Theoretical Level**
  —Substantive Theories
    - Structuralist Theory
    - Post-Structuralist Theory (in Postmodernism)

  —Meta-Theories
    - Epistemic Objectivism vs. Epistemic Historicism
    - Epistemic Subjectivism vs. Epistemic Non-Subjectivism
      –Phenomenology
      –Ethnomethodology
      –Hermeneutics
    - Epistemic Relativism vs. Epistemic Absolutism
    - Epistemic Reductionism vs. Epistemic Emergencism

- **At Other Levels**
  —Structuration Theory
  —Reflexive Socioanalysis

Notes: These examples are solely illustrative (not exhaustive), and some of the items can be reclassified somewhere else. Nor are they always mutually exclusive. Since they are generalities, exceptions are expected.
Source: From many different sources as indicated in *FPHC*.

Table 2.3. The Thematic Issues of Consciousness (and Other Mental States)

- **The Factor of History**
  —Pre-Modernity
  —Modernity
  —Postmodernity
  —After-Postmodernity

- **The Importance of Needs**
  —Having (e.g., the everyday, the technological)
  —Belonging (e.g., the just and the good)
  —Being (e.g., the true, the holy, the sublime/beautiful, and the good)

Notes: These examples are solely illustrative (not exhaustive). Nor are they always mutually exclusive. Since they are generalities, exceptions are expected. Also, some categories overlap with others; for instance, the good is also related with being-ness, just as the everyday can be connected with belong-ness.
Sources: From *FPHC*, based on *FHC* and *FCD*.

Table 2.4. Having, Belonging, and Being in Consciousness

- **Having (e.g., About the Everyday and Technological)**
  —Ex: Physiological needs (e.g., thirst, hunger, sex)
  —Ex: Safety (e.g., stability, freedom from fear and anxiety)

- **Belonging (e.g., About the Good and Just)**
  —Ex: Social interaction
  —Ex: Friendship, acquaintance
  —Ex: Love, family
  —Ex: Self-respect, respect from others

- **Being (e.g., About the True, Holy, Beautiful/Sublime, and Good)**
  —Ex: Understanding of reality about self and world
  —Ex: Spiritual quest for holiness, beauty, sublimity, and goodness

Notes: These examples are solely illustrative (not exhaustive), and some of the items can be reclassified somewhere else. Nor are they always mutually exclusive. Since they are generalities, exceptions are expected.
Sources: From *FPHC*, based on *FHC* and *FCD*

Table 2.5. The Having-Ness of Consciousness (and Other Mental States)

- **At the Micro-Physical Level**
  —Ex: The finer physics of nutrition

- **At the Chemical Level**
  —Ex: Food guide pyramid

- **At the Bio-Psychological Level**
  —Ex: The hierarchy of needs

- **At the Institutional Level**
  —Ex: The production of commodity fetishism

- **At the Organizational Level**
  —Ex: Mass standardization (and customization); bureaucratic rationality

- **At the Structural Level**
  —Ex: The divide between the haves and the have-nots

- **At the Cultural Level**
  —Ex: The bondage of greater expectations

- **At the Systemic Level**
  —Ex: The technological transformation of poverty with transvaluations

- **At the Cosmological Level**
  —Ex: Floating consciousness in deep space without the human physiological needs

Notes: These examples are solely illustrative (not exhaustive), and some of the items can be reclassified somewhere else. Nor are they always mutually exclusive. Since they are generalities, exceptions are expected.
Sources: From *FPHC*. See also *FCD* and *FHC*.

Table 2.6. The Belonging-Ness of Consciousness (and Other Mental States)

- **At the Micro-Physical Level**
  —Ex: Statistical physics and social networks

- **At the Chemical Level**
  —Ex: Olfaction and social relations

- **At the Bio-Psychological Level**
  —Ex: Dual human nature on relationships

- **At the Institutional Level**
  —Ex: Private property and social cleavage

- **At the Organizational Level**
  —Ex: Legal formalism and iron cage

- **At the Structural Level**
  —Ex: Class conflicts and social alienation

- **At the Cultural Level**
  —Ex: Ruthless society and the culture of law

- **At the Systemic Level**
  —Ex: Human extinction and post-human relations

- **At the Cosmological Level**
  —Ex: The transcendence of equality in the cosmos and beyond

Notes: These examples are solely illustrative (not exhaustive), and some of the items can be reclassified somewhere else. Nor are they always mutually exclusive. Since they are generalities, exceptions are expected.
Sources: From *FPHC*. See also *FCD* and *FHC*.

Table 2.7. The Being-Ness of Consciousness (and Other Mental States)

- **At the Micro-Physical Level**
  —Ex: Space-time and matter-energy in classical mechanics, quantum mechanics, and the theory of relativity

- **At the Chemical Level**
  —Ex: Drugs and well being

- **At the Biological Level**
  —Ex: Neuroscience and mystical experiences

- **At the Psychological Level**
  —Ex: Reductionism and emergencism

- **At the Institutional Level**
  —Ex: The proliferation of cults and sects, and the corporate-art industry

- **At the Organizational Level**
  —Ex: The organization of ideas in the scheme of things

- **At the Structural Level**
  —Ex: Disciplinary power and control in the order of things

- **At the Systemic Level**
  —Ex: Mutualism and ecological psychology

- **At the Cultural Level**
  —Ex: The recurrence of competing spirits, and floating consciousness as a climax of evolution

- **At the Cosmological Level**
  —Ex: The search for elsewhere when, and the evolution of other consciousnesses (e.g., the hyper-spatial consciousness)

Notes: These examples are solely illustrative (not exhaustive), and some of the items can be reclassified somewhere else. Nor are they always mutually exclusive. Since they are generalities, exceptions are expected.
Sources: From *FPHC*. See also *FCD* and *FHC*.

Table 2.8. Cognitive Partiality in Different Mental States

- **The Conscious**
  - —*Biased*
    - Ex: Self-overratingness
    - Ex: Self-modesty
    - Ex: Self-fulfilling prophesy
  - —*Shallow*
    - Ex: Attribution error
    - Ex: Heuristics
    - Ex: Illusory thinking
  - —*Short-term*
    - Ex: Deindividuation
  - —*Materialistic*
    - Ex: Hierarchy of needs

- **The Subconscious**
  - Ex: mental reconstruction
  - Ex: stereotyping

- **The Unconscious**
  - Ex: automatic processing
  - Ex: cognitive intuition

Notes: These examples are solely illustrative (not exhaustive), and some of the items can be reclassified somewhere else. Nor are they always mutually exclusive. Since they are generalities, exceptions are expected. And the comparison is relative, not absolute.
Source: From *BCPC*

Table 2.9. Emotional Non-Neutrality and Behavioral Alteration in Different Mental States

- **The Emotional**
  - —*Conscious*
    - Ex: Feelings
  - —*Subconscious*
    - Ex: Moods
  - —*Unconscious*
    - Ex: Empathy
    - Ex: Instincts

- **The Behavioral**
  - —*Conscious*
    - Ex: Foot-in-the-door
    - Ex: Role playing
    - Ex: Saying-is-believing
  - —*Subconscious*
    - Ex: Discrimination
  - —*Unconscious*
    - Ex: Non-Verbal Communication

Notes: These examples are solely illustrative (not exhaustive), and some of the items can be reclassified somewhere else. Nor are they always mutually exclusive. Since they are generalities, exceptions are expected. And the comparison is relative, not absolute.
Source: From *BCPC*

Table 2.10. The Limits of Intuition in Unconsciousness

- **Cognitive Intuition (or Intuitive Thinking)**
  —*Features*
    Ex: mental schemas
    Ex: expertise
    Ex: blindsight
  —*Problems*
    Ex: inaccurate
    Ex: non-explanatory

- **Emotional Intuition**
  —*Features*
    Ex: empathy
    Ex: instincts
  —*Problems*
    Ex: over-generalized
    Ex: non-explanatory

- **Behavioral Intuition**
  —*Features*
    Ex: prosemics
    Ex: kinesics
  —*Problems*
    Ex: unreliable
    Ex: non-explanatory

Notes: These examples are solely illustrative (not exhaustive), and some of the items can be reclassified somewhere else. Nor are they always mutually exclusive. Since they are generalities, exceptions are expected. And the comparison is relative, not absolute.
Source: From *BCPC*

Table 2.11. The Wealth/Poverty Dialectics in Different Mental States: The Case of Cognition

- **The Conscious**
  - —*Biased*
    - Ex: If richer in self-serving bias, then poorer in understanding others
  - —*Shallow*
    - Ex: If richer in heuristic thinking, then poorer in comprehending reality
  - —*Short-term*
    - Ex: If richer in short-term tendency, then poorer in long-term planning
  - —*Materialistic*
    - Ex: If richer in physiological obsession, then poorer in spiritual enlightenment

- **The Subconscious**
  - Ex: If richer in mental reconstruction, then poorer in accuracy of recall
  - Ex: If richer in stereotyping, then poorer in understanding groups

- **The Unconscious**
  - Ex: If richer in automatic processing, then poorer in depth of analysis
  - Ex: If richer in cognitive intuition, then poorer in reliability of judgments

Notes: These examples are solely illustrative (not exhaustive), and some of the items can be reclassified somewhere else. Nor are they always mutually exclusive. Since they are generalities, exceptions are expected. And the comparison is relative, not absolute.
Source: From *BCPC*

Table 2.12. The Wealth/Poverty Dialectics in Different Mental States: The Case of Emotion and Behavior

---

- **Emotion**
  - —*Conscious*
    - Ex: If richer in relying on familiarity and similarity for social attraction, then poorer in having diverse social relations
  - —*Subconscious*
    - Ex: If richer in moodiness, then poorer in sober thinking
  - —*Unconscious*
    - Ex: If richer in empathy, then poorer in task-oriented efficiency
    - Ex: If richer in instincts, then poorer in critical thinking

- **Behavior**
  - —*Conscious*
    - Ex: If richer in foot-in-the-door technique, then poorer in instant gratification
    - Ex: If richer in role playing, then poorer in identity stability
  - —*Subconscious*
    - Ex: If richer in discriminating, then poorer in social harmony
  - —*Unconscious*
    - Ex: If richer in kinesics and proxemics, then poorer in verbal skills, relatively speaking.

Notes: These examples are solely illustrative (not exhaustive), and some of the items can be reclassified somewhere else. Nor are they always mutually exclusive. Since they are generalities, exceptions are expected. And the comparison is relative, not absolute.

Source: From *BCPC*

Table 2.13. The Theoretical Debate on Nature vs. Nurture (Part I)

• **The Environmental Approach**

—*Thesis*: It focuses, relatively speaking, more on the environment (culture and society) in explaining the achievement gap among individuals and for that matter, countries or regions, when contrasted with the natural factors.

—*Discourse*: Examples include Jose Ortega y Gasset ("Man has no nature; what he has is history"), Ashley Montagu ("Man is man because he has no instincts, because everything he is and has become he has learned from his culture, from the man-made part of the environment, from other human beings"), Stephen Jay Gould ("[The] brain [is] capable of a full range of behaviors and predisposed to none"), and Jesse Jackson (who blames white racism for the failure of blacks to close the achievement gap between whites and blacks in America). The works on dependency theory in international political economy (with a Marxian influence) and on the Protestant work ethic (by Max Weber) also point to this environmental direction.

• **The Genetic Approach**

—*Thesis*: It focuses instead, relatively speaking again, on hereditory factors (e.g., genes and evolution) in explaining the achievement gap among individuals and for that matter, countries or regions, when contrasted with the envrionmental factors.

—*Discourse*: Examples are Hans Eysenck and William Sheldon (in constitutional psychology), Konrad Lorenz (in his work on innate aggressive human nature), Gary Marcus (on the complexities of human thought by a tiny number of genes) and Robert Plomin, together with Michael Owen and Peter McGuffin (on the genetic basis of complex human behaviors).

(continued on next page)

Table 2.13. The Theoretical Debate on Nature vs. Nurture (Part II)

- **The Compromise Approach**
  —*Thesis*: It seeks the middle-of-the-road argument in regard to nature and nurture and regards all differences among individuals and groups as the result of the mixture of both nature and nurture, more or less equally.
  —*Discourse*: Examples include C. Murray and R. Herrnstein ("It seems highly likely to us that both genes and environment have something to do with this issue") and Dan Dennett ("Surely 'everyone knows' that the nature-nurture debate was resolved long ago, and neither side wins since everything-is-a-mixture-of-both-and-it's-all-very-complicated....")

- **The Transcendent Approach**
  —*Thesis*: It goes beyond both nature and nurture (without, however, committing the compromise fallacy) in showing their closely intertwined interactions in producing the behavioral differences as often seen in individual human endeavors on the micro scale, and for that matter, in country (or regional) endeavors on the macro one—in the context of my five theses, namely, (a) the compromise fallacy, (b) no oppression without self-oppression, (c) no success without failure, (d) the factor of randomness, and (e) the post-human vision, to be elaborated in Chapter Six.
  —*Discourse*: Peter Baofu proposed this approach on the basis of his "theory of contrastive advantages" (as an original theoretical contribution to the debate, which was first proposed and analyzed in *The Future of Capitalism and Democracy*). In the end, the human genes will not last, to be eventually superseded by post-human life forms, so the debate between genes and memes has obscured something profoundly important about the future that the world has never known. And the debate is also misleading and faulty in its dichotomy.

Source: From *BNN*. See the book for citations and details.

Table 2.14. Physical Challenges to Hyper-Spatial Consciousness

- **The Understanding of a Higher-Dimensional World of Space-Time**
  —Ex: 4 for traditional aspects of space-time (e.g., length, width, breadth and time) plus 6 more new dimensions in theory of hyper-space, with profound implications for practical applications to new forms of consciousness.

- **The Mastering of Dark Matter and Dark Energy**
  —Ex: "ordinary matter" (e.g., atoms, molecules) as a mere 4.4% of the universe, with 23% made of "cold dark matter" and the rest (about 73%) of mysterious "dark energy," with fundamental significance to questions about the limit of the speed of energy (or info), the availability of energy for use, and the nature of space-time, just to cite some examples.

- **The Exploration of Multiverses**
  —Ex: theoretical speculation of other universes (e.g., "baby universes," "gateways" in black holes, "wave function of the universe," "many worlds," "brane worlds"), with potentially seminary discoveries of different physical laws in relation to matter-energy and space-time, and vital differences to the future of post-human conquest of other universes (for the emergence of new forms of consciousness).

Notes: These examples are solely illustrative (not exhaustive), and some of the items can be reclassified somewhere else. Nor are they always mutually exclusive. Since they are generalities, exceptions are expected. The point here is to give a rough picture of the evolution of consciousness to the hyper-spatial consciousness and others totally unknown to current earthlings. As a note of clarification, it makes no difference to my argument as to whether or not the hyper-spatial consciousness may emerge before, during, and after floating consciousness.
Source: From *Table 4.5* of *FPHC*

Table 2.15. The Theory of Floating Consciousness (Part I)

• **At the Micro-Physical Level**
—Ex: intelligent life without the human physical-chemical system

• **At the Chemical Level**
—Ex: space radiation and toxins

• **At the Bio-Psychological Level**
—Ex: exo-biological evolution in deep space
—Ex: genetic engineering of new beings

• **At the Institutional Level**
—Ex: post-capitalism
—Ex: post-democracy

• **At the Organizational Level**
—Ex: less legal-formalistic routines

• **At the Structural Level**
—Ex: alien forms of violence

• **At the Cultural Level**
—Ex: transcending freedom
—Ex: transcending equality

(continued on next page)

Table 2.15. The Theory of Floating Consciousness (Part II)

• **At the Cosmological Level**
—Ex: parallel universes
—Ex: pocket universes

• **At the Systemic Level**
—Ex: space habitats (in zero-gravity)

Notes: Each example draws from the works of different scholars in the field. For instance, at the cosmological level, the idea of parallel universes is from the theoretical speculation in quantum cosmology by Stephen Hawking and others, while the one of pocket universes comes from the theoretical work of Allan Guth at MIT. And at the institutional level, I proposed post-capitalism and post-democracy in *FCD* (and later, from *BDPD* and *BCPC*). In addition, the examples are solely illustrative (not exhaustive), and some of the items can be reclassified somewhere else. Nor are they always mutually exclusive. Since they are generalities, exceptions are expected.
Sources: From *FPHC*—and, originally, from *FCD*

Table 2.16. The Potential of Unfolding Unconsciousness

- **Superior Senses**
  —*Through space*
    - Ex: clair-sentience (in feeling)
    - Ex: clair-voyance (in seeing)
    - Ex: clair-audience (in hearing)
    - Ex: clair-austance (in tasting)
    - Ex: clair-alience (in smelling)
    - Ex: clair-cognizance (in knowing)

  —*Through time*
    - Ex: pre-cognition (in knowing), pre-sentiment (in feeling)
    - Ex: retro-cognition (in knowing), retro-sentiment (in feeling)

- **Superior Contacts**
  —*With living minds*
    - Ex: telepathy

  —*With the dead*
    - Ex: mediumship

  —*With other-living entities*
    - Ex: telekinesis

Notes: The categories and examples are solely illustrative (not exhaustive), and the comparison is relative (not absolute), nor are they necessarily mutually exclusive. And some can be easily re-classified elsewhere. As generalities, they allow exceptions.
Source: A summary of Ch.5 of *FPHU*

Table 2.17. The Future Exploration of Unfolding Unconsciousness

- **In the Context of Nature**
  —Ex: the higher-dimensional space-time in hyperspace theory
  —Ex: the particle-wave interactions in quantum mechanics
  —Ex: the study of brain waves in electromagnetic theory

- **In the Context of the Mind**
  —Ex: the unconscious fantasies in psychoanalysis
  —Ex: the mind-altering drugs in biochemistry
  —Ex: the manipulation of neural activity in neurobiology

- **In the Context of Culture**
  —Ex: the correlation between anomalous experience and moral/religious/aesthetic interests in culture studies
  —Ex: the role of myths and language in epistemology

- **In the Context of Society**
  —Ex: different organizational agendas in anomalous research
  —Ex: the scholarly divide on anomalous study
  —Ex: interests and propaganda in institutioanl research
  —Ex: the transformative power of technology in research on social systems
  —Ex: the natural and non-natural selection of other worlds in exo-biology
  —Ex: the role of the post-human conscious mind in qualitative demography

Notes: The examples in each category are solely illustrative (not exhaustive), and the comparison is relative (not absolute), nor are they necessarily mutually exclusive. And some can be easily re-classified elsewhere. As generalities, they allow exceptions.
Source: A summary of Chs.2-5 of *FPHU*, in conjunction with the rest of the book

• Part Three •

Nature

CHAPTER 3
UNCONSCIOUSNESS AND NATURE

> What are the implications for [natural] science of the fact that psychic functioning appears to be a real effect?...What ideas might be relevant in the context of suitably extending science to take these phenomena into account?
>
> —Brian Josephson (1996)

The Potential of Nature

The understanding of anomalous experience in the domain of unconsciousness (together with its conscious counterpart) can be enhanced, not just from the perspective of the mind (as was analyzed in Chapter Two) but also from other perspectives, like the one of nature (as the topic of this chapter).

The perspective of nature in relation to the issue of anomalous experience in the domain of unconsciousness (together with its conscious counterpart) can be explored in three different interesting fields, namely, (3.2) unconsciousness and chemistry, (3.3) unconsciousness and micro-physics, and (3.4) unconsciousness and cosmology (macro-physics), to be analyzed respectively hereafter.

Unconsciousness and Chemistry

In the field of chemistry, anomalous experience in the domain of unconsciousness (together with its conscious counterpart) can be studied in two major ways for illustration, that is, in relation to (3.2.1) biochemical theory and (3.2.2) physical biochemical theory, to be addressed in the following order, and summarized in *Table 6.4*.

Biochemical Theory

The role of biochemical theory to explain anomalous experience in the context of unconsciousness (together with its conscious counterpart) was already introduced and discussed in *Sec. 2.3.1* (of Chapter Two).

To avoid redundancy, the analysis will not be repeated here, and the reader is advised to revisit *Sec. 2.3.1*, if necessary.

This brief sub-section here serves as a reminder of this overlap between them.

Physical Biochemical Theory

A related but different approach to study biochemistry in relation to anomalous experience in the context of unconsciousness (together with its conscious counterpart) is to add physics into the equation.

Quantum Back Action and Biochemical Molecules

So, a new field, in the absence of better terms, can be called "physical biochemistry" (combining physics, chemistry, and biology).

A good illustration here is of course the study (by some scholars who are interdisciplinary in intellectual orientation) of brain chemistry in relation to some physical occurrences.

For instance, some reasearch projects were carried out, such that "[b]rain chemistry with a Quantum coherence in the nerons, or sensitivity to earth's magnetic fields have been putatively invoked to explain Psychic abilities." (A. Zaman 2004)

Jack Sarfatti (1998), for one, proposed his "quantum back action" (by way of quantum theory) to explain anomalous experience in the context of biochemistry (e.g., biochemical messenger molecules and neuron pulses).

Sarfatti started from "the most basic concepts of physics. According to Newton's third law of motion, every action generates an equal and opposite reaction, so the 'mind-like quantum force'...must generate a 'quantum back action.'" (J. Beichler 1998)

As Sarfatti thus explained, "the term 'back-action' mean[s] that the quantum wave field is 'directly affected by the conditions of the particles.' It is qualitatively obvious that such a direct dependence is the counter-force or reaction to the quantum force. The combination of the quantum force of wave on particle with the counter-force or back-action of particle on wave forms a feed-back control loop which is able to control the formerly uncontrollable guidance of the particle by its wave. This results in a distortion of the statistical patterns of orthodox quantum mechanics. This is the mechanism of intent or free will." (J. Beichler 198)

What Sarfatti was trying to say here is that "consciousness collapses the wave packet to realize or materialize a solid particle as in the normal quantum mechanical point of view, but he has further added the idea that the particle reacts equally and oppositely to the collapsing wave in the form of a 'back action.' Just as consciousness acts physically through an exchange of information which causes the wave collapse, the particle reacts through its 'back action' to pass information on the state of the collapse back to consciousness. Therefore, the solid particle must affect the consciousness which collapsed the wave to create it." (J. Beichler 1998)

The wave-particle duality and its interaction at the quantum level is at full play here, albeit being used for the explanation of anomalous experience. For instance, in the context of psi events, "Sarfatti implies that his theory of 'back action' can serve to explain psi effects by a mutual exchange of information at the quantum level rather than a one-way exchange of information from consciousness to physical particle. He ultimately associates his 'back action' with perception and consciousness." (J. Beichler 1998)

When put in the context of biochemistry, Sarfatti then showed how the interaction between wave and particle is linked with the transformation of sensory data from neuron pulses and bio-chemical messenger molecules into meaningful information: "The back-reaction, not found in orthodox quantum mechanics, completes a feed-back control loop between particle and wave which explains the matter-mind connection in which mind is the quantum wave that not only moves living matter but is, in turn, moved by living matter. The latter is the basis of perception and consciousness. It is how sensory data from neuron pulses and bio-chemical messenger molecules transform their information into meaningful subjective experience (i.e., qualia)." (J. Beichler 1998)

More amazingly, Sarfatti is not alone on this, as some scholars even went so far as to visit "[u]nderwater streams" and "[h]igh voltage electromagnetic fields" (to be further elaborated in the next section, *Sec. 3.3*, on unconsciousness and physics), to the extent of linking them to such phenomena as "hauntings in houses and dowsing" (which are of course rather bizarre forms of anomalous experience).

Plausible Arguments vs. Scientiifc Explanations

These new projects may sound interesting, as they often catch popular attention in the mass media, but a deeper question is how much they really prove and explain, in a way to be accepted by the scientific community.

In the case of Sarfatti, the problem is compounded, since he even went further to link other cognitive states like "[p]urpose, meaning, intention, intuition," and the rest, to the extent that his critics are right to point out that "Sarfatti gives no further physical mechanisms which can help to distinguish between these various types of mental activity. It was perhaps unwise for Sarfatti to have associated his 'back action' with so many different things before he has more fully developed his theory and provided some further verification of his ideas. Sarfatti's concepts are well taken, but so many unsubstantiated claims lend a distinct air of speculation to Sarfatti's theory, rendering his theory, as are so many others, tentative and incomplete." (J. Beichler 1998)

In the end, Aparthib Zaman (2003), for one, was right to the point when he wrote that "[t]hese are not scientific explanations, but still an attempt to explain through plausibility arguments based on natural laws."

The critique notwithstanding—Zaman (2003) had something more positive to say about them as a whole, in the context of anomalous experience as illustrated in the examples aforecited: "Scientists only declare that nothing [in comparable studies of anomalous experience] has as yet been observed that VIOLATES any well established KNOWN natural law. The crucial thing to realize is that VIOLATES is not the same as UNEXPLAINABLE. If something cannot be explained by any known natural law but at the same time does not violate one, then scientists are open minded about it and only try to give plausibility arguments using Occam's Razor as guide to explain it."

So the virtue of these projects is to point out the hidden dimension of anomalous experience in the context of unconsciousness (especially though not exclusively in relation to the deeper layer of the intangible realm, which needs further study).

Thus, this is only to repeat the importance of the two ontologial principles in existential dialectics (e.g., the openness-hiddenness principle and the explicability-inexpliciability principle), to the extent that some portions of anomalous experience (in the examples above) can be open for description and explained (in terms of plausible arguments), although only *to some extent*—but other parts remain hidden (which requires further study) and inexplicable (in the absence of some sound scientific explanations).

Unconsciousness and Micro-Physics

Another relevant field, this time, in relation to micro-physics, has been used to study anomalous experience in the context of unconsciousness (together with its conscious counterpart).

Three good candidates are as follows, namely, (3.3.1) quantum theory, (3.3.2) hyperspatial theory, and (3.3.3) electromagnetic theory, to be analyzed in what follows.

Quantum Theory

Baron Albert von Schrenck-Notzing used the term "paraphysics" more than a century before to refer to the use of physics for the understanding of anomalous experience like psi events (J. Beichler 1998)

E. Douglas Dean, an engineer and president of the Parapsychological Association, followed in his footsteps and introduced "paraphysics in the annual presidential speech before the Association. After 1970, the word began appearing on a more regular basis." (J. Beichler 1998)

The Subquantum Domain

In 1996, Brian D. Josephson, a Nobel Laureate physicist, and his colleague Jessica Utts, wrote in *Physics Today* an article titled "The Paranormal: The Evidence and Its Implications for Consciousness," in which they asked: "What are the implications for science of the fact that psychic functioning appears to be a real effect?...What ideas might be relevant in the context of suitably extending science to take these phenomena into account?"

Josephson (1996) then answered in this way: "Two such concepts are those of the observer, and non-locality. The observer forces his way into modern science because the equations of quantum physics, if taken literally, imply a universe that is constantly splitting into separate branches, only one of which corresponds to our perceived reality. A process of 'decoherence' has been invoked to stop two branches interfering with each other, but this still does not answer the question of why our experience is of one particular branch and not any other. Perhaps, despite the unpopularity of the idea, the experiencers of the reality are also the selectors." (J. Beichler 1998)

They thought that "quantum theory...involves (in ways that in some versions of the idea can be made mathematically precise) the manifestations of a deeper 'subquantum domain.' In just the same way that a surf rider can make use of random waves to travel effortlessly along, a psychic may be able to direct random energy at the subquantum level for her own purposes. Some accounts of the subquantum level involve action at a distance, which fits in well with some purported psychic abilities." (B. Josephson 1996; J. Beichler 1998)

But the problem here is obvious enough, since the idea of "subquantum domain" needs to be more clearly elaborated and explained. It remains too speculative and abstract.

A Single Physically Fundamental Quantity

Some other physicsts took up the challenge and addressed it in a different way.

E. H. Walker (1974), for instance, suggested the existence of "a single physically fundamental quantity" which connects physical reality to consciousness, which is ."a non-physical real entity." (J. Beichler 1998) This single physically fundamental quantity is possible, since, in accordance to the Copenhagen interpretation of quantum theory, "measurement causes the 'collapse' of the wave packet. The act of measurement therefore forms a link between the consciousness and the physical world." (J. Beichler 1998)

This fundamental quantity cannot be any of the four fundamental forces found in nature so far (i.e., gravitational force, strong force, weak force, and electromagnetic force).

To start, "[t]his connecting physical quantity cannot be gravitational fields, nuclear forces nor weak interactions because their magnitudes in the brain are too small thus leaving only electromagnetic forces. The electric currents in the brain are extremely localizable and brain waves fail because of superposition, so electromagnetic waves are likewise ruled out as connectors. This leaves only the single possibility of association by Schrödinger's wave equation." (J. Beichler 1998)

Thus, Walker treated consciousness (in relation to its unconscious counterpart) as "a nonphysical entity connected to the physical world by means of the state vector for a quantum mechanical process linking the synapses of the brain." (E. Walker 1974; J. Beichler 1998)

But the main problem here is that the causal nature of this single physically fundamental quantity is not clearly understood—comparable to the problem encountered in the study on the subquantum domain.

The Hidden Variable

An easy way out for some physicsts is to simply postulate a hidden variable for the causal explanation.

In other words, this hidden variable is introduced, so that it can "make the system causal thereby representing the consciousness of the observer in the Copenhagen Interpretation. This variable is actually the 'hidden variable' which was introduced by Bohm in quantum mechanics to make the 'collapse of the wave packet' both continuous and determinate." (J. Beichler 1998)

This hidden variable has two properties: "Firstly, the 'hidden variable' must interact physically only by means of the measurement process, and secondly, Bell has shown that it must be nonlocal in quantum mechanics. Non-locality means that the 'hidden variable' is independent of time and space and is thus not dependent on physical processes while still affecting the 'collapse of the wave packet.'" (J. Beichler 1998)

These strange properties of the hidden variable, for them, thus make some anomalous experience explainable, so they thought. For instance, "[t]elepathy can be explained as an intersubjective agreement in consciousness or rather a mental act by both the 'sender' and 'receiver' which constrains the wave packet to collapse into a single state. Therefore, a message is no longer sent telepathically and information is no longer conveyed between two or more people. A 'sender' and 'receiver' are no longer needed, since nothing is 'sent' nor 'received.' Only two or more conscious beings are needed. Since no message is sent, but a future state is being agreed upon at a mental level, no sender is needed and clairvoyance becomes the same process as telepathy and precognition. PK [pyschokinesis] involves the same basic process as clairvoyance, only the selection no longer occurs as a quantum mechanical brain process. Instead, it is an accompanying divergent effect of the relevant physical or energetic system. All the aspects of psi are due to the properties of the 'hidden variable' which was introduced into physics to explain consciousness" (in relation to its unconscious counterpart). (J. Beichler 1998)

The critics, however, are not so easily convinced. The most difficult problem here is that not all physicists accept the existence of this so-called "hidden variable," which remains highly speculative, since "[t]he...existence was based upon a need to render quantum theory deterministic and continuous. Many scientists argue that they cannot be 'validly and consistently introduced into the postulates of quantum mechanics.' Using them to explain psi therefore becomes tantamount to introducing an unknown which has been a problem for other physical theories of psi." (C. Chari 1977; J. Beichler 1998)

After all, one can ask: "How do two or more people come to an agreement to simultaneously 'collapse the wave packet' and why do only certain characteristic events (traumatic crises) seem to invoke spontaneous ESP?" (J. Beichler 1998)

Energy from Random Quantum Fluctuations

Richard Mattuck (1977) proposed a way out of this mess concerning the hidden variable, since, for him, "consciousness...can influence a physical system directly by utilizing the quantum mechanical fluctuations in the system properties." (J. Beichler 1998)

In this way, consciousness can be an active agent, in selecting "how the wave packet collapses during any PK [psychokinetic] event, so that the event takes place as determined by consciousness. Energy to sustain the PK event is taken directly from 'quantum fluctuations arising from thermal motions of (local) molecules.' The amount of this energy can be calculated and compared to the amount of energy necessary to move or even levitate an object. Mattuck's calculations indicate that enough 'local' energy is available to accomplish PK phenomena on the macroscopic scale, not just the sub-microscopic level as in Walker's theory. Since the energy in quantum fluctuations is 'uncertain' before the wave packet is collapsed, all mind or consciousness must do is 'select' or 'reorganize' the 'fluctuations in a non-random way so as to produce the PK effect.' By utilizing the energy which is available locally, there is no need for an extraneous 'force' to transmit energy from the subject initiating the PK event to the object acted upon under the influence of psi, thus circumventing one of the major arguments against the existence of PK as well as preserving the conservation of energy." (J. Beichler 1998)

Mattuck's theory offers an improvement on Walker's theory. In the newer theory, Mattuck proposes a "'pulsed information processing rate' which can affect large scale PK power rather than a constant information process rate as did Walker's theory. Walker considers unconsciousness a real but non-physical entity, acting through 'hidden variables,' while Mattuck's concept of consciousness is capable of acting non-locally as a direct part of reality itself." (J. Beichler 1998)

However, recognizing the speculative nature of his idea, Matuck "has also pointed out that his theory has not been finalized, but is merely the first step toward a more complete theory."

In other words, it is still half-baked, with its highly abstract and speculative problem.

Consciousness Waves

This then led others to propose something different. Robert G. Jahn (1987) and Brenda Dunne, for instance, came up with the interesting idea of "consciousnss waves."

Their reasoning is straightforward enough, in that, "if consciousness 'finds wave mechanics a useful complement to particulate physics' then 'consciousness may also find a wave-mechanical metaphor to be conceptually and functionally useful for representing itself.' Since the quantum theoreticians, or rather the 'Copenhagenists,' make use of a 'probability-of-observation' wave, Jahn and Dunne have postulated a similar 'probability-of-experience' wave to be associated with consciousness. Consciousness should then be represented quantitatively by 'generalized consciousness coordinates' just as normal physical quantities are represented in various coordinate systems." (J. Beichler 1998)

These "'consciousness waves' range freely over space and time"; yet, "if a particular consciousness wave is confined to some sort of 'container' or 'potential well,' representative of the environment in which that consciousness is immersed, characteristic patterns of standing waves, or eigenfunctions, will be established that represent the experiences of that consciousness in that situation." (R. Jahn 1987; J. Beichler 1998)

And "[t]hese waves could then escape the potential well in which they are bound, just as ordinary matter waves escape potential wells in quantum physics. In this manner, 'consciousness waves' would not be restricted to act only within the confines or physical limits of the human brain and human consciousness could interact with matter as well as other 'consciousness waves' beyond the normal physical limits of the human body and its five senses, extrasensorally." (R. Jahn 1987; J. Beichler 1998)

In this sense, whenever "the 'consciousness wave' interacts directly with matter, PK [psychokinetics] is attained, and when it interacts with other 'consciousness waves,' PRP [precognitive remote perception] or remote viewing is accomplished." (J. Beichler 1998)

Adding More Questions than Answers

The introduction of "consciousness waves," while adding new hope for the understanding of anomalous experience, yet suffers from some familiar problems facing all other theories of psi so far presented, in that they are highly speculative and complicated, albeit in different ways—although the literature on anomalous experience has already been notorious in this regard, as the critics are quick to point out.

This weakness is all the more serious, since theories afore-cited are "no different from many other theories of psi which suffer from the fact that they add new hypothetical entities to science, even though psi needs simplifications rather than complications." (J. Beichler 1998)

As an illustration, consider this complicatedness in the use of quantum theory for paraphysics, in that "quantum theory may lead to an infinite number of branches of this universe or perhaps an infinite number of universes branching from each event in a single universe. The many worlds interpretation of quantum mechanics was first proposed in the late 1950's by Hugh Everett and followed by the hypotheses of N. Graham and B. DeWitt. Together, they proposed the possibility that there is no single 'collapse' of the wave function in quantum events. All of the infinite possibilities within the wave function are equally real. The measurement which is generally thought to cause the wave 'collapse' might actually only choose which reality of all the possible realities will be observed and a branching of universes takes place." (J. Beichler 1998)

When put in the context of anomalous experience, as I. Good (1965) pointed out, "'we may be dealing with various superpositions of the observer and the observed systems' during various ESP [extra-sensory peceptual] events. A person sensitive to psi may gain knowledge from the infinite number of branched universes which leads to ESP. Abner Shimony argues that all other branches are undetectable, so there is no difference between the philosophy of a 'branching' universe and the 'collapse' of the wave function." (J. Beichler 1998)

The shortcoming of this all is that "this...suffers from an extreme violation of Ockham's principle [or sometimes known as Occam's razor] because it adds unnecessary complications to the quantum theory." (J. Beichler 1998)

But then, four ontological principles in existential dialectics (e.g., the order-chaos principle, the simpleness-complicatedness principle, the openness-hiddenness principle, and the explicability-inexplicabiltiy principle) in existential dialectics become relevant here.

In relation to the order-chaos principle, the search for order to understand the nature of anomalous experience in the scientific theories afore-discussed (especially with the use of quantum mechanics) also encounters its double, in that the random features at the quantum level render it difficult to come up with any explanation which can be so neat, exact, and deterministic (as if things can be chaotic too, when they are orderly).

In relation to the simpleness-complicatedness principle, the analysis of anomalous experience requires some complication to understand its complexity (as revealed in the various physical theories aforecited), but in doing so, it more likely runs the risk of violating the scientific quest for simplicity (as suggested by Ockham's principle).

In relation to the openness-hiddenness principle, anomalous experience reveals its openness (e.g., "consciousness waves"), although only to some extent—while remaining hidden (e.g., the undetectability of different branched universes, other than ours, and other problems aforecited).

And in relation to the explicability-inexplicability principle, it can be explained in some ways (e.g., the use of some hidden variables) but not so in other ways (e.g., the mystery surrouding the simultaneous collapse of the wave packet by different people, and other challenges afoecited).

Hyperspatial Theory

A second approach to use physics for the study of anomalous experience is the growing popularity of field theories of Psi, which in turn make good use of Einstein's theory of relativity, especially in relation to the higher dimensions of space-time (in the context of hyperspatial theory).

Since this issue is related to the one in *Sec. 2.3.3* on hyperspace in relation to unconsciousness and biology, as well as the upcoming *Sec. 3.4* on unconsciousness and cosmology, it will not be repeated here, except advising the reader to visit the two sections if needed.

This sub-section serves as a reminder of this interdisciplinary relationship between paraphysics and parabiology.

Electromagnetic Theory

Another way to show paraphysics in action is the use of electromagnetic theory for the understanding of anomalous experience.

Telepathemic Bit and ESP Events

In the 1970's, I.M. Kogan, for instance, made good use of modern electromagnetic theory and modern information theory and proposed that "with a suitably devised formula we can posit a hypothetical wave yielding a 'telepathemic bit' (i.e. a binary psi unit) of information of specified duration at a specified temperature." (C. Chari 1977)

The reason is that "there is a definite transfer of information during ESP [extrasensory perceptual] events," for instance. (J. Beichler 1998)

Kogan knew physics well enough to understand the importance of ELF (extremely low frequency) electromagnetic waves in his research, since "[t]here is a rule of thumb in physics that the most effectively absorbed waves have nearly the same wavelength as the size of the absorber. The waves produced by the human brain are about ten centimeters long and the brain has a cross-sectional diameter of roughly the same measurement. This would correspond to electromagnetic waves of extremely low frequency. So ELF waves seem to represent the ideal measurable physical quantity for interacting with the human brain producing psi." (J. Beichler 1998)

The Problem about Absorbing Energy

But there is a major problem here, which complicates the research: "While the maximum amount of energy is absorbed from waves of this wavelength, small amounts of energy can be absorbed from waves of all wavelengths, with the amount of energy physically absorbed falling very rapidly the further the wavelength is from that of the ideal. ELFs already carry very little energy since energy is dependent upon frequency. Higher energy waves may not be as well absorbed, but since they have higher energy to begin with, there may be an optimum value of energy which can be absorbed from waves of not quite so ideal wavelength. With the common radio, you can use an antenna of any size and still pick up all frequencies, even those which do not correspond to the antennas length, if you have a proper tuning circuit. So perhaps the brain contains a special tuning circuit, or acts as a tuning circuit itself, which can detect and interpret all electromagnetic waves." (J. Beichler 1998)

Yet, the critics are quick to point out that "[t]his idea is merely speculative"; but the good thing about the research is that "it demonstrates that there is more to the electromagnetic theories of psi than most would care to admit." (J. Beichler 1998)

With this critique in mind, other physicists like Michael Persinger refined this branch of paraphysical research and "added a new element to the ELF [extremely low frequency] argument. He noted that ELF radiation is also emitted during geomagnetic disturbances, lightning and other natural processes. Since these ELF waves are natural, various forms of information could be imprinted by the brain on the common ELF background. This impression could be read by those who are especially sensitive such as telepathic agents." (J. Beichler 1998)

Yet, this improvement is good and bad. It is bad, because it "lacks plausible mechanisms and does not seriously address real psi expressions"—but it is good, because "it does have predictive power and some predictions made by Persinger seem to have been validated." (J. Beichler 1998; H. Edge 1986; J. Mishlove 1994)

So, this also reveals, in a different way, the openness-hiddenness principle and the explicability-inexplicability principle in existential dialectics, in that some aspects of anomalous experience (like ESP events) can be open to outside understanding (e.g., the transmission of telepathemic bit) and explainable to some extent (e.g., the use of modern electromagnetic theory and modern information theory)—but they can also remain hidden (e.g., the speculative nature of the theory) and inexplicable (e.g., the absence of plausible mechanisms).

But this also means that the nature of anomalous experience in relation to the unconscious mind in the intangible realm still has a long way to go, before it is fully understood.

Unconsciousness and Cosmology (Macro-Physics)

Besides the fields of chemistry and micro-physics, there is also the one of cosmology (or macro-physics), which can shed some light on the issue of anomalous experience in the context of unconsciousness (together with its conscious counterpart).

An excellent illustration here concerns, of course, hyperspatial theory.

Hyperspatial Theory

Hyperspatial theory has been used in relation to the issue of biogravity in the context of unconsciousness and biology (as already analyzed in Chapter Two).

In the current context of unconsciousness and cosmology, however, some cosmologists have also used it for the explanation of anomalous experience.

As a start, consider, say, the model concerning "topological folding" by Gertrude Schmeidler.

Topological Folding

In 1972, Schmeidler argued that "our four-dimensional space-time continuum was somehow folded on itself. Distant points or events in space-time are actually quite near for any signals that could travel out of our physical space-time envelope, from one fold to another. If psi could travel unhindered between folds, then ESP [extra-sensory perception] and other such phenomena could be easily explained." (J. Beichler 1998)

This sounds nice enough, needless to say. But the criticis reject it, because her model is highly speculative, with little empirical support. Consider two main problems below.

Firstly, she provided no explanation concerning the underlying mechanisms for signals to travel between folds.

After all, she assumed that "our four-dimensional space-time must be embedded in a fifth dimension for such folding to occur. This assumption may not be so far-fetched as one might imagine in light of the latest theoretical advances in physics. Physical theories utilizing this concept were abandoned by Einstein during the 1940's, but other scientists continued to develop the notion. In the late 1970's, the Kaluza-Klein five-dimensional theory again gained popularity and now many physicists theorize that as many as ten dimensions are needed to explain the various phenomena that are evident on the quantum scale. Within this context, Schmeidler's notions are not so radical as they might seem at first glance. However, she provided no explanations, in the form of mechanisms, of how signals could travel between different points in space-time beyond exiting and reentering different folds" in higher dimensions of space-time (J. Beichler 1998)

Secondly, another problem concerns "our inability to sense or otherwise detect the extra dimension or dimensions. Current theories postulate that the fifth dimension is compactified or curled up in a cylinder of nearly infinitesimal width which circumvents any normal physical detection. The overall extension in the fifth and higher dimensions shrunk to such small sizes during the 'Big Bang,' giving our four-dimensional space-time its present characteristics while guaranteeing that the higher dimensions can only be detected at extremely high states of energy. The enormous amounts of energy needed to detect the higher compacted dimensions are at present and for the foreseeable future unobtainable." (J. Beichler 1998)

In spite of this, her model is not totally useless, since many "hyperspatial/hyperdimensional theories do have a potential for explaining psi. The most obvious advantage comes by way of the fact that these theories utilize a space-time model in which time acts as an extended dimension similar, after a fashion, to our normal spatial dimensions. This model thus allows an easy explanation of precognition in that precognitive events reduce to the same explanation as ESP phenomena. This particular advantage of the space-time model has already been used by other theorists of psi." (J. Beichler 1998)

Universal Consciousness

Saul Paul Sirag (1994) went beyond Schmeidler's model and proposed something more universal, in that "our physical reality is only a 'subrealm of a larger reality' in which all physical forces are unified within a hyperdimensional structure. Using Wigner's interpretation of quantum mechanics whereby consciousness 'projects the state vector onto the eigenvector' during the act of measurement, the non-locality expressed in Bell's theorem suggests the existence of a 'universal consciousness.'" (J. Beichler 1998)

Sirag even boldly claimed that "[t]his consciousness can be represented by a mathematical structure known as a 'reflection space.'" (J. Beichler 1998)

This "universal consciousness" is in fact "a superstructure of which our individual consciousnesses are a small part. It is implied that psi events will eventually be explained via the interaction of the individual consciousness with the 'universal consciousness.'" (J. Beichler 1998)

Of course, this theory is quite interesting indeed. But the main problem is that it is very speculative. Besides, the model is "quite complex and highly technical [mathematical], so any verdict on its validity is far from concluded." (J. Beichler 1998)

The Danger of Reductionism

Even then, there is another problem, which is more serious, that is, the tendency to reduce the explanation of anomalous experience from the narrower viewpoint of physics, chemistry, or else.

The reason for this problem of reductionism is because the consciousness of intelligent life (and its unconscious dimension) cannot be so reductionistic. The focus on quantity (or quantitative measurement) in science often impoverishes scientific progress, especially in the social sciences and the humanities, at the expense of the exploration of quality (or qualitative analysis).

This point is not missed by some critics: "In the past, those studying science have made it a point to study nature in the context of form rather than meaning, thus emphasizing quantity at the expense of quality. But life itself is concerned with meaning rather than form. Life emphasizes the qualitative nature of reality. So, life can not easily be placed within a scientific model even though it has its own 'potentialities' which must eventually be included in any physical model of reality." (J. Beichler 1998)

In the current context of anomalous experience, this is all the more telling, with the use of paraphysics as a notorious example, to the point that Brian Josephson (1991) and Fotini Pallikari-Viras warned us of the danger of reductionism in using science for the explanation of anomalous experience and thereby offering an alternative method (which values qualitative analysis too in a more balanced perspective): "But the...view of knowledge advocated here, an alternative to the conventional view that all knowledge may be reduced to quantum mechanical knowledge, allows life to have its own potentialities, beyond what the constraints of 'good scientific method' will allow, for knowing and for acting on the basis of such knowing. Included in these categories of acting and knowing are psychic functioning" in a non-reductionistic way.

Their view is that "because of the different kind of perceptual and interpretative processes characteristic of life compared with those of science, living organisms can possess knowledge that is more detailed in certain aspects than is the knowledge specified by the quantum theory" and, for that matter, any other hard-core scientific theory. (B. Josephson 1991)

In the end, this shows all the more the relevance of the four ontological principles in existential dialectics, namely, the preciseness-vagueness principle, the opennness-hiddenness principle, the explicability-inexplicability principle, and the symmetry-asymmetry principle.

In relation to the preciseness-vagueness principle, the more precise some theories are in favor of quantitative measurement, the more reductionistic they are in ignoring the importance of qualitative analysis—and vice versa, for that matter.

In relation to the openness-hiddenness principle, reality (like the one of anomalous experience here) is open, to some extent, for external view (e.g., different events in space-time traveling from one fold of physical space-time envelope to another) and yet hidden from deeper analysis (e.g., the underlying mechanisms of these signals traveling between different folds).

In relation to the explicability-inexplicability principle, if anomalous experience (like Psi events) can be explained "via the interaction of the individual consciousness with the 'universal consciousness,'" then its speculativeness with high mathematical technicality has yet to prove anything in nature. (J. Beichler 1998)

And in relation to the symmetry-asymmetry principle, no one denies the importance of the natural sciences (like physics and chemistry here) for the explanation of anomalous experience (more so than, say, the appeal to economics or political science, which do not seem to be much of any use for the explanation of its existence), its use remains limited, however, especially when contextualized within the context of reductionism.

The Weakness of Nature

This, then, is just another way to highlight the limits inherent in the natural sciences for the explanation of anomalous experience, be they in relation to chemistry and physics (as analyzed in this chapter) or in relation to psychology and biology (as already addressed in Chapter Two).

But this does not mean that no progress has been made in understanding the nature of anomalous experience, with newer theories coming to replace older ones over time (as illustrated in this chapter).

The difference between past and present theories on anomalous experience is a sign of some progress, although much remains to be done: "The newer theories are based upon sound physics rather than the mere inventions of new entities or unmeasurable quantities for the sole purpose of explaining psi." (J. Beichler 1998)

For instance, "[h]yperspaces, quantum potentials,...and all the rest are theoretical quantities, variables and entities which exist independent of a theory of psi, if they are proven to exist at all. These were first developed to further theories in physics and the valid use of these new 'things' in mainstream physics will eventually be determined by physicists through a regular application of the scientific method. Should they prove to either exist or become necessary in purely physical theories, then their connections to psi must be seriously discussed." (J. Beichler 1998)

And in the case of electromagnetic theory, however, "[t]he electromagnetic theories of psi...are based upon physical quantities and variables which are already known to exist, rather than hypothetical concepts within physics." (J. Beichler 1998)

In this light, some more ontological principles in existential dialectics become relevent, and two more good instances concern the change-constancy principle and progression-regression principle.

In relation to the change-constancy principle, there is no lack of new (changeable) theories on anomalous experience to replace old ones over time, just as there is the recurrent (constant) guest of science to be invited time and again for its explanation.

And in relation to the progression-regression principle, if there is progress (e.g., the more and more use of new theories on the basis of "sound" science, instead of "the mere inventions of new entities or unmeasurable quantities"), there is also regression, in that "no clear-cut theory has emerged as the front runner to completely explain psi." (J. Beichler 1998)

A better understanding then requires other perspectives, lest any form of reductionism is committed. In other words, to avoid any reductionism in analysis, other perspectives are necessary, and two good candidates are the perspective of culture (in Chapter Four) and the one of society (in Chapter Five).

With this in mind, let's now turn to Chapter Four on unconsciousness and culture, in regard to anomalous experience.

Table 3.1. The Theoretical Debate on Space-Time (Part I)

• **Isaac Newton's Absolutist (Substantivist) Theory of Space-Time**

—space and time are independent from each other. The structure of space-time is $E3 \times E1$ (with the structure of space, *P*, as the set of spatial locations in a three-dimensional Euclidean space, *E3*, and the structure of time as the set of temporal moments, *T*, in the one-dimensional real time, *E1*).

—space and time are also independent from the effects of matter and events. The existence of space and time is possible even in a world absent of matter (and, for that matter, even in a world absent of events), as if they were material objects but with their total unchangingness thorough time.

• **Albert Einstein's Relativist Theory of Space-Time**

—space and time are interchangeable (not absolute), just as matter and energy are equivalent (not independent) with the famous equation, $E = mc^2$ (as in the special theory of relativity in 1905).

—space-time and matter-energy are also relative in a grand union (as in the general theory of relativity in 1915). Thus, each pair affects the other pair, as "matter 'tells' spacetime how to curve [in a non- Euclidean geometry] and curved spacetime 'tells' matter how to behave....Space contracts near mass and dilates away from it. Time dilates near mass and contracts away from it. Clocks positioned farther away from the mass of the earth run faster than clocks closer to the earth." (L. Shlain 1991: 328-330)

(continued on next page)

Table 3.1. The Theoretical Debate on Space-Time (Part II)

• **Peter Baofu's Perspectival Theory of Space-Time**

—space and time can be understood from multiple perspectives, be they in relation to culture, society, nature, and the mind, with each perspective revealing something about the nature of space- time and simultaneously delimiting its view. This is subject to "the regression-progression principle" in existential dialectics.

—each perspective of space and time exists in society and culture with good reasons, with some being more successful and hegemonic (dominant) than others. This is subject to "the symmetry-asymmetry principle" in existential dialectics.

—space and time will not last, to be eventually superseded (altered) by post-humans in different forms (e.g.,stretching/shrinking space-time, engineering more dimensions of space-time, and manipulating multiverses), be they here in this universe or in multiverses. Thus, even the physical existence of space-time cannot last forever, with ever more transformations in the process. This is subject to "the change-constancy principle" in existential dialectics.

—the conventional wisdom (especially by physicists) of treating the physical perspective of space and time as the foundation of all other perspectives (of space and time) and ofregarding them as much less important is a form of reductionism,committing what I call the foundation fallacy, in misleadingly dismissing the multiple perspectives of space and time in relation to culture, society, nature, and the mind.

Notes: The examples in each category are solely illustrative (not exhaustive), and the comparison is relative (not absolute), nor are they necessarily mutually exclusive. Some can be easily re-classified elsewhere. As generalities, they allow exceptions.

Source: A summary of *Sec.1.1*, *Sec.1.2*, and *Sec.1.3* of *FPHST*—and, for that matter, the rest of *FPHST*

Table 3.2. The Technological Frontiers of the Micro-World

- **Type I-Minus**
  —Ex: building structures and mining
- **Type II-Minus**
  —Ex: playing with the genetic makeups of living things
- **Type III-Minus**
  —Ex: manipulating molecular bonds for new materials
- **Type IV-Minus**
  —Ex: creating nanotechnologies on the atomic scale
- **Type V-Minus**
  —Ex: engineering the atomic nucleus
- **Type VI-Minus**
  —Ex: restructuring most elementary particles
- **Type Ω-Minus**
  —Ex: altering the structure of space-time

Notes: As already indicated in *Sec.4.4.2.2* of *FPHC*, the problem with this micro-classification (from Barrow's work) is that the civilization types (with the exception of Type Ω-Minus, for example) are not quite distinct, since many of them can be achieved more or less in a civilization, to the extent that Type II-minus and Type III-minus, just to cite two plausible types, can be historically contemporaneous, relatively speaking, unlike the vast historical distance between, say, Type O and Type I (or Type I and Type II) civilizations. In other words, the micro-classification here is not very useful to understand civilization types but is revealing to see the technological frontiers of the micro-world.
Sources: A reconstruction from J.Barrow (1998:133), as originally shown in *Table 4.7* of *FPHC*. See *FPHC* for more info.

Table 3.3. Theoretical Speculations of Multiverses

- **"Baby Universes" (Ex: Andre Linde and others)**
  —Ex: In a flat universe theory, "even if our part of it eventually collapses,...some spots in the cosmos would suddenly start inflating on their own, creating brand-new 'baby universes.'" (P. Baofu 2000: 623)

- **"Parallel Universes" (Ex: Stephen Hawking and others)**
  —Ex: In quantum cosmology, there allows the existence of infinite numbers of parallel universes, with tunneling among them. (M. Kaku 1994: 256) Hawking later revised his views on this.

- **"Pocket Universes" (Ex: Alan Guth)**
  —Ex: "As the pocket universes live out their lives and recollapse or dwindle away, new universes are generated to take their place....While life in our pocket universe will presumably die out, life in the universe as a whole will thrive for eternity." (A. Guth 1997: 248; P. Baofu 2002: 482)

- **"Brane Worlds" (Ex: Warren Siegel, Lisa Randall, and others)**
  —Ex: Our universe is stuck on a membrane of space-time embedded in a larger cosmos, with different brane worlds connecting and/or colliding with each other.

Notes: These examples are solely illustrative (not exhaustive), and some of the items can be reclassified somewhere else. Nor are they always mutually exclusive. Since they are generalities, exceptions are expected.
Source: From *Table 4.8* of *FPHC*

Table 3.4. Main Reasons for Altering Space-Time

- **The Need to Make New Energy-Matter**
  —Ex: manipulating molecular bonds for new materials
  —Ex: creating nanotechnologies on the atomic scale
  —Ex: engineering the atomic nucleus
  —Ex: restructuring most elementary particles
  —Ex: inventing new forms of matter and energy

- **The Need to Create New Space-Time**
  —Ex: creating "warp drive" (as in science fiction) for space travel
  —Ex: creating "pocket universes"

- **The Need to Conquer the Cosmos unto Multiverses**
  —Ex: spreading floating consciousness and hyper-spatial consciousness, besides other forms that humans have never known, in the cosmos and beyond unto multiverses for ultimate conquest

Notes: The examples in each category are solely illustrative (not exhaustive) nor necessarily mutually exclusive, and the comparison is relative (not absolute). As generalities, they allow exceptions. Also, it should be stressed that the three reasons are all related, in that they all contribute to the evolution of intelligent life in the cosmos unto multiverses in the most distant future beyond our current knowledge.
Sources: A summary of *Sec.6.2* of *FPHST*. See also *FHC*, *FCD*, and *FPHC*.

• PART FOUR •

Culture

CHAPTER 4
UNCONSCIOUSNESS AND CULTURE

> [I]nterest in artistic creativity was positively correlated with the number of paranormal experiences.
> —J.Kennedy (1995) & H.Kanthamanil

The Control of Culture

The analysis of anomalous experience in the domain of unconsciousness (together with its conscious counterpart) can be provided in a very different way, something that natural scientists (be they in chemistry and physics, especially—but also biology and psychology, as addressed in Chapter Two and Chapter Three) often dismiss as irrelevant or superficial.

This form of reductionism (as warned in the last part of Chapter Three) to favor quantitative analysis at the expense of qualitative one is unfortunate for the advance of knowlege but can be avoided, however, if a better understanding of the perspective of culture (as the topic of this chapter) and the one of society (as the topic of the next chapter) is offered and appreciated, in the context of anomalous experience in relation to unconsciousness (and its conscious counterpart).

With this goal in mind—the perspective of culture in relation to the issue of anomalous experience in the domain of unconsciousness (together with its conscious counterpart) can be appreciated in four different ways, namely, (4.2) unconsciousness and morality, (4.3) unconsciousness and religion, (4.4) unconsciousness and aesthetics, and (4.5) unconsciousness and epistemology, to be elaborated in the following order (and summarized in *Table 6.5*).

Unconsciousness and Morality

An interesting way to examine anomalous experience in the context of unconsciousness (together with its conscious counterpart) is to link it with the quest for moral rectitude.

Consider, say, the research projects by J. E. Kennedy (1994, 1995 & 1995a) and H. Kanthamanil.

Anomalous Experience and Character Discipline

J. E. Kennedy (1995a) and H. Kanthamanil, for instance, conducted some surveys with respondents on the relationship between their moral rectitude and their encounter with anomalous experience—among other things too (as will be clear in the next two sections on religion and aesthetics).

Specific Research Questions

For instance, in their research involving the use of questionaires with respondents, some questions were asked, and good examples are "I have had one or more experiences that I am certain were paranormal, and not just coincidence or imagination," "One or more paranormal experiences played a role in helping me meet someone with whom I formed an important personal or professional relationship," and the like.

Sample Selection

Kennedy (1995a) and Kanthamanil then selected a specific sample for the research, on the basis of the following criteria: "The questionnaires were administered to a convenience sample of people who were likely candidates to have had anomalous experiences. The great majority were actively interested in parapsychology and were typical of people who volunteer for parapsychological research."

There were 120 respondents, who include "7 drop-in visitors to the Institute for Parapsychology, 9 people who contacted the Institute by mail or phone, 9 participants in the 1994 summer study program at the Institute, 3 staff members of the Institute, 3 members of the Association for Research and Enlightenment who attended a talk on parapsychology, 13 college students from the mail survey that was described previously…, and 76 respondents to questionnaires mailed to 1200 names on a mailing list of people who had ordered books or other products related to paranormal phenomena." (J. Kennedy 1995a)

Some Positive Findings

An interesting result is that there was a positive correlation between the desire for moral rectitude and the encounter with anomalous experience, for instance.

The following figures reflected an increase reported by different respondents in relation to a specific belief or feeling after some (alleged) previous encounters with anomalous experience.

- "Motivation to maintain my health" (53%)
- "Tolerance for others" (46%)
- "Ability to express love" (45%)
- "Desire to help others" (42%)

These are related to moral rectitude, since these beliefs and feelings are related to some of the most fundamental moral virtues celebrated in many cultures (e.g., love, friendship, generosity, temperance, and fairness).

Some Inconvenient Findings

But the other side of the story needs to be told too, in that some other findings are not so encouraging in relation to the correlation in question.

For instance, the following figures show no change reported by different respondents in relation to the same specific belief or feeling after some (alleged) previous encounters with anomalous experience.

- "Motivation to maintain my health" (44%)
- "Tolerance for others" (48%)
- "Ability to express love" (53%)
- "Desire to help others" (57%)

So, the relationship between moral rectitude and anomalous experience, while positive in correlation for some people, yet shows no correlation for some others. Yet, an interesting note to add here is that there is only a little negative correlation between the two variables in the findings.

But then, two ontological principles in existential dialectics (e.g., the symmetry-asymmetry principle and the progression-regression principle) are useful here.

In relation to the symmetry-asymmetry principle, if there are respondents who all believe in anomalous experience, there are likewise some who report some positive changes afterwards in the context of some spiritual beliefs or feelings, whereas others do not.

And in relation to the progression-regression principle, if there are some progress in understanding better the nature of anomalous experience (e.g., the relationship between moral rectitude and the encounter with anomalous experience), there is likewise some regression (e.g., the not-so-encouraging findings about the alleged positive correlation).

Unconsciousness and Religion

In fact, the question about the relationship between moral rectitude and anomalous experience leads us to a related correlation, that is, the one between religion and anomalous experience.

For illustration, just consider two case studies below, namely, in relation to (4.3.1) mystical experience, TLE, and religious messages, and (4.3.2) anomalous experience and religious conviction, respectively in that order.

Mystical Experience, TLE, and Religious Messages

The first case study concerns the use of neurophysiological theory to explain anomalous experience and religion, which is, however, something already addressed in *Section 2.3.4*.

A Good Source of Material for Religion (and Art)

Without repeating what was written there in *Sec. 2.3.4*, it suffices to add further here that more and more works on temporal lobe epilepsy (or TLE) and its linkage to anomalous experience, which in turn contribute later to further religious activity in life, have been advanced over time.

For instance, Clifford Pickover (1999) thus wrote: "Hidden or diagnosed, admitted or unknown, the mental states that occur in TLE seizures are more than simply neurological symptoms. In people like Tennyson, Saint Paul, and van Gogh these states may have provided material for religion and art. People with TLE, whether or not they know the physiological cause of their seizures, often incorporate their symptoms into poems, stories and myths."

A story, as an illustration, was told about Mohammad, who vividly remembered some scenes from his mystical experiences in his younger days and later used them for his religoius (Islamic) crusade.

Pickover (1999) thus told us: "The religious prophets most often thought to have had epilepsy are Mohammad, Moses, and St. Paul. Dostoevsky, another famous epileptic whose works are filled with ecstatic visions of universal love (and terrible nightmares of uncanny fear and radical evil), thought it was obvious that Mohammad's visions of God were triggered by epilepsy."

More specifically, "[w]hen Mohammad first had his visions of God, he felt oppressed, smothered, as if his breath were being squeezed from his chest. Later he heard a voice calling his name, but when he turned to find the source of the voice, no one was there. The local Christians, Jews, and Arabs called him insane. When he was five years old, he told his foster parents, 'Two men in white raiment came and threw me down and opened up my belly and searched inside for I don't know what.' This description is startling similar to the alien abduction experience described by people with TLE." (C. Pickover 1999)

Mohammad, however, made good use of these mystical encounters in his younger days and later transformed them for religious development, especially in the form of universal love (not hatred), as Doestevsky once wrote of him: "Mohammad assures us in this Koran that he had seen Paradise. He did not lie. He had indeed been in Paradise—during an attack of epilepsy, from which he suffered, as I do." (C. Pickover 1999)

More Difficult Questions

But this is far from telling us in detail how and why these individuals incorporated "their symptoms into poems, stories, and myths" in the way that they did, not in other ones—or in the case of Mohammad in the above story, how and why exactly he transformed his mystical encounters in his younger days for the ultimate sublimation of universal love in the way that he did, not for a more vindictive quest for revenge or hatred in a different way.

Surely, to thus ask may be demanding, but the stake in question is vitally important for the future of intelligent life.

This only says, in a different way, the relevance of the ontological principle in existential dialectics, namely, the openness-hiddenness principle, in that anomalous experience can be revealed about its nature in some ways (e.g., mystical experience, TLE, and religious messaging) but not so in other ones (e.g., the difficult questions afore-raised).

Anomalous Experience and Religious Conviction

In another study, J. E. Kennedy (1995) and H. Kanthamanil carried out some more surveys with respondents on the relationship between religious conviction and anomalous experience.

More Research Questions

In this survey, respondents were asked questions like the following: "Have you ever had a[n]...overwhelming feeling of peace and unity with the entire creation, or profound inner sense of Divine presence...?" "Have you ever had a psychic experience (ESP, precognition, telepathy, or mind over matter) or out of body experience?" And "to what extent do the following values and motivations give your life meaning and purpose," which include, for instance, "observe spiritual or religious beliefs."

Sample Selection

Kennedy and Kanthamanil selected two major samples.

In Sample 1, there were "98 people in a diverse sample that included: 9 older adults who attended a talk on parapsychology at a recreation center, 8 members of the Association for Research and Enlightenment (Edgar Cayce group) who attended a talk on parapsychology, 19 retirees attending classes on parapsychology, 4 people who contacted the Institute for Parapsychology by phone or mail, 15 members of the Institute staff or their family or friends, 9 drop-in visitors to the Institute, 22 college students taking a course on psychological research methods, 6 college students attending a talk on parapsychology, and 6 college students from the previous college student survey...who returned their questionnaires late." (J. Kennedy 1994 & 1995)

And in Sample 2, there were "114 people in a diverse sample that included: 9 participants in the 1994 Summer Study Program at the Institute for Parapsychology, 12 college students in a psychology class that visited the Institute, 7 people who contacted the Institute by phone or mail, 2 Institute staff members, 2 drop-in visitors to the Institute, and 82 respondents to a mailing to 1200 names on a list of people who had ordered books or other products related to paranormal phenomena."

Some Confirmations

One interesting result is that there was a positive correlation between those who claimed to encounter anomalous experience and those who were also engaged in certain forms of transcendent (or religious, in the current context) activities.

In fact, the correlation was 0.39 (for psychic events in Sample 1) and 0.31 (for paranormal events in Sample 2).

Kennedy (1995) and Kanthamanil thus concluded: "The occurrence of transcendent [or more narrowly, religious in the current context] experiences and psychic/paranormal experiences was positively and significantly correlated in all...groups."

Lest any misunderstanding occurs, one should not confuse the word "transcendent" in their usage, as opposed to the word "transcendental" as used for the second category of anomalous experience as introduced in *Sec. 1.2*.

Inconsistent Findings

Yet, there are some troublesome findings which do not fit in well with the previous ones. Consider two of them below.

Firstly, in a paradoxical way, those who experienced anomalous experience were correlated with their spiritual interests (broadly speaking, in their definition) only in a minor way.

The (assumed positive) correlation was only 0.04 for psychic events in Sample 1 and only slightly better (0.17) for paranormal events in Sample 2.

And secondly, even more consistenty so (but in an embarassing way for their research), another paradoxical finding revealed very little negative correlation between those who claimed to encounter anomalous experience and their interest in acquiring material wealth.

In fact, the (assumed negative) correlation was only –0.19 for psychic events in Sample 1 and slightly better (–0.19) for paranormal events in Sample 2.

Kennedy (1995) and Kanthamanil had this rather unconvincing excuse to offer: "The failure to confirm the negative relationship between interest in obtaining wealth and psychic and transcendent experiences suggests that the previous result may have been a statistical fluke or a peculiarity of that particular college population. However, the data also could be consistent with a very weak effect that has little practical significance."

Once more, the two ontological principles (i.e., the symmetry-asymmetry principle and the progression-regression principle) which were relevant in the previous sub-section on anomalous experience and morality can be repeated here for the same reasons, which were already afore-indicated.

Unconsciousness and Aesthetics

In the field of aesthetics, there are also some studies on the association between anomalous experience and artistic creativity.

Just consider two recent research findings on this relationship, namely, one on anomalous belief and associative creativity in *Sec. 4.4.1* and the other on anomalous experience and artistic creativity in *Sec. 4.4.2*—hereafter, in that order.

Anomalous Belief and Associative Creativity

The first experiment concerns a joint research by Lorena Gianotti (2001), Christine Mohr, Diego Pizzagalli, Dietrich Lehmann, and Peter Brugger, whose findings were published in an article titled "Associative Processing and Paranormal Belief" in *Psychiatry and Clinical Neurosciences*.

Research Method

In this experiment, the researchers used "a novel task for the quantitative assessment of both originality and speed of individual associations. This 'BAG' (Bridge-the-Associative-Gap) task was used to investigate the relationships between creativity and paranormal belief. Twelve strong 'believers' and 12 strong 'skeptics' in paranormal phenomena were selected from a large student population (n > 350). Subjects were asked to produce single-word associations to word pairs. In 40 trials the two stimulus words were semantically indirectly related and in 40 other trials the words were semantically unrelated. Separately for these two stimulus types, response commonalities and association latencies were calculated."

A Main Finding

A crucial result was undoubtedly the one which showed that "for unrelated stimuli, believers produced associations that were more original (had a lower frequency of occurrence in the group as a whole) than those of the skeptics. For the interpretation of the result we propose a model of association behavior that captures both 'positive' psychological aspects (i.e., verbal creativity) and 'negative' aspects (susceptibility to unfounded inferences), and outline its relevance for psychiatry." (L. Gianotti 2001)

A Tough Question

A tentative explanation of this difference in associative creativity between the two groups (the skeptics and the believers in the experiment) was that "believers adopt a looser response criterion than skeptics when confronted with 'semantic noise.' Such a signal detection view of the presence/absence of judgments for loose semantic relations may help to elucidate the commonalities between creative thinking, paranormal belief and delusional ideation." (L. Gianotti 2001)

But this explanation may not satisfy the critics, since creativity is a complicated process, and there may well be many other factors involved in accounting for the outcome of an artistic expression. (N. Holt 2006 & 2007)

For instance, some scholars have pointed out that there are "other factors that have been associated with success in ESP studies, such as experimenter effects, belief in the paranormal, self-confidence, extraversion, the ability to shift easily into or between states of consciousness or to 'creativity.'" (N. Holt 2007)

Anomalous Experience and Artistic Creativity

With this tough questioning in mind, there is another experiment which is worth mentioning here.

For instance, J. E. Kennedy (1995) and H. Kanthamanil also wrote in "Association Between Anomalous Experiences and Artistic Creativity and Spirituality" (which was published in *The Journal of the American Society for Psychical Research*) in relation to this issue, that is, on how "artistic purpose in life will correlate positively with psychic or paranormal experiences."

Research Method

Their research method was the same as discussed in the previous section on anomalous experience and religious conviction—both in relation to survey questions and sample selection.

The reason is that the two topics were both discussed and investigated in the same article—except that, in the current context on artistic creativity, some more specific questions relevant to this topic were added, such as "to what extent do the following values and motivations give your life meaning and purpose," which includes, say, "express artistic or literary creativity," and so on.

Some Confirming Findings

Some of the research findings are rather interesting here.

For instance, "psychic or paranormal experiences were positively and significantly correlated with interest in artistic creativity....[T]he correlation was 0.29 for both Samples 1 and 2, which compares with 0.20 for the previous college student sample." (J. Kennedy 1995)

A related finding also showed that "[t]he correlation between transcendent experiences and artistic interest was significant for the high school sample (r=.29) and Sample 2 (r=.45), and was suggestive (r=.17) for Sample 1." (J. Kennedy 1995)

In another finding, "interest in artistic creativity was positively correlated with the number of paranormal experiences (r=.30) and with the number of transcendent experiences (r=.33)." (J. Kennedy 1995)

In fact, these findings are also comparable with "previous studies that found positive correlations between belief in psychic phenomena and creativity scores or artistic studies," such as the works by M. Moon (1975), as well as G. Davis (1973), J. Peterson, and F. Farley. (J. Kennedy 1995)

These scholars also discussed "[t]he apparent relationship between artistic creativity and psi." (J. Kennedy 1995)

This, of course, is useful "for finding talented psi subjects...as well as for understanding the psychological aspects of psi," as the work by M. Schlitz and C. Honorton precisely pointed out. (J. Kennedy 1995)

Some Remaining Questions

A deeper question here, of course, concerns the explanation of the correlation. Does this mean a causal relationship? If so, how is this to be explained?

The authors were cautious enough, however, to not provide any definitive answer—given the history of failed explanations boldly claimed by others before them.

Not surprisingly, they also did not offer any insight on how exactly artistic creativity is related with anomalous experience, other than pointing out a statistical correlation between them.

Or, in the language of the ontological principles in existential dialectics, if there is progress in the research (e.g., the finding of the correlation), there is likewise regression (e.g., the remaining questions unanswered and some embarassing results aforecited)—just as if there is symmetry (e.g., the relevance of artistic creativity to the study of anomalous experience), there is likewise asymmetry (e.g., the greater use of paraphysics and parabiology for the analysis of anomalous experience than the equivalent dependence on para-aesthetics, so to speak).

Unconsciousness and Epistemology

In the field of epistemology (or the theory of knowledge), the study of anomalous experience in the context of unconsciousness (together with its conscious counterpart) can be carried out in another way, this time, in relation to how our knowledge can be shaped by our anomalous experience in the unconscious realm.

Consider three case studies hereafter, namely, (4.5.1) archetypes and myths, (4.5.2) metonymy, metaphor and the structure of language, and (4.5.3) mystical experience and deautomatization—respectively in that order.

Archetypes and Myths

Carl Jung, following in the footsteps of Freud's "psychoanalysis" but rebelling against the latter for his own "analytical psychology", proposed the idea of the "collective unconscious."

Personal and Collective Unconscious

Jung "divided the unconscious into two parts: the personal unconscious and the collective unconscious. The personal unconscious is a reservoir of material that was once conscious but has been forgotten or suppressed." (WK 2007e)

Yet, "[t]here is a considerable two way traffic between the ego and the personal unconscious. For example, our attention can wander from this printed page to a memory of something we did yesterday." (WK 2007e)

When contrasted with the "personal unconscious"—the "collective unconscious is the deepest level of the psyche containing the accumulation of inherited experiences," which include, for instance, variouss forms of "archetypes, dreams, and intuition." (WK 2007e & 2007f)

One major way to explore the collective unconscious is through the study of mythology, from which some patterns can be discovered, which can then be organized into different features of archtetype, intuition, and other things. (WK 2007h)

Although Jung did not specifically analyze anomalous experiences in myths, it is not unusual for many myths to contain events or states of affairs which include unusual (or extraordinary) forces, perception, or happenings beyond the normal expectations in everyday life.

And the collective unconscious, for Jung, can be regarded as an objective phenomenon, for two reasons: "it is common to everyone; and it has a better sense of the self's ideal than the ego or conscious self does." (WK 2007f)

The Danger of Overdependence on Logic and Science

One of Jung's main concerns here with the unconscious mind is precisely to target the modern obsession with scientific rationality, to the extent that what logic and science tell us constitutes only one essential part of reality.

Human knowledge can be more fully developed in a more balanced way, if a deeper effort is made to "integrat[c]...spirituality" for the "appreciation of the unconscious realm." (WK 2007g).

In the current context of anomalous experience, a different way to put it is that the further exploration of unconsciousness in relation to anomalous experience may well open up the deeper layers of the collective unconscious (in Jung's way of speaking).

An Ambivalent Note

But Jung's idea of the collective unconscious is controversial enough, since it has been criticized as unscientific or too speculative.

Edward Glover, for one, "ridiculed the idea of 'thought-images' [in archetypes] as unscientific. (G.Lindzey 1985)" (P. Baofu 2004)

With this challenge in mind, some researchers proposed something slightly different, say, "the existence of unconscious mechanisms that are very different from the Freudian [and Jungian] ones. They speak of a 'cognitive unconscious' [J. Kihlstrom 2002 & 2002a], an "adaptive unconscious" [T. Wilson 2002], or a 'dumb unconscious' [E. Loftus 1992]."

Others (like Pawel Lewicki and D. Schachter) linked the unconscious instead to "implicit memory, and nonconscious acquisition of knowledge." (WK 2006e)

Yet, the scientific critique, while quite appropriate in one way, can be irrelevant in another, since it commits the opposite extreme of "scientism."

After all, Jung's point here is to point us away from the overdependence on logic and science as the dominant rationality of our time.

Metonymy, Metaphor, and the Structure of Language

Jacques Lacan approached the study of the unconscious differently, in connection with something more observable, that is, in treating the unconscious as a form of language.

"The unconscious," for Lacan, "was not a more primitive...part of the mind separate from the conscious, linguistic ego, but rather, a formation every bit as complex and linguistically sophisticated as consciousness itself." (WK 2007e)

Let's consider this interesting idea a bit further.

The Priority of the Signifier over the Signified

Lacan's idea, however, was influenced by Freud's psychoanalysis and "the structural linguistics of Ferdinand de Saussure and Roman Jakobson, based on the function of the signifier and signified in signifying chains." (WK 2007e)

In relation to de Saussure and Jakobson, Lacan then "applied the[ir] ideas...to psychoanalytic practice. For example, while de Saussure described the linguistic sign as a relationship between a signified and an arbitrary signifier, Lacan inverted the relationship, putting in first place the signifier as determining the signified, and so being closer to Freud's position that human beings know what they say only as a result of a chain of signifiers, a-posteriori." (WK 2006e)

But what is the relevance of this talk of the signified and the signifier to the issue concerning the unconscious mind?

An answer points to Lacan's reinterpretation of Freud's interpretation of dreams, in the context of the structure of language so understood (that is, the relationship between the signified and the signifier).

Let's pursue this further below.

Metonymy and Metaphor

In relation to Freud's psychoanalysis, Lacan reinterpreted "Freud's *The Interpretation of Dreams*. There, Freud identifies two mechanisms at work in the formation of unconscious fantasies: condensation and displacement. Under Lacan's linguistic reading, condensation is identified with the linguistic trope of metonymy, and displacement with metaphor." (WK 2006e)

Although Lacan, like Jung, did not explicitly focus on anomalous experience when discussing the unconscious mind, his linguistic reading of metonymy and metaphor (in his re-interpretation of Freud's analysis of condensation and displacement) can still be useful here.

A major reason, so I argue, is that the unconscious mind can be explored further in the future, in the context of the varieties of anomalous experience when humans try to use metonymies and metaphors to imagine different horizons for their senses and other faculties in the quest of understanding reality better.

In this sense, so I want to argue further, the use of metonymies and metaphors in anomalous experience can reveal something about the formation of unconscious fantasies.

Such metaphors like "I want to fly like a bird," or such metonymys like "Mind can travel in higher dimensions of space-time" can say something about unconscious fantasies in relation to anomalous experience, since the examples here involve some unusual abilities or forces which are not available to humans in the present.

Moderntiy and the Dependence on Language

Unlike Jung, who criticized the moderns as too dependent on logic and science for the pursuit of knowledge—Lacan looked at the problem of modernity differently, in that it "is the era when humans begin to grasp their essential dependence on language." (WK 2006e)

But the problem here for Lacan is that, because of his dependence on structural linguistics and psychoanalysis, his "entire model of mental functioning open to severe critique, since in mainstream linguistics, Saussurean models have largely been replaced," and Freud's psychology has not been less subject to a variety of criticisms (some of which were already discussed in Chapter Two).

And even "[t]oday, there are still fundamental disagreements within psychology about the nature of the unconscious mind. It may simply stand as a metaphor that ought not to be reified." (WK 2007e)

Yet, the virtue of this academic exercise reveals an ontological principle in existential dialectics, that is, the openness-hiddenness principle, in that, when the unconscious realm is further explored (e.g., in relation to the unconscious fantansies by use of metonymies and metaphors), so that the huge portion below the tip of the mental iceberg becomes increasingly known—it has its limits (e.g., the dependence on language, and the bias for science and logic).

Mystical Experience and Deautomatization

A different way to explore the realm of the unconscious in the context of anomalous experience in relation to epistemolgy is to study the nature of "contemplative meditation" in some forms of mystic anomalous experience.

Three Basic Categories of Mystical Experience

To start, Arthur Deikman (2007) described "the basic characteristic of mystical experience as the intuitive perception that we are part of a universe that is a unified whole. As William James and others have remarked, such an experience is usually accompanied by feelings of reverence and awe; it is highly valued and is felt to be a more direct perception of reality than is possible ordinarily. Such an intuitive experience is called mystical because it is considered beyond the scope of language to convey."

Mystical experience can be classified in terms of three groups, from the shallow form to the most trained one, namely, (a) "untrained-sensate," (b) "trained-sensate," and (c) "trained-transcendent." (A. Deikman 2007)

Firstly, the "untrained-sensate" category "applies to experiences occurring in persons not regularly engaged in meditation, prayer, or other spiritual exercises. Apparently, anyone can have a sensate-mystical experience. Such states feature intense affective, perceptual, and/or congnitive phenonema that appear to be extensions of familiar psychological processes." (A. Deikman 2007)

Secondly, the "trained-sensate" category goes a bit further and has in mind "the same phenomena occuring in...persons who have deliberately sought 'grace' and 'enlightenment' by means of long practice in meditation and religious discipline. The untrained sensate and the trained-sensate states are phenomenologically indistinguishable, but the reports of trained mystics are usually expressed in the language of the religious system in which they are trained." (A. Deikman 2007)

Thirdly, the "trained-transcendent" category is more advanced than the first two, since it goes into "a higher experience—the ultimate goal—that goes beyond affect or ideation. It is the latter experience, occuring almost always in association with long training, that characterizes the 'trained-transcedent' group. Poulain describes the state as follows: 'Then the spirit is transported high above all the faculties into a void of immense solitude whereof no mortal can adequately speak. It is the mysterious darkness wherein is concealed the limitless good. To such an extent are we admitted and absorbed into something that is one, simple, divine, and illimitable, that we seem no longer distinguishable from it....In this unity, the feeling of multiplicity disappears. When, afterwards, these persons come to themselves again, they find themselves possessed of a distinct knowledge of things, more luminous and more perfect than of others....This state is called the ineffable obscurity....This obscurity is a light to which no created intelligence can arrive by its own nature.' In 'The Heart Sutra' what is apparently the same state is expressed as follows: 'And no feeling, thought, impression, understanding, and no eye, ear, nose, tongue, body, mind, No form, sound, smell, taste, touch or thought....'" (A. Deikman 2007)

Meditation and Renunication

In order to reach this highest stage, one needs to practice, practice, and practice two essential techniques, namely, (a) renunication and (b) meditation.

(a) While renunciation often requires a form of physical asceticism to sacrifice all materalistic desires of the flesh and others, it is the first technique (viz., meditation) which is most relevant here for the analysis of anomalous experience in relation to the unconscious in the context of epistemology.

(b) The technique of "meditation" often makes use of a special form of contemplation which is "a nonanalytic apprehension of an object or idea—nonanalytic because discursive thought is given up and with it the ordinary attempt psychologically to grasp or manipulate the object of atention. 'Nondemanding attention' suggests the appropiate attitude. Ordinary thougth is considered an interference; it hinders the direct contact that yields essential knowledge through perception alone." (A. Deikman 2007)

Deautomatization

In this special state of looking at reality, Deikman (2007) "hypothesized that these changes were a consequence of 'deautomatization,' an undoing of the usual ways of perceiving and thinking due to the special way that attention was being used. In particular, he proposed that there seemed to be a deautomatization of the psychological structures that organize, limit, select, and interpret perceptual stimuli.

In "de-automatization," a concept as developed by Gill and Brennan, refers to the undoing, as the name suggests, of automatization—"both means and goal structures—directed toward the environment. De-automatization is, as it were, a shake-up which can be followed by an advance or a retreat in the level of organization...." (A. Deikman 2007)

The technique of contemplative meditation, a special form of mediation, is precisely "just such a manipulation of attention as is required to produce deautomatization. The percept receives intense attention while the use of attention for abstract categorization and thought is explicitly prohibited. Attention is reinvested in perception. Since automatization normally accomplishes the transfer of attention from a percept of action to abstract thought activity, the meditation procedure exerts a force in the reverse direction. Cognition is inhibited in favor of perception, since the active intellectual style is replaced by a receptive perceptual mode. Automatization is a hierarchically organized developmental process, and one would expect a deautomatization to produce a shift towards a perceptual and cognitive experience, involving a mode developmentally preceding the more analytic abstract intellectual mode typical of present-day adult thought. The shift would be to a process lower in hierarchy, rather than a complete cessation of the particular function involved." (A. Deikman 2007)

In a concrete research, Heinz Werner "studied the perceptual and cognitive function of children and members of primitive cultures" and "went on to describe the imagery and thought of primitive cultures and of children as (1) relatively more vivid and sensuous, (2) syncretic, (3) physiognomic and animated, (4) less differentiated with respect to the distinction between self and object and between objects, and (5) characterized by a lack of differentiation and a fusion of sense modalities." (A. Deikman 2007)

The state of deautomatization is sometimes referred to as "primitive" and "regressive" because "the undoing of automatic perceptual and cognitive structures permits a gain in sensory intensity and richness at the expense of abstract categorization and differentiation. One might call the direction regressive in a developmental sense, but the actual experience is probably not within the psychological scope of any child. It is a deautomatization occurring in an adult mind, and the experience gains its richness from adult memories and functions now subject to a different mode of consciousness." (A. Deikman 2007)

The Poverty of Scientific Knowledge

Deikman's conclusion (2007) is that "scientific research has neglected the study of mystical experiences not only because of their association with organized religion, but because scientists have applied such terms as 'regressive,' 'immature,' and 'childish' to an area of function that may be of value".

More specially, science has molded our contemporary way of thinking into a certain way for acting on the world (instead of being receptive to, or taking in, it), which is especially more revealing when examining it in the context of our use of language: "We tend ordinarily to use language to analyze, discriminate, and divide the world into pieces or objects which we can then grasp—psychologically and physically—in order to act upon them. The richness and subtlety of our language for any particular area of our lives reflects the extent to which we apply the action mode to that sector." (A. Deikman 2007)

As an illustration, "a monk working in a garden or lovers in embrace ideally would be given up to the receptive mode. However, if the monk or nun are worried about how soon they will gain enlightenment or experience mystical union, or if the lovers are preoccupied about how well they are performing, quite a different kind of experience will result." (A. Deikman 2007)

This receptive mode in deautomatization in relation to mystic experience has profound implications for understanding what knowledge is.

In the case of the mystics on anomalous experience of a special religious type, Deikman's conclusion (2007) is that science has delimited our grasping of the world for its highly selective process in looking at reality: "Studies in perception and developmental psychology indicate that typically we exercise a significant selection process over the array of stimuli with which we are presented. For efficiency's sake, we have to pay attention to some things and not to others, and we automatize that selection process to such an extent that it becomes difficult to recover our perceptual and cognitive options."

The virtue of learning from mystic experience, especially of an anomalous type, is to allow us to "make use of a variety of means to bring about a deautomatization so that a new, fresh perception can occur....As in the case of creative intuition, descriptions of such 'enlightenment' experiences indicate that they are sudden, involuntary, and present the 'answer' in a flash. They tend to follow a long period of struggle and are often triggered by something of an irrelevant nature—the same pattern noticed for creative intuition. Futhermore, accounts of enlightenment often stress that additional work was needed before the new knowledge was fully 'realized.' One might say that it had to be integrated through use of the action mode." (A. Deikman 2007)

Thus, the point here is not that one should choose either the receptive mode (in mystical experience) or the action mode (in scientific experience), but that they are "complementary" in giving us a fuller understanding of the world, if used both.

But to appreciate this requires the overcoming of our cultural bias for the action mode, which used to suggest that "'mystical states' are unreal, pathological, crazy, or regressive. Without knowing it, under the banner of the scientific method, our thinking has been constricted." (A. Deikman 2007)

And this barrier has thus impoverished our thinking, especially in relation to "defenses aginst reliquishing conscious control, defenses against the unexpected and the unknown, defenses against the blurring and loss of boundaries defining the self." (A. Deikman 2007)

In this light, "mystics have been the guardians of a potentiality that has been ours and that it is now time for us to reclaim. We can integrate this realm with our present knowledge, making it less exotic and less alien. By doing so, we can explore and regain a functional capacity that we may now need for our very preservation." (A. Deikman 2007)

The Limited Relevancy of a Special Type

But the essential problem here is that the kind of mystical religious experience as a case study has limited implications for the current context of the unconscious in the context of anomalous experience.

Consider, for instance, three important points.

Firstly, not all kinds of mystical experience belong to the category of anomalous experience, as already clearly delineated in *Sec. 1.2.*

Secondly, not all forms of meditation refer to contemplative meditation, which is a special type of meditation.

And lastly, de-automatization does not aim to eliminate the scientific way of looking at the world but only adds further to the multiple ways of seeking knowledge.

In this regard, one of the ontological principles in existential dialectics, namely, the openness-hiddenness principle, becomes relevant—because the study of mystical experience can open up our grasping of reality in a different way (e.g., deautomatization), and yet it is hidden in another way (e.g., the alternative scientific option).

The Limitation of Culture

This limitation of the exploration of the unconscious mind in the context of anomalous epxerience can be further studied, this time, in relation to another perspective (that is, the perspective of society), not just in relation to the perspective of the mind (as analyzed in Chapter Two), of nature (as discussed in Chapter Three), and of culture (as the topic of this chapter).

With this in mind, let's now turn to Chapter Five on unconsciousness and society, in relation to anomalous experience.

Table 4.1. The Theoretical Debate on Civilization

- **The Progressive Theory of Civilization**
  —*Thesis*: The "civilizing" process is "good," as opposed to the "barbarizing" process as something "bad," relatively speaking.
  —*Discourse*: Especially, though not exclusively, in the Enlightenment era and a bit before. Example: Thomas Hobbes—in that the tribes in primitive societies were "savages."

- **The Romantic Theory of Barbarity**
  —*Thesis*: The "civilizing" process is "bad," as opposed to the "barbarizing" process as something "good," relatively speaking.
  —*Discourse*: Especially, though not exclusively, in the Counter-Enlightenment circle. Example: Jean-Jacques Rousseau—in that civilization "corrupts" men, and the "savages" are in fact "noble."

- **The Moderate Theory of Civilization**
  —*Thesis*: The "civilizing" process is "good," but there is a price to pay, especially in systematic (compulsive) self-control.
  —*Discourse*: Especially, though not exclusively, in some late modern and postmodern circles. Example: Norbert Elias—in that social manners become more refined in the civilizing process, but self-control also becomes more systematic.

- **The Theory of Post-Civilization**
  —*Thesis*: The civilizing process is as evil and good as barbarity, and each cannot exist without the other, to be eventually superseded by post-civilization unto the post-human age.
  —*Discourse*: Proposed by Peter Baofu. See the rest of *BCIV* for more analysis.

Source: From *BCIV* on the theoretical debate

Table 4.2. No Freedom Without Unfreedom in the Civilizing Processes (Part I)

- **The Rationalizing Process (at the Level of Culture)**
  - —if freer from the dominance of unreason (as in barbarism) in the civilizing process, then less free from the rationalizing process (be it in the form of the principle of either transcendence or immanence)
  - —if freer from the principle of immanence in the rationalizing process, then less free from the inclination to commit terror in the name of reason and the relative underdevelopment of non-reason (e.g., in relation to yoga and meditation)
  - —if freer from the principle of transcendence in the rationalizing process, then less free from the relative underdevelopment of reason (e.g., in relation to systematic methodology) and the occurrence of oppression in the name of non-reason

- **The Pacifying Process (at the Level of Society)**
  - —if freer from the dominance of pillage (as in savagery) in the civilizing process, then less free from the pacifying process (be it in the form of external control or self-control)
  - —if freer from self-control in the pacifying process, then less free from the temptation of expansionist oppression and rebellious mindset in external control
  - —if freer from external control in the pacifying process, then less free from the gruesome psychological self-torture and conformism in self-control

(continued on next page)

Table 4.2. No Freedom Without Unfreedom in the Civilizing Processes (Part II)

- **The Stewardizing Process (at the Level of Nature)**
  —if freer from the dominance of nature (as in the state of nature) in the civilizing process, then less free from the stewardizing process (be it in the form of the stewardship of creation or the covenant with nature)
  —if freer from the stewardship of creation in the stewardizing process, then less free from material underdevelopment, relatively speaking, and spiritual exclusion in the covenant with nature
  —if freer from the covenant with nature in the stewardizing process, then less free from ecological degradation and spiritual disconnection from nature in the stewardship of creation

- **The Subliming Process (at the Level of the Mind)**
  —if freer from the dominance of spontaneity (as in the wild state of the mind) in the civilizing process, then less free from the subliming process, be it in the form of (cyclical-centric) self-refinement or (linear-centric) self-discipline
  —if freer from (cyclical-centric) self-refinement in the subliming process, then less free from the (linear-centric) self-regimen (as a form of neurosis)
  —if freer from (linear-centric) self-discipline in the subliming process, then less free from the (cyclical-centric) self-torture (equally as a form of neurosis)

Notes: The examples in each category are solely illustrative (not exhaustive), and the comparison is relative (not absolute), nor are they necessarily mutually exclusive. And some can be easily re-classified elsewhere. As generalities, they allow exceptions.
Sources: From *BCIV*. See also *FHC*, *FCD*, *FPHC*, *BDPD*, and *BCPC*.

Table 4.3. No Equality Without Inequality in the Civilizing Processes (Part I)

- **The Rationalizing Process (at the Level of Culture)**
  —if more equal for the role of rationalization in the rationalizing process (of civilizational making), then less equal for that of mythicization (as in barbarism)
  —if more equal for the principle of transcendence in (linear-centric) rationalizing process, then less equal for the principle of immanence
  —if more equal for the principle of immanence in (cyclical-centric) rationalizing process, then less equal for the principle of transcendence

- **The Pacifying Process (at the Level of Society)**
  —if more equal for pacification in civilizational making, then less equal for the institution of pillaging and others (as in savagery)
  —if more equal for external control, relatively speaking, in pacifying process, then less equal for self-control
  —if more equal for self-control, relatively speaking, in pacifying process, then less equal for external-control

- **The Stewardizing Process (at the Level of Nature)**
  —if more equal for stewardship in the stewardizing process (of civilizational making), then less equal for reverent (submissive) existence (as in barbarism)
  —if more equal for the stewardship of creation in (linear- centric) stewardizing process, then less equal for the (cyclical-centric) covenant with nature for harmonious co-existence
  —if more equal for the (cyclical-centric) covenant with nature in the stewardizing process, then less equal for the (linear-centric) stewardship of nature for domination

(continued on next page)

Table 4.3. No Equality Without Inequality in the Civilizing Processes (Part II)

- **The Subliming Process (at the Level of the Mind)**
  —if more equal for the role of reason in the subliming process, then less equal for that of unreason (as in the natural state of wildness)
  —if more equal for the primacy of reason in (linear-centric) subliming process, then less equal for other faculties (e.g., intuition, existential feelings, and analogous thinking) in cyclical-centric one
  —if more equal for the exercise of other faculties (e.g., intuition, existential feelings, and analogous thinking) in cyclical-centric subliming process, then less equal for the role of reason in linear-centric counterpart

Notes: The examples in each category are solely illustrative (not exhaustive), and the comparison is relative (not absolute), nor are they mutually exclusive. And some can be easily reclassified else-where. As generalities, they allow exceptions.
Sources: From *BCIV*. See also *FHC*, *FCD*, *FPHC*, *BDPD*, and *BCPC*.

Table 4.4. Five Theses on Post-Civilization

• Post-civilization no longer treats civilization as good and barbarity as evil (relatively speaking), nor does it nostalgically regard barbarity as good and civilization as evil (relatively speaking again). Civilization is as evil and good as barbarity.

• Post-civilization also no longer accepts the dichotomy between civilization and barbarity. Civilization cannot exist without barbarity. It is no longer necessary to preserve civilization, any more than it is imperative to destroy barbarity. To go beyond civilization and barbarity is to acknowledge the co-existence of both, although the degree of scaling one over the over varies from case to case—but is not to be extreme in largely favoring one over the other, *on average* (subject to the constraints of existential dialectics).

• Post-civilization is thus subject to the constraints of existential dialectics. There is no freedom without unfreedom, and no equality without inequality, for instance. There will be no utopia; even should there be one, there would be dystopia embedded within it.

• Post-civilization will eventually replace civilization (as a form of life settlement), to be dominated by post-capitalist and post-democratic lifeforms here on earth and in deep space (besides other alien lifeforms that we have never known), unto the post-human age in multiverses. Those few post-humans who keep civilization will live in a "post-human civilization," while the rest (the majority), who choose post-civilization, will evolve towards the state of "post-human post-civilization." One therefore should not confuse "post-human civilization" with "post-human post-civilization," as the two are not the same.

• Post-civilization will confront psychosis as a primary problem in the culture of virtuality unto the post-human age, just as civilization has neurosis as a primary one of its own (although both neurosis and psychosis are major problems in both).

Notes: The comparison in each category is relative (not absolute), nor are they necessarily mutually exclusive. And some can be easily re-classified elsewhere. As generalities, they allow exceptions.
Sources: From *BCIV*. See also *FHC*, *FCD*, *FPHC*, *BDPD*, and *BCPC*.

Table 4.5. Barbarity, Civilization, and Post-Civilization

- **The Rationalizing Process (at the Level of Culture)**
  —*Barbarity*
    - More mythicizing than rationalizing, relatively speaking
  —*Civilization*
    - More rationalizing than mythicizing, relatively speaking
  —*Post-Civilization*
    - Beyond the dichotomy, subject to existential dialectics

- **The Pacifying Process (at the Level of Society)**
  —*Barbarity*
    - More pillaging than pacifying, relatively speaking
  —*Civilization*
    - More pacifying than pillaging, relatively speaking
  —*Post-Civilization*
    - Beyond the dichotomy, subject to existential dialectics

- **The Stewardizing Process (at the Level of Nature)**
  —*Barbarity*
    - More revering than stewardizing, relatively speaking
  —*Civilization*
    - More stewardizing than revering, relatively speaking
  —*Post-Civilization*
    - Beyond the dichotomy, subject to existential dialectics

- **The Subliming Process (at the Level of the Mind)**
  —*Barbarity*
    - More impulsing than subliming, relatively speaking
  —*Civilization*
    - More subliming than impulsing, relatively speaking
  —*Post-Civilization*
    - Beyond the dichotomy, subject to existential dialectics

Notes: The comparison in each category is relative (not absolute), nor are they necessarily mutually exclusive. And some can be easily re-classified elsewhere. As generalities, they allow exceptions.
Sources: From *BCIV*. See also *FHC*, *FCD*, *FPHC*, *BDPD*, and *BCPC*.

Table 4.6. Types of Super Civilization in the Cosmos (Part I)

- **Type I**
  —a civilization which gains control of and uses the total energy output "falling on its planet from its sun for interstellar communication" (or, in general, space colonization). For N. Kardashev, who proposed the first three types, human civilization is currently Type Zero (Type O), which is below even Type I, since its present energy consumption for all purposes, let alone for interstellar communication, is still 10,000 times less.

- **Type II**
  —a civilization which gains control of and uses directly the total energy output of its sun for interstellar communication (or, in general, space colonization).

- **Type III**
  —a civilization which gains control of and uses the total energy output of its galaxy for interstellar communication (or, in general, space colonization).

- **Type IV**
  —a civilization which gains control of and uses the total energy output of its cluster of galaxies for interstellar communication (or, in general, space colonization).

- **Type V**
  —a civilization which gains control of and uses the total energy output of its supercluster of galaxies for interstellar communica-tion (or, in general, space colonization).

(continued on next page)

Table 4.6. Types of Super Civilization in the Cosmos (Part II)

- **Type…n**
  —So continues the series in what I call the cyclical progression of hegemony in the cosmos and beyond.

Notes: The Russian astrophysicist Nikolai Kardashev proposed the first three types of super civilization in terms of total energy out-put for interstellar communication. (CSM 1979) I extend his argument further to propose Type IV, Type V, Type VI, and Type…n, in the context of my claim about the cyclical progression of he-gemony in the cosmos and beyond.
Sources: From *Table 9.4* of *FCD*. See *FHC*, *FCD*, and *FPHC* for more info.

Table 4.7. The Civilizational Project from Pre-Modernity to After-Postmodernity (Part I)

	Pre-Modern	*Modern*	*Postmodern*	*After-Postmodern*
Main narratives	•Sacralness •Courtliness •Vitalism •Animism	•Freedom •Equality •Fraternity	•Multiplicity •Hybridization	•Naked contingency •Cyclical progression of hegemony
Main institutions	•Monarchy •Aristocracy •Feudalism •Holy order •Primitivism	•Capitalism •Liberalism •Socialism •Nazism •Fascism	•Capitalism •Liberalism •Postmodern politics of difference	•Post-Capitalism •Post-Democracy •Others
Main techno-logical and economic revolutions	•Agricultural	•Service •Industrial	•Informational	•Biological •Material •Energy •Space •Others

(continued on next page)

Table 4.7. The Civilizational Project from Pre-Modernity to After-Postmodernity (Part II)

	Pre-Modern	*Modern*	*Postmodern*	*After-Postmodern*
Main agents	•Males •Upper strata •Mini-states	•Males •Upper strata •Whites •Empires	•Males •Upper strata •Whites •Others •Supra-states •IO's	•Post-humans •Humans •Others
Main impacts	•Local	•Inter-national	•Global	•Outer-space •Multiverse
Main outcomes	•Towards moderntiy •Rise of linear- & cyclical-centric civiliza-tions	•Towards post-modernity •Dominance of linear-centric civilization	•Towards after-post-moderntiy •Linear-centric civiliza-tion in crisis	•Towards human (& maybe post-human) extinction •Rise of post-civiliza-tion, especially in post-human forms of space-time

Notes: The examples in each category are solely illustrative (not exhaustive) nor necessarily mutually exclusive, and the comparison is relative (not absolute). As generalities, they allow exceptions.
Sources: From *Table 10.16* of *FCD*—and also from *BCIV* on post-civilization (and *FPHST*)

Table 4.8. Civilizational Holism (Part I)

- **At the Micro-Physical Theoretical Level**
  —Ex: Mastering of quantum mechanics, electromagnetism, and other fields for the understanding of a broad range of anomalous experiences and theapplication for artificial intelligence (*Sec.1.4.1* of *FPHC*)

- **At the Chemical Theoretical Level**
  —Ex: Unprecedented expansion of (and violence to) the mind through ever new forms of drugs (and virtual technologies, for that matter) (Ch.9 of *FCD*)

- **At the Biological Theoretical Level**
  —Ex: Humans are not biologically equal, on the basis of race, gender, ethnicity, age, and whatnot. (*Sec.2.6* & Ch.10 of *FCD*; *BNN*) And post-humans will experience the same fate, in an even more amazing way.

- **At the Psychological Theoretical Level**
  —Ex: Human cognitive impartiality and emotional neutrality are quite limited. (*Secs.2.4-2.5* of *FCD*)
  —Ex: Rise of Floating Consciousness (Ch.10 of *FCD*; Chs.1 & 4 of *FPHC*)

- **At the Organizational Theoretical Level**
  —Ex: Administrative colonization of deep space, with less legal-formalism in some corners. (Chs.9-10 of *FCD*)

- **At the Institutional Theoretical Level**
  —Ex: Both capitalism and democracy will not last, to be superseded by different versions of post-capitalism and post-democracy in after-postmodernity. (Ch.10 of *FCD*)

- **At the Structural Theoretical Level**
  —Ex: Social stratification reappears in ever new forms, also with new causes and new players in the cyclical progression of hegemony. (Chs.8-10 of *FCD*)
  —Ex: The world of hyper-empires, and the union of the unions (*BWT*)

(continued on next page)

Table 4.8. Civilizational Holism (Part II)

- **At the Systemic Theoretical Level**
  —Ex: Outerspace expansion: local → regional → global → solar → galactic → clustery → multiversal (Ch.9 of *FCD*)
  —Ex: Demographic transition: human extinction, and the rise of post-humans (e.g., cyborgs, thinking machines, thinking robots, genetically altered superior beings, floating consciousness, hyper-spatial consciousness) (Ch.4 of *FPHC*; Ch.10 of *FCD*; & Ch.7 of *FHC*)
  —Ex: New technological forces in material sciences, electronic and communication sciences, energy sciences, biosciences, manufacturing and engineering sciences, and space sciences (Ch.10 of *FCD* & Ch.7 of *FHC*)
  —Ex: Systematic dominance towards nature for space colonization (Chs.9-10 of *FCD*; Chs.2 & 7 of *FHC*)

- **At the Cultural Theoretical Level**
  —Ex: The post-human transcendence of freedom and equality (Ch.10 of *FCD*)
  —Ex: Methodological Holism (Ch.1 of *FCD*; Ch.1 of *FPHC*; *Sec.2.1* & *Sec.2.5* of *BCPC*)
  —Ex: The Evolution from Barbarity to Post-Civilization (*BCIV*)

- **At the Cosmological Theoretical Level**
  —Ex: Mastering of dark matter and dark energy, and the exploration of multiverses (Ch.4 of *FPHC*; Ch.10 of *FCD*; & Ch.7 of *FHC*)
  —Ex: Alternation of space-time (*FPHST*)
  —Ex: The emergence of hyper-spatial consciousness (*FPHC*)

- **At Other Levels**
  —Ex: Historical: pre-modernity → modernity → postmodernity → after-postmodernity (human distinction, and the rise of post-humans, including floating consciousness) (Ch.7 of *FHC* & Ch.10 of *FCD*)

Notes: These examples are solely illustrative (not exhaustive), and some of the items can be reclassified somewhere else. Nor are they always mutually exclusive. Since they are generalities, exceptions are expected. And the comparison is relative, not absolute.
Sources: From *Table 5.1* of *FPHC*—with details from *FHC*, *FCD*, and the rest

Table 4.9. Theories on Civilizational Holism
(Part I)

I. Theories in Relation to Nature

—At the Macro-Physical (Cosmological) Theoretical Level

• 26. Theory of Hyper-Spatial Consciousness (Peter Baofu) (Ch.4 of *FPHC*)

(• 24). Perspectival Theory of Space-Time (Peter Baofu) (*FPHST*)

(• 23). Dialectic Theory of Complexity (Peter Baofu) (*FC*)

(• 20). Theory of Floating Consciousness (Peter Baofu) (Ch.10 of *FCD*; Chs.1 & 4 of *FPHC*)

• 25. Theory of the Geopower of Nature (Peter Baofu) (Ch.4 of *ALD*)

—At the Micro-Physical Theoretical Level

• 24. Perspectival Theory of Space-Time (Peter Baofu) (*FPHST*)

• 23. Dialectic Theory of Complexity (Peter Baofu) (*FC*)

II. Theories in Relation to the Mind

—At the Biological Theoretical Level

• 22. Theory of Contrastive Advantages (Peter Baofu) (*Sec.2.6* & Ch.10 of *FCD; BNN*)

—At the Psychological Theoretical Level

• 21. Theory of Unfolding Unconsciousness—also known as the Unfolding Theory of Anomalous Experience (Peter Baofu) (*FPHU*)

• 20. Theory of Floating Consciousness (Peter Baofu) (Ch.10 of *FCD*; Chs.1 & 4 of *FPHC*)

• 19. Theory of Cognitive Partiality (Peter Baofu) (*Sec.2.4* of *FCD*; *Sec.4.5.1.1* of *BCPC*)

• 18. Theory of Emotional Non-Neutrality (Peter Baofu) (*Sec.2.5* of *FCD*; *Sec.4.5.2* of of *BCPC*)

• 17. Theory of Behavioral Alteration (Peter Baofu) (*Sec.4.5.3* of *BCPC*)

(continued on next page)

Table 4.9. Theories on Civilizational Holism (Part II)

III. Theories in Relation to Society

—*At the Organizational Theoretical Level*

- 16. Theory of E-Civic Alienation (Peter Baofu)
  (Ch.7 of *FCD*)
- 15. Combinational Theory of Organizational Behavior (Peter Baofu)
  (Ch.6 of *ALD*)

—*At the Institutional Theoretical Level*

- 14. Theory of Post-Capitalism (Peter Baofu)
  (Ch.10 of *FCD*; Chs.2 & 4 of *FPHC*; *BCPC*)
- 13. Theory of Post-Democracy (Peter Baofu)
  (Ch.10 of *FCD*; Chs.3 & 4 of *FPHC*; *BDPD*)
- 12. Dynamic Theory of Comparative Political Systems (Peter Baofu)
  (*ALD*)

—*At the Structural Theoretical Level*

- 11. Theory of the Cyclical Progression of Hegemony (Peter Baofu)
  (Chs.9-10 of *FCD*; Chs.1, 3 & 4 of *FPHC*; *BDPD*)
- 10. Theory of the Cyclical Progression of Empire-Building
  (Peter Baofu)
  (*BWT*)

—*At the Systemic Theoretical Level*

- 9. Theory of Post-Humanity (Peter Baofu)
  (Ch.7 of *FHC*; Chs.3, & 10 of *FCD*; Chs.1, 3 & 4 of *FPHC*; and other books of mine)
- 8. Theory of the Cyclical Progression of System Integration and Fragmentation (Peter Baofu)
  (Chs.9-10 of *FCD*)
- 7. Synthetic Theory of Information Architecture (Peter Baofu)
  (*FIA*)

(continued on next page)

Table 4.9. Theories on Civilizational Holism (Part III)

IV. Theories in Relation to Culture

—At the Cultural Theoretical Level

- 6. Theory of Post-Civilization (Peter Baofu) (*BCIV*)
- 5. Theory of the Trinity of Modernity to Its After-Postmodern Counterpart (Peter Baofu) (*FHC*; Ch.10 of *FCD*)
- 4. Transformative Theory of Aesthetic Experience (Peter Baofu) (*FAE*)

V. Theories in Relation to the Rest

—At Other Levels (Historical)

- 3. Theory of the Evolution from Pre-Modernity to After-Postmodernity (Peter Baofu) (*FHC*; Ch.9-10 of *FCD*; *FPHC*)

VI. Meta-Theories (in Relation to Theories)

—At the Methodological Meta-Theoretical Level

- 2. Theory of Existential Dialectics (Peter Baofu) (*FHC*; *FCD*; *FPHC*; *BDPD*; *FC*; *FAE*; *ALD; FIA*)

—At the Ontological Meta-Theoretical Level

- 1. Theory of Methodological Holism (Peter Baofu) (Ch.1 of *FCD*; Ch.1 of *FPHC*; *Sec.2.1* & *Sec.2.5* of *BCPC*; *FC*)

Notes: All these theories are my constructions, as some of the main contributions of my grant project on civilization and its future. These examples are solely illustrative (not exhaustive), and some of the items can be reclassified somewhere else. Nor are they always mutually exclusive. Since they are generalities, exceptions are expected.
Sources: From *FHC*, *FCD*, *FPHC*, *BDPD*, *BCPC*, *BCIV*, *FPHST*, *BNN*, *BWT*, *FC*, *FAE*, *ALD*, *FIA*, and *FPHU*

• PART FIVE •

Society

CHAPTER 5
UNCONSCIOUSNESS AND SOCIETY

> In "The Secret Sales Pitch: An Overview of Subliminal Advertising"... August Bullock argues...that subliminal messages do affect behavior and are commonly employed in media....For example, [in] the cigarette slogan 'If you got crushed in the clinch with your soft pack, try our hard pack'...[a]n alternate interpretation...is 'If you are anxious about impotency, smoke our cigarettes to compensate.' The secondary 'impotency' interpretation is repressed because it is disturbing, just at the viewer's sexual apprehensions are likely repressed. The repressed meaning activates unconscious anxieties and induces consumption—because people smoke more when they are uncomfortable.
>
> —Wikipedia (2007i)

The Discipline of Society

The understanding of anomalous experience in the domain of unconsciousness (together with its conscious counterpart) takes a different turn, when examined from the perspective of society.

This is, again, something which is often dismissed as irrelevant or superficial in a reductionistic way by hard-core natural scientists (be they in chemistry and biology, especially—but also physics and psychology, as addressed in Chapter Two and Chapter Three).

This reductionistic fallacy is unfortunate (as already so warned in the last part of Chapter Three), since the perspective of society has much to illuminate the working of anomalous experience in the unconscious domain (together with its conscious counterpart).

With this caveat concerning reductionism in mind—the perspective of society can reveal its power in relation to the issue of anomalous experience in the domain of unconsciousness (together with its conscious counterpart) in four different ways, namely, (5.2) unconsciousness and social organizations, (5.3) unconsciousness and social institutions, (5.4) unconsciousness and social structure, and (5.5) unconsciousness and social systems, to be addresed hereafter, respectively, and summarized in *Table 6.6*.

Unconsciousness and Social Organizations

The nature of social organizations can tell us something interesting too in regard to anomalous experience, be it in conscious and unconscious domains.

How anomalous experience is to be understood, in a major way, depends, to certain extent, on what social organizations carry out the analysis (although this section here overlaps a bit with *Sec.5.4* on unconsciousness and social structure).

The Varieties of Social Organizations

Those social organizations which champion the existence of anomalous experience are more likely to have positive things to say about it, whereas those who are skeptical toward it are more likely to do the reverse.

Consider a few instances below.

The Negative Side

There is no lack of social orgnizations which filter information with the aim to question the existence of anomalous experience. (YH 2007)

Hereafter are four random examples.

For instance, *Australian Skeptics* (<http://www.skeptics.com.au/>) want to "[i]nvestigates the paranormal and pseudo-science from a responsible scientific viewpoint," as a way to question the beliefs in anomalous experience.

Bay Area Skeptics (<http://www.baskeptics.org/>) aims to "[[e]ncourage critical thinking, and accuracy in the media and schools," especially on issues related to "paranormal, pseudoscience, fraud, and psychotherapeutic practices."

Cincinnati Skeptics (<http://www.cincinnatiskeptics.org/>) is "[c]ommitted to encouraging rational, well-informed evaluation of fringe-science, pseudo-science and paranormal claims."

And *East Bay Skeptics Society* (<http://www.eb-skeptics.org/>) strives to "[a]dvocative philosophical and social organization promoting skeptical inquiry of paranormal claims and of any manner of thinking or movement that claims a scientific basis."

The Affirmative Side

On the other side of the fence are some social organizations which are more open to the study of anomalous experience.

Hereafter are a few random instances. (YH 2007a)

Atlantic Paranormal Society (<http://www.the-atlantic-paranormal-society.com/>) has its offical mission "to help anyone with questions pertaining to paranormal phenomena and ghost hunting, as featured on the series, Ghost Hunters."

Association for the Scientific Study of Anomalous Phenomena (<www.assap.org>) is a "[s]ociety of ghosthunters, UFO spotters, and serious researchers."

Tri-State Paranormal Research (<http://www.tsprghosts.com/>) is "a Northern New Jersey paranormal research group, working to bring paranormal study into the mainstream of modern science."

The Enigma Project (<http://userpages.umbc.edu/~frizzell/tep.html>) is an "[a]ssociation of technically oriented individuals who investigate and document unexplained phenomena and paranormal claims."

Even some university laboratories exist to conduct parapsychological research, and good examples include "the Koestler Parapsychology Unit at the University of Edinburgh,...the Parapsychology Research Group at Liverpool Hope University,...the VERITAS Research Program at the University of Arizona,...the Consciousness and Transpersonal Psychology Research Unit of Liverpool John Moores University,...the Center for the Study of Anomalous Psychological Processes at the University of Northampton,...and the Anomalistic Psychology Research Unit at Goldsmiths University of London." (WK 2007l)

Other research organizations on anomalous experience are "the Parapsychological Association,...the Society for Psychical Research,...the American Society for Psychical Research,...the Rhine Research Center and Institute for Parapsychology,...the Parapsychology Foundation,...and the Australian Institute of Parapsychological Research." (WK 2007l)

Different Organizational Agendas

The list on each side of the fence can be added to *ad infinitum*, but the important point to remember here is that social organizations are not innocent in their analysis of anomalous experience, in the context of the theoretical debate (among, say, the skeptics, the agnostics, and the defenders of anomalous claims) as already introduced in *Sec.1.4*

These different organizational agendas constitute respective organizational interests for the understanding of anomalous experience.

But this only reveals an ontological principle in existential dialectics, namely, the symmetry-asymmetry principle, in that if social organizations are allowed to have different research agendas, they are not necessarily equal in acceptance.

In the scientific mind of our time, for instance, those who are skeptical and critical to anomalous claims are more accepted in the mainstream scientific community than those who claim their existence.

By contrast, in the older days of antiquity, anomalous claims receveid a more favorable atmosphere of attention.

Unconsciousness and Social Institutions

A closely related issue concerns social institutions—not just on the basis of social organizations.

Two good instances for illustration concerns the use of anomalous experience for two institutional interests, namely, (5.3.1) the use and misuse of subliminal message in the economic institution and (5.3.2) remote viewing and psychic warfare in the military institution.

The Use and Misuse of Subliminal Message

Consider, say, the nature of "subliminal message," which, by definition, is "a signal or message embedded in another object, designed to pass below the normal limits of perception. These messages are indiscernible by the conscious mind, but allegedly affect the subconscious or deeper mind. " (WK 2007i)

Although subliminal messages are subconscious, they have implications for the understanding of the unconscious realm (as will be clear below).

The Study of Subliminal Messages

Scientists had done some research works on this anomalous phenomonon over the years.

For instance, E.W. Scripture (1898) in *The New Psychology* first "described the basic principles of subliminal messages." (WK 2007i)

Later, Knight Dunlap carried out another research, in which he "flashed an 'imperceptible shadow' to subjects while showing them a Müller-Lyer illusion containing two lines with pointed arrows at both ends which create an illusion of different lengths. Dunlap claimed that the shadow influenced his subjects subliminally in their judgment of the lengths of the lines." (WK 2007i)

And Harry Hollingworth even wrote "in an advertising textbook that such subliminal messages could be used by advertisers" and others. (WK 2007i; A. Pratkanis 1992)

The Threat of Subliminal Seduction

Hollingworth's warning later became true, as subliminal messages were later used (and misused) by different social institutions.

For instance, "[d]uring World War II, the tachistoscope, an instrument which projects pictures for an extremely brief period, was used to train soldiers to recognize enemy airplanes. Today the tachistoscope is used to increase reading speed or to test sight." (WK 2007i; A. Pratkanis 1992)

In 1957, "market researcher James Vicary claimed that quickly flashing messages on a movie screen in Fort Lee, New Jersey had influenced people to purchase more food and drinks. Vicary coined the term subliminal advertising and formed the Subliminal Projection Company based on a six-week test. Vicary claimed that during the presentation of the movie Picnic he used a tachistoscope to project the words 'Drink Coca-Cola' and 'Hungry? Eat popcorn' for 1/3000 of a second at five-second intervals. Vicary asserted that during the test, sales of popcorn and Coke in that New Jersey theater increased 57.8 percent and 18.1 percent respectively." (WK 2007i)

Shortly afterwards, Vance Packard (1957) promoted Vicary's idea in *The Hidden Persuaders*, which "led to a public outcry, and to many conspiracy theories of governments and cults using the technique to their advantage." (WK 2007i)

In 1958, "Vicary conducted a television test in which he flashed the message 'telephone now' hundreds of times during a Canadian Broadcasting Corporation program, and found no increase in telephone calls. In 1962, Vicary admitted that he fabricated his claim, the story itself being a marketing ploy. Efforts to replicate the results of Vicary's reports have never resulted in success." (WK 2007i; A. Boese 2002)

In 1973, commercials in the United States and Canada for the game *Hūsker Dū?* flashed the message 'Get it.' During the same year, Wilson Bryan Key's book *Subliminal Seduction* [1973] claimed that subliminal techniques were widely used in advertising. Public concern was sufficient to cause the FCC to hold hearings in 1974." (WK 2007i)

In 2000, "[d]uring the…U.S. presidential campaign, a television ad campaigning for Republican candidate George W. Bush showed words (and parts thereof) scaling from the foreground to the background on a television screen. When the word BUREAUCRATS flashed on the screen, one frame showed only the last part, RATS." (WK 2007i; C. Crowley 2000)

The Debate on Subliminal Effectiveness

Yet, the question here is: Is sublimal seduction effective?

As usual, the debate has been hotly carried out by two opposing sides: "One of them argues that only the simpler features of unconscious signals could be perceived. The second school of thought argues that unconscious cognition is comprehensive and that much more is perceived than can be verbalized." ("WK 2007i)

On the positive side are those who "claim they gain influence or power from the fact that they circumvent the critical functions of the conscious mind, and therefore subliminal suggestions are potentially more powerful than ordinary suggestions. This route to influence or persuasion would be akin to auto-suggestion or hypnosis, wherein the subject is encouraged to be (or somehow induced to be) relaxed so that suggestions are directed to deeper (more gullible) parts of the mind; some observers have suggested that the unconscious mind is incapable of critical refusal of hypnotic or subliminal suggestions." (WK 2007i)

On the negative side, however, are the critics who "have suggested that the effect of subliminal messages would at best be no more than that of a glimpse of a billboard in the corner of an eye. Controlled experiments that attempt to demonstrate the influence of subliminal messages generally find little to no effect."

More contemporary works point to a middle position, in which subliminal seduction has some effectiveness.

For instance, Tom Stafford (2004) and Matt Webb in *Mind Hacks* argued that "subliminal messages are effective in 'priming' (putting a half-processed idea in the mind, leading to increased familiarity or a 'tip of the tongue' situation where the idea is present but is not articulated until triggered). It also states that for this reason it has limited application in persuasion, and only slightly more use in advertising. The text states that additionally only one word or image is perceived subliminally most of the time, and that the primary way in which it can be used in advertising is by creating a familiarity with a product that has not been seen before, familiarity that could be misinterpreted as preference. The text references an experiment in which faces were flashed subliminally before the test subject rated a group of faces as to which were preferable." (WK 2007i)

In another research, Johan Karremans at the University of Nijmegen in 2006 found out that "subliminal messaging may have an effect when the message is goal-relevant. In their experiments, half of the participants was subliminally primed with Lipton Ice (i.e., 'Lipton Ice' was repeatedly flashed on a computer screen for 24 milliseconds), while the other half was primed with a control non-word. Subsequently, the prime positively influenced participants' choice for Lipton Ice over another soft drink, but only for participants who already were thirsty. Participants who were not thirsty were not influenced by the subliminal messages. " (WK 2007i)

Later, August Bullock in "The Secret Sales Pitch: An Overview of Subliminal Advertising" argued that "subliminal messages do affect behavior and are commonly employed in media," with his "The Ambiguity Principle," which is to say that "carefully constructed ambiguities can be tools of subliminal persuasion. When a stimulus has two meanings, and one of the meanings resonates with a repressed emotion, the disturbing meaning is repressed the same way that the emotion is repressed. The repressed meaning influences the viewer on a subliminal or unconscious level." (2006i)

As an example, "the cigarette slogan 'If you got crushed in the clinch with your soft pack, try our hard pack' has two meanings. On the surface it says 'Our cigarettes are better because they come in hard packages rather than soft ones.' An alternate interpretation, however, is 'If you are anxious about impotency, smoke our cigarettes to compensate.' The secondary 'impotency' interpretation is repressed because it is disturbing, just at the viewer's sexual apprehensions are likely repressed. The repressed meaning activates unconscious anxieties and induces consumption—because people smoke more when they are uncomfortable. If the ad directly challenged the viewer by proclaiming 'You are impotent, aren't you?' the viewer would be offended and would avoid the product. Because the message is presented as a subliminal ambiguity, however, the viewer is influenced by the stimulus without becoming aware of it." (WK 2007i)

Bullock then specified three types of subliminal ambiguities, that is, "in the meaning of text, in the meaning of a picture, and in the form of an optical illusion (where, for example, ice cubes in a liquor ad might be interpreted as skulls or death images). In the cigarette ad discussed above, the backbone of a female model appears to have been airbrushed to resemble an erect phallus. Bullock maintains that modern media often contain these three forms of subliminal messages." (WK 2007i)

In the end, the analysis so far reveals something didactic about two ontological principles in existential dialectics in action here, namely, the symmetry-asymmetry principle and the progression-regression principle.

In relation to the symmetry-asymmetry principle, if there is symmetry (e.g., the availability of different claims about subliminal messages), there is like asymmetry (e.g., the plausible work by E.W. Scripture and the questionable one by James Vicary).

In relation to the progression-regression principle, if there is progress in the study of anomalous experience (e.g., the work by August Bullock), there is likewise regression to be noticed (e.g, the misuse of subliminal messages for advertising and propaganda).

Remote Viewing and Psychic Warfare

A second illustration involves the use of remote viewing in psychic warfare by the U.S. military, as a case study here.

The Nature of Remote Viewing

To start, "remote viewing," a form of psychic power in anomalous experience, "is the projection of human consciousness through space and time, allowing for access to information that may be unavailable by any other means. Some remote viewers claim to be able to travel into the past or future, and can traverse vast distances and penetrate any walls or defenses. A few have claimed accuracy rates of 80 percent or higher." (G. Knapp 2003)

Perhaps more than anyone else, Ingo Swann "is most responsible for the development of RV, and Thompson Smith (1998), a discipline of Swann, wrote "a book about the technique, *Remote Perceptions*, and recently opened a school for remote viewing in Boulder City. Students are taught the basics in Smith's home office, then quickly get started giving it a try." (G. Knapp 2003)

And the "first serious studies of the technique were conducted in secrecy in the '70s. Discreet contractors such as Stanford Research Institute and Science Applications International Corp. (SAIC) found that the ability is real and that, with training, remote viewers can accomplish what would seem impossible." (G. Knapp 2003)

It did not take long, however, before the research was used for institutional interests, this time, by the U.S. military for psychic warfare.

The Application of Remote Viewing

For instance, "[b]ased on the Stanford Research Institute studies, the Army started its own remote viewing program, and in the years since RV teams have assisted the FBI, DEA, DOE and numerous other alphabet agencies, with varying degrees of success." (G. Knapp 2003)

John Alexander (1990), a retired Army intelligence officer in the U.S. military, personally testified the application, since he "was involved in the Army's psychic research program dating to the early '80s, and he co-authored *The Warrior's Edge*, a book about government research into psychokinesis and 'remote viewing.' Overall, the U.S. government spent nearly 30 years and tens of millions of dollars trying to unlock psychic secrets, spurred in part by the perception that America was well behind the Soviets in psychic research." (G. Knapp 2003)

Some specific examples concerning the application of anomalous experience for military purposes involved the U.S. military trying to locate and kill Saddam Hussein during the Gulf War, with the use of "a secret panel of 'psychics' for information about his whereabouts"—and other military operations. (G. Knapp 2003)

Although the attempt against Hussein was not successful, "remote viewers had more success during Desert Storm in helping to locate hidden Scud missiles, as well as stashes of chemical and biological weapons. The same psychic technique had been used years earlier in U.S. attempts to bomb Libyan dictator Muammar Khadafy, who narrowly escaped being blown to bits. Remote viewers have also successfully tracked Russian submarines, kept tabs on Soviet nuclear missiles and leaders, were right on the money in locating the American hostages in Iran, and have achieved other successes, many of which remain classified." (G. Knapp 2003)

The Effectiveness of Remote Viewing

But how effective is remote viewing, when applied for institutional interests, for instance?

Frankly enough, the answer is quite mixed.

John Alexander's comment is well taken, in the current context: "Is it [remote viewing] real? The answer is yes. Does it work 100 percent of the time? The answer is no. We've had some spectacular hits and some spectacular misses." (G. Knapp 2003)

After all, it is not easy to acquire remote viewing, as it requires special training—although the ability is open to all.

Angela Smith, for instance, "who earned her doctorate in psychology, says the scientists who've studied remote viewing think it works by tapping into something akin to a gigantic universal database. She contends that everyone has the ability to remote view to some extent but says it requires training and practice. Col. Alexander agrees that everyone has some ability to remote view, but he cautions against blanket acceptance of the claims of some RV practitioners. 'The skills are universal,' Alexander says. 'But it's kind of like photography. Everyone can take pictures, but not everyone is photographer.'" (G. Knapp 2003)

So, this only reinforces the progression-regression principle in existential dialectics, in that, if there is progress in the study of anomalous experience (e.g., the works on remote viewing afore-cited), there is likewise regression (e.g, the dangerous application of remote viewing for psychic warfare).

Unconsciousness and Social Structure

These conflicting features in the study of anomalous experience can even be clearer, when examined from the perspective of social structure.

An illustrative case study here concerns the divided opinions on the validity of anomalous claims among the humanists, natural scientists, and social scientists.

The Scholarly Divide

Just consider a few surveys among different scholars on anomalous experience, and this social divisiveness on the anomalous scholarship is all the more revealed (and shown in *Table 5.1*).

Surveys of the Scholarly Community

For instance, in commenting a 1979 scientific survey on clairvoyance, Daryl J. Bem (1994) and Charles Honorton in "Does Psi Exist? Replicable Evidence for an Anomalous Process of Information Transfer" had this refreshing observation to make: "A survey of more than 1,100 college professors in the United States found that 55% of natural scientists, 66% of social scientists (excluding psychologists), and 77% of academics in the arts, humanities, and education believed that ESP is either an established fact or a likely possibility. The comparable figure for psychologists was only 34%. Moreover, an equal number of psychologists declared ESP to be an impossibility, a view expressed by only 2% of all other respondents." (M. Wagner 1979)

In another survey of natural scientists in the National Academy of Sciences, this time on extrasensory perception, "96% described themselves as 'skeptical' of ESP, although 2% believed in psi and 10% felt that parapsychological research should be encouraged." (WK 2007k; R. McConnell 1991)

The Contention on Scholarship

The hard-core natural scientists, consequently, are less likely to be supportive of anomalous claims than their colleagues in the social scientists. And the humanists are most likely to be more open-minded about the claims, since they are less obsessed with the overdependency on scientific rationality which has so much dominated the scientific community since the modern era.

The specific reasons for the schism among the researchers on anomalous experience are not hard to find.

Here are a few often cited reasons, with ESP as a case study here: "A scientific methodology that shows statistically significant evidence for ESP with nearly 100% consistency has not been discovered. The lack of a viable theory of the mechanism behind ESP is also frequently cited as a source of skepticism. Historical cases in which flaws have been discovered in the experimental design of parapsychological studies, and the occasional cases of fraud marred the field." (WK 2007k)

Moreover, "[c]ritics of experimental parapsychology hold that there are no consistent and agreed-upon standards by which 'ESP powers' may be tested, in the way one might test for, say, electrical current or the chemical composition of a substance. It is argued that when psychics are challenged by skeptics and fail to prove their alleged powers, they assign all sorts of reasons for their failure, such as that the skeptic is affecting the experiment with 'negative energy.'" (WK 2007k)

A Lesson from the Scholarly Divide

This scholarly divide reveals all the more a major ontological principle in existential dialectics, namely, the symmetry-asymmetry principle, in that, if there are myriad researchers on anomalous experience, not all of them are equally influential and persuasive, as some are more so than others.

In the present context, using the first survey as an illustration, the humanists are the mostly likely to accept them, but the natural scientists are the least, with the social scientists somewhere in between.

Unconsciousness and Social Systems

But something even more tremendous has yet to happen, when examined from the perspective of social systems, in relation to anomalous experience in the context of unconsciousness (and its conscious part).

Three illustrations hereafter, in three main domains of social systems, suffice to clarify this essential point, namey, (5.5.1) the transformative power of technology, on the issue concerning technology, (5.5.2) the natural (and non-natural) selection of other worlds, on the issue concerning the environment, and (5.5.3) unfolding unconsciousness and the post-human conscious mind, on the issue concerning demography.

The Transformative Power of Technology

A good way to start is by way of a brief introduction to my past works on the transformative power of technology.

My Past Works

Let me introduce a few books of mine for illustration, although the list is not exhaustive.

For instance, in the two volumes of *The Future of Human Civilization* (or *FHC*) in 2000, I already showed the transformative power of technology to create what I visionarily called the "post-humans" (e.g., thinking machines, thinking robots, cyborgs, genetically altered superior beings, and the like) in the future world.

In the subsequent book titled *The Future of Capitalism and Democracy* (o *FCD*) in 2002, I further elaborated the different technologies and environments in deep space unto multiverses for the further development of this post-human world that we have never known.

In another book titled *The Future of Post-Human Consciousness* (or *FPHC*) in 2004 (and also *FCD*), I went further to introduce other post-human lifeforms like "floating consciousness" and "hyperspatial consciousness."

In still another book titled *The Future of Post-Human Space-Time* (or *FPHST*) in 2006, I proposed how technology will be used again, this time, to change space and time for the post-human world.

In another subsequent book titled *Beyond Nature and Nurture* (or *BNN*) in 2006, I showed, in greater details, the biological origins of this technological transformation of the coming post-human species.

In the following book titled *The Future of Aesthetic Experience* (o *FAE*) in 2007, I analyzed how technology will be used again, this time for the tremendous transformation of aesthetic experience in the post-human world in a way that we have never known. In this work, I even introduced the so-called "evolution-transformation principle" in existential dialectics, in specifically giving credit to the transformative role of technology for the change in the world and beyond, and thus the word "transformation" in the principle is suggestive.

Thus is the transformative power of technology.

The Rise of Unfolding Unconsciousness

In the current context of anomalous experience in the context of unconsciousenss and its conscious counterpart, technology will have its role to play as well, in contributing to the rise of what I originally call, in the absnece of better words, *unfolding unconsciousness* in the future world to come.

This should not be surprising, in light of my previous visionary works on the transformative role of technology.

What is more specific in the current context of anomalous experience is that, although the numerous case studies so far introduced in this book for the analysis of the different perspectives of understanding and exploring anomalous experience in relation to unconsciousness and its conscious counterpart are not exhaustive, nor are they perfect (since all of them, in one way or another, have been subject to different criticisms as shown in the previous chapters)—many of them have the virtue to point us to the right direction of making a prediction of what is to come in the future world of exploring the unconscious mind.

The important point to remember here is not whether or not the case studies are valid beyond doubt (since none of them is completely so), but that they show us different imaginative possibilities of a still very much speculative world that we have never clearly understood.

All of their specific arguments are most likely to be falsified in future studies, just as no anomalous claim has ever been conclusively proved in all human history hitherto existing. After all, what has?

But to dismiss them on this ground errs on an extremely ignorant and naïve basis in relation to the future world to come, to which technology will steadily and eventually contribute, in *unfolding* the nature of the unconscious mind for the future human world (and, especially though not exclusively, its post-human successor) to master.

As a summary, the case studies so far, illustrative as they merely are, already show us the direction that technology will take to unfold the unconscious mind, even if the specific details and arguments that current scientists and scholars provide are not entirely convincing.

Good examples, as summarized in *Table 2.17*, include, say, the higher-dimensional space-time in hyperspace theory, the particle-wave interactions at the quantum mechanical level in quantum mechanics, the unconscious fantasies in psychoanalysis, the mind-altering drugs in biochemistry, the manipulation of neural activity in neurobiology, the study of brain waves in electromagnetic theory, the correlation between anomalous experience and moral/religious/aesthetic interests in culture studies, the role of mythology and language in epistemology, different organizational agendas in organizatonal studies, the scholarly divide in social structural study, interests and propaganda in institutioanl research, the transformative power of technology in social system research, the natural and non-natural selection of other worlds in exo-biology, and the rise of post-humans in qualitative demography.

These fields will be important to the future unfolding of the unconscious mind for the better understanding of anomalous experience in a way that we have never known, although the specific arguments and details provided by many of the scholars in the literature in all human history hitherto existing are most likely to be falsified in the distant future scientific world.

The coming post-humans will make use of the speculative fantasies that humans have so far imagined since time immemorial, in order to expand their senses and faculties in a way that humans can only so far dream of.

In *FHC*, *FCD*, *FPHST*, and *FPHC*, for instance, I already gave some examples of the extraordinary powers of future post-humans that we current humans do not have. They can see, smell, touch, taste, hear, run, jump, think, communicate, and do many other things faster and better that we humans can only fantasize in science fiction and fraudulent anomalous claims.

To dismiss anomalous claims on the simplistic basis of the lack of conclusive scientific evidences so far in human history really miss this important point for the coming future world of post-humans that we have never known, especially in the context of the rise of the unfolding unconsciousness.

Our often fraudulent anomalous claims only give them the foundation of imaginative creativity to build superior intelligent life in the future world, both in deep space and beyond unto multiverses.

The Expansion-Contraction Principle in Existential Dialectics

Consequently, the rise of this unfolding consciousness constitutes a tremendous turning point for the future of unconsciousness and its conscious counterpart.

Freud made good use of his imagination when he treated the domain of unconsciousness metaphorically as the huge portion of the mental iceberg lying beneath its tip, which has remained hidden from full understanding but has much potential to be actualized.

In the post-human world, as the domain of unconsciousness is further unfolden and better understood, its vast storage of information (be it about fantasies or not) in the intangible realm will be more fully utilized in a way that the human world so far has never known.

The transformation of the human brain will undergo a tremendous change in utilization. It is interesting to note a recent work by Daniel Pink (2005) in *A Whole New Mind*, in which he claims the evolution of "the Information Age" to "the Conceptual Age," so that the human brain is shifting from the previous focus on the left brain to the right brain in this new era.

As Pink put it himself, "[w]ell, the scales are tipping away from what it used to take for people to get ahead—logical, linear, left-brain, and spreadsheet-type abilities—in favor of abilities like artistry, empathy, and big-picture thinking, which are becoming more valuable. Left-brain skills are still absolutely necessary in our complex world. They're just not sufficient anymore." (MCN 2007)

Whether or not Pink is correct or not about this major shift is subject to debate, for sure. But the more important point here is not about the certainty of this shift (as Pink falsely assumed)..

Rather, what Pink does not realize is that this shift is minor, when contrasted with something more tremendous to come, in that the function of the brain will shift further and further to the fuller exploitation of the unconscious realm, or that huge portion of the mental iceberg beneath the surface, which has yet to be fully understood and utitlized.

The post-humans will more fully study, understand, and exploit the different capacities and fantasies in the unfolding unconsciousness, and the examination of anomalous experience in this book precisely points to the direction of this coming transformation of the brain that humans have never known.

In so doing, a new ontological principle in existential dialetics, that is, the expansion-contraction principle, can be introduced, in that just as entities can expand in some ways over time, they can also contract in different ways.

This principle, although not so explicitly identified, was already used, however partially, in relation to different topics in my previous works (e.g., the theory of floating consciousness in *FCD* and *FPHC*, the union of the unions in *BWT*, and the cyclical progression of system fragmentation and integration in *FCD*).

In the current context of anomalous experience in relation to unconsciousness, the brain will undergo a major shift towards the fuller exploitation of the unconscious domain.

The future of the conscious mind will have to deal with this paradigmatic shifting of the unfolding unconsciousness. So, the further exploitation of anomalous experience by post-humans to expand further their extraordinary senses and other capacities on the basis of the human history of anomalous imagination is coming.

But expansion will have its double, that is, contraction. In other words, not every single capacity and imagination in the history of anomalous experience as claimed by humans will be fully studied and exploited by post-humans. Some will be ignored, and their influence will contract, whereas others will be given more attention, and their influence will expand.

But why? To understand "why" requires the understanding of the natural (and non-natural) selection of other worlds.

The Natural (and Non-Natural) Selection of Other Worlds

In Chapter 7 of *FHC,* I already analyzed the impact of a radically different environment on the coming emergence of the post-human lifeforms on earth and later in deep space until multiverses.

In Chapter 10 of *FCD*, I further developed the thesis, especially (though not exclusively) in *Sec.10.4.4* titled "The Next Frontier: Deep Space in Multiverses."

In *FPHC* (and also *FCD*), I explored further how the mind will undergo changes towards the direction of "floating consciousness" and "hyperspatial consciousness," in relation to these radically different environments.

In *BNN*, I further explored the interactions between nature and nurture in transforming intelligent life in all history hitherto existing, and its post-human future.

In *FPHST*, I showed how space-time will also be changed in relation to this post-human world.

All these reminders, illustrative (non-exhaustive) as they merely are, are to show how much the transformation of living environments in highly different forms will change intelligent life in a new way, which is subject to both natural selection and, for that matter, non-natural selection (as expressed in the evolution-transformation principle).

In the current context of anomalous experience in the unconscious realm (and its conscious counterpart), how the unconscious mind is unfolded in more specific details in the distant future will be in large part dependent on the contingent worlds that the post-humans will live for their utilization on earth and soon, in deep space until multiverses.

Some portions of the unconscious mind in relation to some specific capacities and fantasies will be expanded further by post-humans for their uses, while others will not be so much used—contingent on the specific environments in question.

And these can be about superior senses (be they through space, as in clair-sentience, clair-voyance, clair-audience, clair-austance, clair-alience, or clair-cognizance—or through time, as in pre-cognition, re-sentiment, retro-cognition, and retro-sentiment), or about superior contacts (be they with living minds as in telepathy, with the dead as in midiumship, or with other non-living entities as in telekinesis), as shown in *Table 2.16*.

Already, some scholars start speculating on the coming world that humans have never known so far in history, especially (though not exclusively) in relation to anomalous experience.

For instance, Kevin Warwick proposed "techlepathy," on the basis of "his recent cybernetics research around developing practical, safe devices for directly connecting human nervous systems together with computers and with each other. He believes techno-enabled telepathy will in the future become the primary form of human communication." (WK 2007m)

Others like Thea Alexander (1976) in the novel *2150 A.D.* speculated the possibility of using telekinesis, telepathy, and precognition in future societies.

In a different way, Moravec proposed the "Bush Robot" in a future world, in which "a postbiological being with many numbers of arms, legs, and other flexible limbs, each of which is connected with photoreceptors far more sensitive than those ever had before on Earth. And its limbs could branch out into smaller and finer limbs, like the twigs of a tree, whenever needed.(E.Regis 1990:169-70)" (P.Baofu 2000: Ch.7)

More daringly, "Pynchon came up with the idea of an automaton (sewn into the flesh with 'a miniature electric switch' connected to electric wires running 'from its terminals up the arm, disappearing under the sleeve'), who can even absorb X-rays, gamma rays, and neutrons, or take the worst falls without suffering damage. (D.Porush 1985:119) In John Barth's universe of machines, these superior beings can take human mannerisms and physiognomies but perform superhuman deeds (e.g., seeing in the dark, hearing unusual noise, walking on water, flying, and changing colors).(D.Porush 1985:149-50)" (P. Baofu 2000: Ch.7)

The list can go on, of course, but the point here is the contingent selection, be it natural or non-natural, of other worlds to come that humans have never known.

Their contingent selection will greatly shape the specific forms of capacities and fantasies of the unconscious mind to come in the post-human world.

Unfolding Unconsciousness and the Post-Human Conscious Mind

But there is one more business left to do, that is to say, that the unfolding unconscious mind so understood, be it about its expansion and contraction in relation to anomalous experience in the intanglible realm, will be developed in close connection with the post-human conscious mind to come that humans have never known.

After all, Freud is right, to the extent that both the conscious mind and the unconscious mind interact with each other in different ways.

In the coming post-human world, I already proposed in *FCD* and later in *FPHC*, two radically different forms of the conscious mind, namely, "floating conssciousness" in deep space and "hyperspatial consciousness" in higher dimensional space-time.

And in *FHC* (and also *FCD*), I also suggested that other forms of the post-human conscious mind include thinking machines, thinking robots, cyborgs, genetically altered superior beings, and the like.

The rise of the unfolding unconsciousness (or more broadly, the unfolding unconscious mind) will be developed in conjunction with the guidance and influence of floating consciousness, hyper-spatial consciousness, and these other forms of the post-huaman conscious mind.

Unfolding unconsciousness is thus closely related to floating consciousness, hyper-spatial consciousness, and these other forms of post-human consciousness in the distant future.

In the short-term, however, unfolding consciousness starts being explored by the human mind, just as in the medium-term, it will be examined by other forms of the post-human mind (like those of thinking machines, thinking robots, cyborgs, genetically altered superior beings, and the like—even before the emergence of floating consciousness and hyper-spatial consciousness in the distant term).

The history of unconsciousness and its future can therefore be summarized in what follows:

———

primordial unconsciousness → human unconsciousness →
post-human unconsciousness (with unfolding unconsciousness as a climax in the evolution of unconsciousness)

———

By the same logic, but in a different context, the history of consciousness and its future can be summarized in what follows (as already introduced in Chapter 1, based on my previous books):

———

primordial consciousness → human consciousness →
post-human consciousness (with floating consciousness and hyper-spatial consciousness as a climax in the evolution of consciousness)

———

In this sense, the analysis of the history of unconsciousness and its future so understood (in *FPHU*) is a logical sequence to my previous work on the history of consciousness and its future (in *FPHC*).

The two are thus closely related and complement each other.

The Drawback of Society

Needless to say, one should not try to understand the nature of anomalous experience in the context of unconsciousness (and its conscious counterpart) solely from the perspective of society (as the subject matter of this chapter).

Rather, the fuller nature of anomalous experience in the context of unconsciousness and its conscious counterpart should be broadly examined in relation to other perspectives too, be they in relation to the mind (in Chapter Two), nature (in Chapter Three), and culture (in Chapter Four).

With this caveat against reductionism in mind, what then can we conclude, at the end of this long intellectual journey?

This is the question to be answered in the following chapter, Chapter Six titled "Conclusion: The Future of Unconsciousness"—to which we now turn.

Table 5.1. The Scholarly Divide on Anomalous Experience

- **A 1979 scientific survey on scholars believing in ESP**
  - —34% of psychologists
  - —55% of natural scientists
  - —66% of social scientists (excluding psychologists)
  - —77% of academics in the arts, humanities, and education

- **A 1991 survey of natural scientists (inside NAS) believing in ESP**
  - —96% were "skeptical"
  - —2% believed in psi
  - —10% supported parapsychological research

Source: From Ch.5 of *FPHU*, based on the data from D. Bem (1994), M. Wagner (1979), WK (2007k), and R. McConnell (1991)

Table 5.2. The Theory of Post-Democracy I: The Priority of Freedom over Equality (Part I)

- **Differences**
  - —*For the aggressive Lions (the strong Elitists)*
    - •Setting up rank distinctions among unequals (e.g., between inferior humans and superior post-humans, or later among inferior post-humans and superior ones, relatively speaking)
    - •Yearning for being not only distinguished from unequals, but also the first among equals (the best of the very best)
    - •Soul-searching for a high spiritual culture (not the trashy one for the masses). Mass culture is a dirty joke for them.
  - —*For the manipulative Foxes (the weak Counter-Elitists)*
    - •Seeking a gentle hegemony by way of more communitarian concerns (for inferior humans and, later, inferior post-humans)
    - •Being more sympathetic to less formal-legalistic institutions and values

- **Similarities**
  - —*For both Lions and Foxes*
    - •Exploring different spheres of non-human consciousness in the cosmos (something vastly superior than the human one)
    - •Recognizing the democratic illusions (e.g., no freedom without unfreedom, no equality without inequality, or simply no justice without injustice, and vice versa)

(continued on next page)

Table 5.2. The Theory of Post-Democracy I: The Priority of Freedom over Equality (Part II)

Notes: The two callings and examples in each category are solely illustrative (not exhaustive), since there will be many different post-human value ideals in the distant future of post-human civilization. The comparison is also relative (not absolute) towards post-democracy, so this is not just a version of free-market democracy (nor Fascism/Nazism, as shown in the table later on democracy, non-democracy, and post-democracy). Nor are they mutually exclusive. As generalities, they allow exceptions. And the specific forms of post-human post-democratic ideals need to be further developed in future after-postmodern history, as they will be different from the ones we now know. The point here is to solely give an extremely rough picture of a small part of the world to come that we have never known.
Source: From Ch.10 of *FCD*. Refer to text for more info and references.

Table 5.3. The Theory of Post-Democracy II: The Priority of Equality over Freedom

- **Hybrid Versions of**
  —Ex: the Trans-Feminine Calling
  —Ex: the Trans-Sinitic Calling
  —Ex: the Trans-Islamic Calling
  —Ex: the Trans-Outerspace Calling

- **Qualifications**
  —These four versions of post-capitalist value ideals need not automatically be post-democratic, just as capitalism does not necessarily mean democracy. They are two different entities—though closely related.
  —But up to a certain threshold of elevating equality at the farther expense of freedom, the democratic ideals will be overcome and cease to exist.
  —The overcome will not be socialist or communist, but post-democratic with no freedom without unfreedom and no equality without inequality, subject to the constraints of existential dialectics.

Notes: The callings are solely illustrative (not exhaustive), since there will be many different post-human value ideals in the distant future of post-human lifeforms. The comparison is also relative (not absolute), nor are they mutually exclusive. As generalities, they allow exceptions. And the specific forms of post-human post-democratic ideals need to be further developed in future after-postmodern history, as they will be different from the ones we now know. The point here is to solely give an extremely rough picture of a small part of the world to come that we have never known.
Source: From Ch.10 of *FCD*. Refer to text for more info and references.

Table 5.4. The Theory of Post-Democracy III: The Transcendence of Freedom and Equality (Part I)

- **Transcending Freedom in Floating Existence**
  —*Freedom*: seeking an ultimate elimination of the body. Being without the body. The aim is to transcend freedom in the end into a metaphysical state (i.e., beyond the physique).
  —*Unfreedom*: yet facing difficult trade-offs. The sacrifice of bodily existence and its joyfulness. An eternal boredom in floating existence in dark deep space, though with alternative pleasures. There is no free lunch even in the state of transcending freedom.

- **Transcending Equality in the Rivalry of Cosmic Hegemony**
  —*Inequality*: competing to outlast other lifeforms in floating existence, or just marginalizing them for one's hegemonic expansiveness in the rest of the cosmos (and even beyond). Universalism is only for the mediocre.
  —*Equality*: accepting only those of one's rank as equal partners in the vast spacetime for cosmic supremacy. Even here, the aim is to transcend equality into a metaphysical state.

(continued on next page)

Table 5.4. The Theory of Post-Democracy III: The Transcendence of Freedom and Equality (Part II)

Notes: Do not confuse this transcendence of freedom and equality (as one version of post-democracy) with the naïve temptation to transcend the freedom/unfreedom and equality/inequality dialectics. Existential dialectics hold true for freedom and equality in all cultures and societies—past, present, or future (i.e., democracy, non-democracy, and post-democracy), regardless of whether freedom and equality are conventionally understood as "negative" or "positive."

Also, the two features and examples in each are solely illustrative (not exhaustive), since there will be many different post-human value ideals in the distant future of post-human lifeforms. The comparison is also relative (not absolute), nor are they mutually exclusive. As generalities, they allow exceptions. And the specific forms of post-human ideals even for these radically alien floating lifeforms (and others unknown to us) need to be further developed in future after-postmodern history, as they will likely be different from the ones herein illustrated. The point here is to solely give a very rough picture of a small part of the extremely alien world to come that we have never known.

Source: From Ch.10 of *FCD*. Refer to text for more info and references.

Table 5.5. Democracy, Non-Democracy, and Post-Democracy (Part I)

- **Democracy**
  - —*Theoretical Constructs*
    - •The pursuit of freedom and equality (in various degrees), regardless of whether freedom and equality can be understood as "negative" or "positive"
      - (1) more equality than freedom: The relative priority of the good over the right
      - (2) more freedom than equality: The relative priority of the right over the good
  - —*Types*
    - •Only (1): Different versions of communitarian moral universalism
    - •Only (2): Different versions of liberal moral universalism
    - •(1) or (2): Different versions of anarchic (non-nation-state) moral universalism
    - •(1) or (2): Different versions of postmodern moral localism

- **Non-Democracy**
  - —*Theoretical Constructs*
    - •The focus on (1') equality or (2') freedom, but not both, regardless of whether freedom and equality can be understood as "negative" or "positive"
  - —*Types*
    - •Only (1'): Different versions on the Far Left (e.g., Stalinism, Robespierrianism)
    - •Only (2'): Different versions on the Far Right (e.g., Nazism, absolute monarchism)

(continued on next page)

Table 5.5. Democracy, Non-Democracy, and Post-Democracy (Part II)

- **Post-Democracy**
  - *—Theoretical Constructs*
    - •The priority of (1'') equality over freedom, or (2'') freedom over equality, or (3'') the transcendence of freedom and equality, regardless of whether freedom and equality are "negative" or "positive." In degree, (1'') or (2'') is less than (1') or (2') but more than (1) or (2)—respectively.
    - •Like democracy and non-democracy, post-democracy is also subject to the freedom/unfreedom and equality/inequality dialectics (or existential dialectics in general). Unlike them, post-democracy acknowledges the constraints of existential dialectics and no longer value freedom and equality as sacred virtues. There is no utopia, in the end; even were there one, dystopia would exist within it.
  - *—Types*
    - •(1''): Different versions of trans-Sinitic value ideals
    - •(1''): Different versions of trans-feminine value ideals
    - •(1''): Different versions of trans-Islamic value ideals
    - •(1''): Different versions of trans-outerspace value ideals
    - •(2''): Different versions of post-human elitist value ideals
    - •(3''): Different versions of the value ideals of floating consciousness (etc.)

(continued on next page)

Table 5.5. Democracy, Non-Democracy, and Post-Democracy (Part III)

Notes: The examples are solely illustrative (not exhaustive), nor are they mutually exclusive. As generalities, they allow exceptions. "Negative" freedom is freedom "from" (e.g., freedom from poverty), whereas "positive" freedom is freedom "to" (e.g., freedom to the state of enlightenment). "Negative" equality is "procedural" equality (e.g., equality of opportunity), while "positive" equality is "substantive" equality (e.g., equality of outcome). Existential dialectics impose constraints on freedom and equality in democracy, non-democracy, and post-democracy, regardless of whether freedom and equality can be understood as "negative" or "positive" in conventional discourse. Therefore, do not confuse the transcendence of freedom and equality in (3'') with the naïve temptation to transcend existential dialectics. There is no utopia, in the end; even should there be one, it would not exist without dystopia embedded within it.
Sources: A summary, based on my previous works, especially Ch.5 of *FHC*, Chs.5-10 of *FCD*, Chs.2-4 of *FPHC*, and Chs.1 & 7 of *BDPD*. The reader should consult the books for more analysis, as this is only a summary here.

Table 5.6. Multiple Causes of the Emergence of Post-Democracy (Part I)

• **At the Micro-Physical Level**
—Ex: intelligent life without the human physical-chemical system
—Sources: Ch.7 of *FHC*; Chs.9-10 of *FCD*; Ch.1 of *FPHC*

• **At the Chemical Level**
—Ex: space radiation and toxins
—Sources: Ch.7 of *FHC*; Chs.9-10 of *FCD*

• **At the Bio-Psychological Level**
—Ex: exo-biological evolution in deep space
—Ex: genetic engineering of new beings
—Ex: limits of cognitive partiality
—Ex: illusions of emotional neutrality
—Ex: human biological inequality
—Sources: Ch.2 & Chs.9-10 of *FCD*; Ch.7 of *FHC*; Ch.4 of *BCPC*

• **At the Institutional Level**
—Ex: the flawed logic of equality
—Ex: the conflicting nature of governance
—Sources: Ch.5 of *FHC*; Chs.6 & 10 of *FCD*; Ch.3 of *FPHC*; Chs.2-5 of *BDPD*

• **At the Organizational Level**
—Ex: e-civic alienation
—Ex: the dark sides of formal-legalistic routines
—Sources: Ch.3 of *FHC*; Ch.7 of *FCD*; Ch.3 of *FPHC*

• **At the Structural Level**
—Ex: ever new forms of inequities, at home and abroad
—Ex: the emergence of China, women, and Islam as major actors
—Sources: Chs.5-6 of *FHC*; Chs.7, 9 & 10 of *FCD*; Chs.4-5 of *BDPD*

(continued on next page)

Table 5.6. Multiple Causes of the Emergence of Post-Democracy (Part II)

- **At the Cultural Level**
  - —Ex: freedom/unfreedom dialectics
  - —Ex: equality/inequality dialectics
  - —Ex: system fragmentation and integration
  - —Sources: Ch.5 of *FHC*; Chs.3, 9 & 10 of *FCD*; Ch.4 of *FPHC*; Ch.1 of *BDPD*; Ch.4 of *BCPC*

- **At the Systemic Level**
  - —Ex: space habitats (in zero-gravity) and colonization
  - —Ex: ultra advanced future info systems
  - —Ex: qualitative demography
  - —Sources: Ch.7 of *FHC*; Chs.9 &10 of *FCD*

- **At the Cosmological Level**
  - —Ex: the colonization of multiverses
  - —Ex: the expansion of floating consciousness
  - —Ex: the spread of hyper-spatial consciousness
  - —Sources: Ch.7 of *FHC*; Chs.9 &10 of *FCD*; Ch.4 of *FPHC*

Notes: The examples in each category are solely illustrative (not exhaustive), and some of the items can be reclassified somewhere else. Nor are they always mutually exclusive. Since they are generalities, exceptions are expected.
Sources: From *FHC*, *FCD*, *FPHC*, *BCPC*, and *BDPD*. See also *Table 1.13* and *Table 1.14* of *BCIV* on my perspectives on civilizational holism (or *Table 1.17* and *Table 1.18* of *FAE*).

Table 5.7. Some Clarifications about Post-Capitalism and Post-Democracy (Part I)

• The prefix "trans-" in the first category of post-capitalism (with its four versions) refers to something "going beyond" (not "uniting" or "combining").
Ex: *Sec.10.3.3* of *FCD*; *Sec.2.4* & *Sec.4.4* of *FPHC*; *Sec.7.2* of *BCPC*

• Such terms like "post-democracy," "post-capitalism," "post-human elitist," "trans-feminine calling," and the like as used in my works are more for our current intellectual convenience than to the liking of future humans and post-humans, who will surely invent more tasteful neologisms to call their own eras, entities, and everything else, for that matter. But the didactic point here is to use the terms to foretell what the future might be like, not that its eras and entities must be called so exactly and permanently.
Ex: *Sec.11.1* of *FCD*; *Sec.7.2* of *BCPC*

• The four versions in the first category of post-capitalist value ideals need not automatically be post-democratic, just as capitalism does not necessarily mean democracy. They are two different entities—though closely related. But up to a certain threshold of elevating equality at the farther expense of freedom, the democratic ideals will be overcome and cease to exist. The same is true for the post-human elitist calling in the second category of post-capitalism in relation to post-democracy, depending on the extent to which freedom is elevated at the expense of equality.
Ex: *Sec.10.4.3.3* of *FCD*; *Table 3.9* of *FPHC*; *Table 7.6* of *BDPD*

• The comparison in each of the three realms of existence in all forms of post-capitalism is not absolute, but relative. Examples include "communal" vs. "individualistic," and the like.
Ex: Notes in *Table 10.8*, *Table 10.9*, *Table 10.10*, & *Table 10.11* of *FCD*; Chs.2-4 of *FPHC*; *Sec.7.2* of *BCPC*

• The emergence of post-capitalism (and post-democracy, for that matter) has multiple causes (to not be reduced to one or only a few).
Ex: Ch.10 of *FCD*, Chs.2-4 of *FPHC*; *Sec.1.3* & *Sec.7.2* of *BCPC* (or *Table 1.8* & *Table 7.11*)

(continued on next page)

Table 5.7. Some Clarifications about Post-Capitalism and Post-Democracy (Part II)

• The specific forms of post-capitalism (and post-democracy, for that matter) need to be further developed in future after-postmodern history, as they will be different from the ones we now know. The point here is to solely give an extremely rough sketch of a world to come that we have never known.
Ex: *Sec.10.3.3* & *Sec.10.4.3.3* of *FCD*; *Table 10.14* & *Table 10.15* of *FCD*; *Sec.7.2* of *BCPC*

• All forms of post-capitalism are not part of a "teleological law," but of "historical trends" only. The same is also true for all forms of post-democracy.
Ex: *Sec.7.1* of *FHC*; *Sec.9.5.3.2* & *Sec.10.3.4.2* of *FCD*; *Sec.7.2* of *BCPC*

• Post-capitalism is not better than capitalism in an "absolute" sense but only fits in better, on the basis of the historical contingency of culture, society, nature, and the mind in some future eras. The same is true for post-democracy in relation to democracy. The term "better" is historically relative.
Ex: *Sec.10.3.3* of *FCD*; *Sec.1.7* of *BDPD*; *Sec.1.5* of *BCPC*

• All forms of post-capitalism and post-democracy are subject to the constraints of existential dialectics. In the process, the dialectic direction is to go beyond the conventional "either-or" dichotomies (e.g., freedom vs. unfreedom, equality vs. inequality, freedom vs. equality, individuality vs. communality, spirituality vs. materiality, formal legalism vs. informal legalism, etc.). As is true in post-civilization, to go beyond the dichotomies is to acknowledge the co-existence of both in each dichotomy, although the degree of scaling one over the over varies from case to case (e.g., the theory of post-capitalism I, the theory of post-capitalism II, the theory of post-democracy I, the theory of post-democracy II, etc.)—but is not to be extreme in largely favoring one over the other, *on average* (all things considered). There is no utopia to be had in the end; even should there be one, dystopia would exist within it.
Ex: Ch.5 of *FHC*; *Sec.10.4.4.2* of *FCD*; *Sec.1.5* of *BDPD*; *Sec.1.3* of *BCPC*; *BCIV*

(continued on next page)

Table 5.7. Some Clarifications about Post-Capitalism and Post-Democracy (Part III)

• All forms of post-capitalism, however different from each other though they are, share one common feature, in that they all inspire for a higher spiritual culture. The same is also true for post-democracy.
Ex: *Sec.10.3*, *Sec.10.4* & *Sec.10.5* of *FCD*; *Chs.2-4* of *FPHC*; *Sec.7.2* of *BCPC*

• All forms of post-capitalism try to avoid the excess in capitalist consumerism by favoring more basic than artificial needs in having, but the quality and quantity of these "basic" needs will be measured by future standards, not by our current ones. Standards are historically relative.
Ex: *Sec.10.3*, *Sec.10.4* & *Sec.10.5* of *FCD*; Ch.2 of *FPHC*; *Sec.7.2* of *BCPC*

• All forms of post-capitalism make use of a different degree of political authority with advanced info systems in future history and strives for higher spiritual cultures (especially in the post-human age), while acknowledging the constraints of existential dialectics and no longer valuing free market (as in capitalism) and economic control (as in non-capitalism) as sacred virtues.
Ex: *Sec.10.3.4.2*, *Sec.10.3*, *Sec.10.4* & *Sec.10.5* of *FCD*; Chs.2-4 of *FPHC*; *Sec.1.5* of *BDPD*; *Sec.7.2* of *BCPC*

Notes:: The main points here are solely illustrative (not exhaustive) nor necessarily mutually exclusive, and the comparison is relative (not absolute). As generalities, they allow exceptions. The sections as cited are only illustrative (not exhaustive).
Sources: From *FHC*, *FCD*, *FPHC*, and *BDPD*

Table 5.8. The Theory of Post-Capitalism I.1: By Group— Ex: Spiritual/Communal in the Trans-Feminine Calling

- **More Communal Than Individual**
  —*Sharing*: learning from others, as different ideas mutually enrich
  —*Cooperative*: encouraging a sense of shared leadership and teamwork

- **More Informal-Legalistic Than Formal-Legalistic**
  —*Specific*: listening more from the heart than from the head, to know a person as a concrete, not as an abstract, unit
  —*Affective*: thinking and acting with others on a more affective tone. Business can mix with an emotional touch.
  —*Ascriptive*: hiring (or firing) can be done on the basis of merit (or lack of it), but deep solidarity (sisterhood) is important too.
  —*Particularistic*: making decisions on the basis of cost-benefit analysis, but a given group relationship is vital

- **More Spiritual Than Secular**
  —*Long-Term Looking*: sharing for a long-term relationship (e.g., love, friendship), not just for a short-term gain
  —*Loving/Caring*: showing compassion for the sufferings of others, without quickly blaming and pre-judging
  —*Respectful*: showing acceptance about others' feelings (and thoughts)

Notes: The categories and examples are solely illustrative, since there can be different versions, and the comparison is relative (not absolute), nor are they mutually exclusive. As generalities, they allow exceptions. The specific forms of the trans-feminine version need to be further developed in future after-postmodern history, as they will be different from the ones we now know, since the prefix "trans-" here means going beyond or deconstructing the feminine values, while using them as the inspirational point at the beginning.
Source: From Ch.10 of *FCD*. Refer to text for more info and references.

Table 5.9. The Theory of Post-Capitalism I.2:
By Nation-State—
Ex: Spiritual/Communal in the Trans-Sinitic Calling

- **More Communal Than Individualistic**
  —*Centralized*: being more top-down in management
  —*Collective*: encouraging more group cooperation
  —*Social*: investing in trust and connection

- **More Informal-Legalistic Than Formal-Legalistic**
  —*Specific*: knowing more of those related or connected
  —*Affective*: behaving in a paternalistic, hierarchical way
  —*Ascriptive*: favoring family members and those related
  —*Particularistic*: building connection (guanxi) as imperative

- **More Spiritual Than Secular**
  —*Expansionist*: diffusing civilizational values (e.g., the superiority complex of civilizationalism)
  —*Holistic*: synthesizing things into a panoramic horizon
  —*Historical*: learning from the lessons of the ancient past
  —*Respectful*: deferential to elders and superiors

Notes: The categories and examples are solely illustrative, since there can be different versions, and the comparison is relative (not absolute), nor are they mutually exclusive. As generalities, they allow exceptions. The specific forms of the trans-Sinitic version need to be further developed in future after-postmodern history, as they will be different from the ones we now know, since the prefix "trans-" here means going beyond or deconstructing the Sinitic values, while using them as the inspirational point at the beginning.
Source: From Ch.10 of *FCD*. Refer to text for more info and references.

Table 5.10. The Theory of Post-Capitalism I.3: By Region— Ex: Spiritual/Communal in the Trans-Islamic Calling

---

- **More Communal Than Individualistic**
  —*Collective*: building the webs of relationships to bind individuals
  —*Sharing*: cultivating the established "wisdom" through common experience
  —*Cooperative*: stressing harmony, solidarity, and commonality

- **More Informal-Legalistic Than Formal-Legalistic**
  —*Specific*: making efforts to know well the participants (family and larger community) in matters of common concern
  —*Affective*: mixing work with language and ritual on explicit religious (Islamic) ideals, texts, stories, and examples
  —*Ascriptive*: privileging local history and custom on relationships among kinship groups
  —*Particularistic*: preferring an unbiased insider with ongoing connections to all parties

- **More Spiritual Than Secular**
  —*Historical*: learning from the lessons of the past as a source of stability and guidance
  —*Deferential*: showing respect for age, experience, status, and leadership in communal affairs
  —*Honorable*: emphasizing face, dignity, prestige, and fairness
  —*Compassionate*: giving mercy and charity ("Zahah") to others

---

Notes: The categories and examples are solely illustrative (not exhaustive), and the comparison is relative (not absolute), nor are they mutually exclusive. As generalities, they allow exceptions. The specific forms of the trans-Islamic version need to be further developed in future after-postmodern history, as they will be different from the ones we now know, since the prefix "trans-" here means going beyond or deconstructing the Islamic values, while using them as the inspirational point at the beginning.
Sources: From Ch.10 of *FCD*. Refer to text for more info and references, especially from the works by George Irani (2000) and C. Murphy (September 19, 2001).

Table 5.11. The Theory of Post-Capitalism I.4: By Universe— Ex: Spiritual/Communal in the Trans-Outerspace Calling

- **More Communal Than Individual**
  —*Cooperative*: requiring teamwork in small space habitats
  —*Sharing*: learning from, and enjoying being with, each other in a small group in outer space

- **More Informal-Legalistic Than Formal-Legalistic**
  —*Specific*: knowing more about each other to facilitate living and working together in space, both as fellow astronauts and space-mates
  —*Affective*: being friendly and social to each other as vital to working and living in small space quarters
  —*Ascriptive*: nurturing comaraderie among fellow astronauts as if they are family members over time
  —*Particularistic*: building work relationship with enduring memory in a space mission

- **More Spiritual Than Secular**
  —*Long-Term*: looking beyond selfish materialistic concerns in a precarious space environment with potential life or death
  —*Loving/Caring*: cultivating deep bondage for the success of a long term space mission
  —*Transcendent*: searching for life meaning in outer space

Notes: The calling and examples in each category are solely illustrative (not exhaustive), since there will be many different outer-space value ideals in the distant future of space colonization. The comparison is also relative (not absolute), nor are they mutually exclusive. As generalities, they allow exceptions. And the specific forms of trans-outer-space calling need to be further developed in future after-postmodern history, as they will be different from the ones we now know, since the prefix "trans-" here means going beyond or deconstructing the current outer-space values, while using them as the inspirational point at the beginning. The point here is to solely give an extremely rough picture of a small part of the world to come that we still do not know much about.
Source: From Ch.10 of *FCD*. Refer to text for more info and references.

Table 5.12. The Theory of Post-Capitalism II: Spiritual/Individualistic in the Post-Human Elitist Calling (Part I)

- **More Individualistic Than Communal**
  —Setting up rank distinctions among unequals (e.g., between inferior humans and superior post-humans, or later among inferior post-humans and superior ones, relatively speaking)
  —Yearning for being not only distinguished from unequals, but also the first among equals (the best of the very best)
  —Recognizing the constraints of equality/inequality dialectics (or existential dialectics in general)

- **More Spiritual Than Secular**
  —Soul-searching for a high spiritual culture (not the trashy one for the masses). Mass culture is a dirty joke for them.
  —Exploring different spheres of non-human consciousness in the cosmos (something vastly superior than the human one)
  —Recognizing the constraints of freedom/unfreedom dialectics (or existential dialectics in general)

- **Qualifications**
  —Although post-human elitist post-democracy is comparable to post-human elitist post-capitalism in some respects, the former does not necessarily imply the latter (post-human elitist post-capitalism), just as democracy does not have to entail capitalism. They are two different (though related) entities.
  —But up to a certain threshold of incorporating government intervention with advanced info systems in future civilizations for higher spiritual concerns at the expense of the free market and materialist pursuit, the capitalist ideal will be overcome.
  —The overcome will not be Fascist or feudalistic, but post-capitalist, subject to the constraints of existential dialectics.

(continued on next page)

Table 5.12. The Theory of Post-Capitalism II: Spiritual/Individualistic in the Post-Human Elitist Calling (Part II)

Notes: The calling and examples in each category are solely illustrative (not exhaustive). The comparison is also relative (not absolute), nor are they mutually exclusive. As generalities, they allow exceptions. And the specific forms of post-human elitist post-capitalism need to be further developed in future after-postmodern history, as they will be different from the ones we now know, while using them as the inspirational point at the beginning. The point here is to solely give an extremely rough picture of a small part of the world to come that we still do not know much about.
Sources: From Ch.10 of *FCD* (and also *FPHC*, *BDPD*, and *BCPC*). Refer to the text for more info and references.

Table 5.13. Capitalism, Non-Capitalism, and Post-Capitalism (Part I)

• **Capitalism**

—*Theoretical Constructs*

- •Allocation of scarce resources among alternative wants largely by free market for competition (whose characteristics in its ideal form include, for instance, no barrier to entry or exit, homogeneity, perfect information, a large number of buyers/sellers, and perfect factor mobility)
- •More formal-legalistic than informal-legalistic, more individualistic than communal, and more material (secular) than spiritual
- •Either (1) minimal government or (2) relatively active government

—*Types*

- •Only (1): Different versions of market capitalism (e.g., the U.S.)
- •Only (2): Different versions of welfare capitalism (e.g., Sweden)

• **Non-Capitalism**

—*Theoretical Constructs*

- •Allocation of scarce resources among alternative wants mainly by political authority for policies (which can be regulative, redistributive, symbolic, and participatory)
- •More informal-legalistic than formal-legalistic
- •Either (1') more individualistic (for the elites), often (though not always) for material (secular) concerns, or (2') more communal (for the masses), often (though not always) for spiritual concerns

—*Types*

- •Only (1'): Different versions on the Right (e.g., Fascist corporate-state economy for the glory of the new Rome, medieval lord-vassal-serf economy for the power of the feudalistic order)
- •Only (2'): Different versions on the Left (e.g., Soviet command economy for the creation of the New Socialist Man)

(continued on next page)

Table 5.13. Capitalism, Non-Capitalism, and Post-Capitalism (Part II)

- **Post-Capitalism**
  - —*Theoretical Constructs*
    - •Allocation of scarce resources among alternative wants largely by political authority with advanced info systems in future civilizations, subject to existential dialectics. In degree of allocating by authority, post-capitalism is more than capitalism but less than non-capitalism.
    - •More spiritual than secular (material)
    - •Either (1'') more individualistic or (2") more communal
    - •Like capitalism and non-capitalism, post-capitalism is also subject to the freedom/unfreedom and equality/inequality dialectics (or existential dialectics in general). There is no utopia, in the end; even were there one, dystopia would exist within it.
    - •Unlike capitalism and non-capitalism, post-capitalism makes use of a different degree of political authority with advanced info systems in future civilizations and strives for higher-spiritual cultures (especially in the post-human age), while acknowledging the constraints of existential dialectics and no longer valuing free market (as in capitalism) and economic control (as in non-capitalism) as sacred virtues.
  - —*Types*
    - •Only (1"): Different versions of post-human elitist value ideals
    - •Only (2''): Different versions of trans-Sinitic value ideals
    - •Only (2''): Different versions of trans-feminine value ideals
    - •Only (2''): Different versions of trans-Islamic value ideals
    - •Only (2''): Different versions of trans-outerspace value ideals

(continued on next page)

Table 5.13. Capitalism, Non-Capitalism, and Post-Capitalism (Part III)

Notes: The calling and examples in each category are solely illustrative (not exhaustive). The comparison is also relative (not absolute), nor are they mutually exclusive. As generalities, they allow exceptions. And the specific forms of each calling need to be further developed in future after-postmodern history, as they will be different from the ones we now know, while using them as the inspirational point at the beginning. The point here is to solely give an extremely rough picture of a small part of the world to come that we still do not know much about.

Source: From Ch.10 of *FCD*. Refer to the text for more info and references.

Table 5.14. Multiple Causes of the Emergence of Post-Capitalism (Part I)

• **At the Micro-Physical Level**
—Ex: intelligent life without the human physical-chemical system
—Ex: mastering of quantum mechanics, electromagnetism, and other fields for the understanding of a broad range of anomalous experiences and the application for artificial intelligence for spiritual quest
—Sources: Ch.7 of *FHC*; Chs.9-10 of *FCD*; Ch.1 of *FPHC*

• **At the Chemical Level**
—Ex: space radiation and toxins
—Sources: Ch.7 of *FHC*; Chs.9-10 of *FCD*

• **At the Bio-Psychological Level**
—Ex: exo-biological evolution in deep space
—Ex: genetic engineering of new beings
—Ex: limits of human cognition
—Sources: Ch.2 & Chs.9-10 of *FCD*; Ch.7 of *FHC*

• **At the Institutional Level**
—Ex: the flawed logic of the free market
—Ex: the need of a post-autistic economics
—Sources: Ch.10 of *FCD*

• **At the Organizational Level**
—Ex: the dark sides of formal-legalistic routines
Sources: Ch.3 of *FHC*; Ch.7 of *FCD*; Ch.3 of *FPHC*

• **At the Structural Level**
—Ex: ever new forms of inequities, at home and abroad
—Ex: the emergence of China, women, and Islam as major actors
—Sources: Chs.5-6 of *FHC*; Chs.7, 9 & 10 of *FCD*; Chs.4-5 of *BDPD*

(continued on next page)

Table 5.14. Multiple Causes of the Emergence of Post-Capitalism (Part II)

- **At the Cultural Level**
  —Ex: freedom/unfreedom dialectics
  —Ex: equality/inequality dialectics
  —Sources: Ch.5 of *FHC*; Chs.3 & 10 of *FCD*; Ch.4 of *FPHC*; Ch.1 of *BDPD*

- **At the Systemic Level**
  —Ex: space habitats (in zero-gravity) and colonization
  —Ex: ultra advanced future info systems
  —Ex: qualitative demography
  —Sources: Ch.7 of *FHC*; Chs. 9 & 10 of *FCD*

- **At the Cosmological Level**
  —Ex: multiverses
  —Sources: Ch.7 of *FHC*; Chs. 9 & 10 of *FCD*; Ch.4 of *FPHC*

Notes: The examples in each category are solely illustrative (not exhaustive), and some of the items can be reclassified somewhere else. Nor are they always mutually exclusive. Since they are generalities, exceptions are expected.
Sources: From *FHC*, *FCD*, *FPHC*, *BCPC*, and *BDPD*. See also *Table 1.13* and *Table 1.14* of *BCIV* on my perspective on civilizational holism (or *Table 7.12* and *Table 7.13* in *ALD*).

• PART SIX •

Conclusion

CHAPTER 6
CONCLUSION—THE FUTURE OF UNCONSCIOUSNESS

> What is the range of consciousness in the universe?....How is consciousness related to other aspects of the world [like anomalous experience]?
> —Gerald Feinberg (1994)

The Fascinating Unconscious Mind

Unconsciousness, or that large portion of the mental iceberg beneath its tip, already starts unfolding, albeit slowly but steadily. Yet, its future course has a long way to go.

In this sense, the three different theoretical approaches in the theoretical debate concerning the nature of anomalous experience in relation to unconsciousness and its concscious counterpart as introduced in Chapter One are inadequate.

Firstly, the "skeptical" argument is a bit too dismissive, since, so the skeptics think, if "there is no scientific evidence supporting [anomalous] abilities," they "are nothing more than intentional trickery or self delusion." (WK 2007)

The skeptical argument is not convincing, because those who claim to have personally encountered anomalous experience do not accept the skeptical rejection. Moreover, for the believers, to believe or not can be a matter of faith, not on the basis of conclusive empirical evidences.

Secondly, the "agnostic" argument, though a bit better, is still weak, since it does not say anything more than just maintaining an open-minded attitude about anomalous claims.

Thirdly, the "anomalous" argument is equally not quite plausible, since they are too enthusiastic about their claims, often without adequately providing substantive empirical evidences.

Lastly, my "unfolding" argument, unlike the previous three, is different, in accepting partially each of the three arguments, without, however, wholly siding with any one of them.

Yes, the skeptics are right to the extent that many anomalous claims are questionable—but, contrary to what they think, we cannot rule them out solely on that basis.

Yes, the agnostics are right to the extent that we should maintain an open-minded attitude about the anomalous claims—but, contrary to what they think, this by itself does not say much.

Yes, the defenders of anomalous claims are right to the extent that anomalous experience can be plausible in certain ways (although not exactly proven)—but, contrary to what they think, much more work remains to be done, just as its future course has yet to be fully predicted.

To understand better the nature of anomalous experience and its future course requires a holistic methodology (to incorporate all fields of human knowledge, in accordance to the partiality-totality principle in existential dialectics), just as it also needs an appreciation of the six theses in my theory of unfolding unconsciousness, as explained in what follows, respectively, and summarized in *Table 6.2*.

A reminder needs to be made here, however, in that, if I do not list all the ontological principles in existential dialectics (fifteen of them so far) in the six theses, it is not because the other ones are not important.

The important point to remember is that the six theses are the main concerns here, although the rest of the fifteen principles will be introduced too in the context of summarizing the six theses as shown below.

1st Thesis: The Openness-Hiddenness Principle

With this reminder about the rest of the fifteen principles in mind—the first thesis concerns the openness-hiddenness principle in the category of "structure" in existential dialectics, in that reality has its hidden face, just as it is open to outside view in some other ways.

In the current context of anomalous experience in relation to unconsciousness and its conscious counterpart, it can be shown in different ways.

For instance, certain aspects of reality concerning anomalous experience can be open for examination (e.g., the experiment with SPECT images in *Sec. 2.3.2*, the linkage to TLE in *Sec. 2.3.4*, the transmission of telepathemic bit in

Sec. 3.3.3, the analysis of higher dimensional space-time in *Sec. 3.4*, and the use of metonymies and metaphors in *Sec. 4.5*).

Other aspects, however, remain hidden, and examples include the elusive deeper nature of spiritual reality in the intangible realm in *Sec. 2.2.2*, the deeper nature of the anomalous experience itself in *Sec. 2.3.4*, the undetectability of different branched universes in *Sec. 3.3.1*, the underlying mechanisms of signals traveling between different folds of physical space-time in *Sec. 3.4*, and the dependence on language and the bias for science and logic in *Sec. 4.5*.

This principle should be used in conjunction with two other principles, also in the category of structure (which were already developed in my previous works), that is, the simpleness-complicatedness principle and the preciseness-vagueness principle.

For instance, in relation to the simpleness-complicatedness principle, the analysis of anomalous experience, on the one hand, requires some complication to understand its complicatedness (as revealed in the various physical theories in Chapter Three), but, on the other hand, runs the risk of violating the scientific quest for simplicity (as required by the Ockham's principle, also known as Occam's razor).

And in relation to the preciseness-vagueness principle, the more precise some theories are with the use of quantitative measurement, the more reductionistic they are in ignoring the importance of qualitative analysis (as shown in *Sec. 3.4*).

2nd Thesis: The Expansion-Contraction Principle

The second thesis is the expansion-contraction principle in the category of "process" in existential dialectics, in that entities in the world can both expand in some ways and contract in other ones, as part of their nature.

This principle, although not so explicitly called, was already used in my previous works on different topics (e.g., the theory of floating consciousness in *FCD* and *FPHC*, the union of the unions in *BWT*, and the cyclical progression of system fragmentation and integration in *FCD*).

In the current context of anomalous experience in relation to unconsciousness and its conscious counterpart, one of the most fascinating expressions of this is none other than the analysis of different causes of the slow but steady expansion (and, furthermore, if put in a different way, unfolding) of unconsciousness in this book.

In other words, the brain will undergo a major transformation towards the fuller exploitation of the unconscious domain—in conjunction with floating consciousness, hyper-spatial consciousness, and other forms of the post-human conscious mind in the conscious domain.

This principle should be used in conjunction with three other principles, also in the category of process (which were already introduced in my previous works), namely, the change-constancy principle, the slowness-quickness principle, and the order-chaos principle.

In relation to the change-constancy principle, if the unconscious mind remains constantly potent in shaping intelligent life, it also undergoes changes, be they in terms of being more fully understood and of being more radically transformed later in the process.

In relation to order-chaos principle, if there is order (say, in relation to different patterns of metaphor and metonymy in unconscious fantasies), there is also chaos in the nature of anomalous experience, since, for instance, the use of quantum mechanics in paraphysics also encounters its double, in that randomness at the quantum level defiles any explanation which can be so exact and deterministic.

And in relation to the slowness-quickness principle, while some nature of anomalous experience is known as fast (e.g., subliminal messages), its deepest layer of reality remains extraordinarily slow to be fully unfolded and understood (e.g., the difficult problems confronted by different theories so far introduced).

3rd Thesis: The Symmetry-Asymmetry Principle

The third thesis, the symmetry-asymmetry principle in the category of "agency," is not new, since it was already identified and used in different works of mine.

But, when used in the current context of anomalous experience in relation to unconsciousness and its conscious counterpart, four illustrations can be provided below.

Firstly, while all fields of human knowledge have their say on anomalous experience, the research works in the natural sciences (especially physics and chemistry—and, to a secondary extent, biology and psychology) are often more cited than the comparable ones like political science or economics (as shown in Chs.2-3 and *Sec. 5.4*). To avoid reductionism, however, it should be mentioned that even the use of the natural sciences remains limited, especially when contextualized within the context of reductionism (as shown in *Sec. 3.4*).

Secondly, if there are numerous individuals who claim to have encountered different forms of paranormal experience, they do not react to them in the same ways (as shown in *Sec. 4.2*, *Sec. 4.3* and *Sec. 4.4*).

Thirdly, although diferent social organizations can have different research agendas on anomalous experience, they are not necessarily equal in acceptance (as shown in *Sec. 5.2*).

And fourthly, while there are numerous paranormal research findings, they are not equal in validity, like the plausible work by E.W. Scripture and the questionable one by James Vicary (in *Sec. 5.3*).

This principle should be used in conjunction with two other principles, also in the category of "agency" (which were already developed and used in my previous works), namely, the evolution-transformation principle and the softness-hardness principle.

In relation to the evolution-transformation principle, the best way to illustrate its relevance to the current context of anomalous experience is the discussion of natural evolution (as in the context of different worlds) and its non-natural transformation (as in the development of highly advanced technology)—which were especially, though not exclusively, discussed in *Sec. 5.5*).

And in relation to the softness-hardness principle, the use of anomalous experience can occur not just in a soft (seductive) way but also in a hard (violent) one. One good illustration here concerns the "soft" use of subliminal seduction in advertising (as analyzed in *Sec. 5.3*) and the "hard" use of psycho- and bio-warfare for the alternation of the conscious and the unconscious mind (as discussed in *Sec. 9.2.5* on "the hi-tech forms of warfare and violence" in *FCD*) and, for that matter, for military training and propaganda (as addressed in *Sec. 5.3*).

4th Thesis: The Progression-Regression Principle

The fourth thesis, the progression-regression principle in the category of "outcome," is also not new, since it was already used in different works of mine. It refers to the ambivalent reality that, if there is progress, there is likewise regression.

In the current context of anomalous experience in relation to unconsciousness and its conscious counterpart, it is revealing in different ways.

For instance, on the one hand, there are some progress in understanding the nature of anomalous experience (e.g., the relationship between moral rectitude and the encounter with anomalous experience in *Sec. 4.2*, the use of sound physics in new paraphysical theories in *Sec. 3.3* and *Sec. 3.4*, since these "newer theories are based upon sound physics rather than the mere inventions of new entities or unmeasurable quantities for the sole purpose of explaining psi"). (J. Beichler 1998)

On the other hand, there is likewise regression (e.g., the embarrassing work of James Vicary and the misuse of subliminal advertising and propaganda in *Sec. 5.3*).

In the end, as already indicated in Chapter Five, in spite of the problems confronting the numerous works afore-cited in the last four chapters—the virtue of using them as case studies in this book is to point out the direction of unfolding consciousness in a way that humans have never known before, although the specific details and arguments have yet to be fully worked out, which constitute a tall task for future humans (and especially in the more distant future, for post-humans).

In fact, even the American Psychological Association published a report in 2000 which admitted that now is time long overdue to acknowledge the progress made in the study of anomalous experience: "Psychology has achieved enough maturity and breadth it can take a serious look at these unusual but important experiences." (F. MacHovec 2002)

That said—this principle should be used in conjunction with another principle, also in the category of "outcome," namely, the same-difference principle, in that an entity does not have to change over time only in order to be more different from its opposing alternatives, as it can be more similar.

In the current context of anomalous experience (as discussed in *Sec. 5.5*), while unfolding unconsciousness will be more utilized by post-humans for different extraordinary capacities (different from the conscious mind), it is also subject to the influence and guidance of the post-human conscious mind (e.g., the post-human conscious mind in the medium term, and floating consciousness as well as hyper-spatial consciousness in the distant term).

5th Thesis: The Explicability-Inexplicability Principle

The fifth thesis is about the explicability-inexplicability principle in the category of "method," which tells us the duality of the research dilemma, in that, if reality can be explained in some ways, it also has its other ways which are not quite explainable, at a given point in time.

This principle is not very new, since it was already used in my previous works, although it was not so explicitly identified. For instance, in *Sec. 5.1.3* of *FPHC* on "Epistemological and Ontological Inexplicability," I already pointed out some reality (like the one concerning consciousness in that book), which may not be explicable in some fundamental ways, although it can be explained in other ones.

In the current context of anomalous experience in relation to unconsciousness and its conscious counterpart, this principle is useful here.

For instance, on the one hand, certain reality in relation to unconsciousness and its conscious counterpart in *Sec. 3.3* and *Sec. 3.4* can be explained, though only to an extent (e.g., the use of different field theories like the curvature of space in Einstein's theory of relativity and the use of some hidden variables).

On the other hand, other aspects are not so readily explainable, and good examples concern the works in *Sec. 2.3.3* by Toben, Wolf, and Sarfatti on biogravity, and the mystery surrounding the simultaneous collapse of the wave packet by different people in *Sec. 3.3.1*).

This principle should be used in conjunction with another principle, also in the category of "method," namely, the predictability-unpredictability principle, in that while some features of reality are readily predictable, others are not, at any given point of time (especially, though not exclusively, in my previous works like *FPHC* and *FC*).

In the current context of anomalous experience, the work by Michael Persinger on ELF waves (in *Sec. 3.3.3*) is a good example, since "it does have predictive power and some predictions made by Persinger seem to have been validated," and yet other aspects are yet to be predictable, as Persinger did not provide any "plausible mechanisms and does not seriously address real psi expressions." (J. Beichler 1998; H. Edge 1986; J. Mishlove 1994)

6th Thesis: The Post-Human Mastery

The sixth thesis gives a major role to post-humans for their future transformation of the unconscious mind, especially in relation to its unfolding in the context of different anomalous capacities that humans have never had.

These extraordinary capacities may involve, just to cite some major examples here for illustration, superior senses (be they through space, as in clair-sentience, clair-voyance, clair-audience, clair-austance, clair-alience, or clair-cognizance—or through time, as in pre-cognition, re-sentiment, retro-cognition, and retro-sentiment), and superior contacts (be they with living minds as in telepathy, with the dead as in midiumship, or with other non-living entities as in telekinesis), as shown in *Table 2.16*.

The rise of the unfolding unconscious mind will be played out in conjunction with the post-human conscious mind (especially, though not exclusively, with floating consciousness and hyper-spatial consciousness—

together with other post-humans forms like thinking machines, thinking robots, genetically altered superior beings, cyborgs, and the rest), subject to the natural (and non-natural) selection of other worlds in deep space unto multiverses.

The Unfolding Unconscious Mind

The unconscious mind, when fully unfolded, will mark a tremendous milestone for intelligent life, since it will unleash the extraordinary powers of anomalous experience that humans in their entire history so far can only dream or fantasize about, or, in more than occasional cases, have to resort to fraudulent claims to sustain their (at times notorious) credibility.

In this sense, even if the entire human history of anomalous experience so far had been a shameful chapter full of "intentional trickery or self delusion," so the skeptics are quick to point out—this criticism would miss something tremendously important for future intelligent life, in that this (allegedly) fraudulent history reveals an enormously imaginative exploration of a different world for post-humans to entertain and develop, with their superior resources and different lifeworlds which render the transformation of the unconscious mind possible in a way which has so far denied the human race. (WK 2007)

Since the varieties of anomalous experience also include some (not all) forms of spiritual (at times religious) quest for a supernatural entity (conventionally known, in different meanings of course, as "god"), a different way to understand the future of religion is to thus visionize the distant transformation of the post-human mind in the direction of floating consciousness, hyper-spatial consciousness, and unfolding unconsciousness both on earth, and even more tremendously so later, in deep space until multiverses.

Thus is the future of anomalous experience, in a small sense—or of the mind (or intelligent life), both conscious and unconscious, in a large sense.

Table 6.1. The Theoretical Debate on Anomalous Experience (Part I)

- **The Skeptical Argument**
  —A major theoretical approach to the study of anomalous experience can be understood, in the absence of better terms, as the *skeptical argument*.
  —The skeptics argue, with psychic claims as an illustration, that, since "there is no scientific evidence supporting such abilities," it is thus "apparent [that] psychic phenomena are nothing more than intentional trickery or self delusion." (WK 2007)
  —For instance, the skeptic James Randi once went so far as to offer "a $1 million prize to any individual who can, under controlled circumstances, demonstrate any paranormal or supernatural ability. As of yet no one has passed the preliminary challenge." (WK 2007) And thus, anomalous experience, for the skeptics, is not believable.
  —And Jonathan P. Dowling once even wrote that "[a]rticles dealing with parapsychology should not be published in *PRA* [viz., *Physical Review A*]—period."
  —But the skeptic argument is not convincing to those who claim to have personally experienced it. Besides, to believe or not can be a matter of faith, and the requirement of conclusive evidences may not be relevant to the believers.

(continued on next page)

Table 6.1. The Theoretical Debate on Anomalous Experience (Part II)

• **The Agnostic Argument**

—An alernative theoretical approach is less extreme than the skeptical argument, so it can be called, in the absence of better terms, *the agnostic argument.*

—An agnostic, unlike a skeptic, does not think that anomalous experience can simply be dismissed on the basis of the lack of some conclusive evidences concerning its general existence. Instead, so they think, one should be more open-minded to the possibility of its existence.

—Henry Stapp (1995), for one, argued that one "cannot rationally rule out the possibility" of anomalous experience, "when they can be accounted for by plausible physical models," even if not conclusively proven. (J. Beichler 1998)

—Another good illustration of the agnostic argument is the one by Aparthib Zaman (2003) in the quotation at the beginning of this chapter, in that, since "Psi phenomena…are yet not conclusively proven to exist….[t]he only reasonable view would be to not permanently rule out the existence of any paranormal events."

—But for the believers, although the agnostic argument is welcome, it remains too weak.

(continued on next page)

Table 6.1. The Theoretical Debate on Anomalous Experience (Part III)

• **The Anomalous Argument**

—Another theoretical approach is undoubtedly most supportive of the existence of anomalous experience, when contrasted with those of the skeptics and the agnostics, so it can be labeled, in the absence of better terms, as *the anomalous argument.*

—Unlike the skeptics and agnostics, those who defend the anomalous argument genuinely think that anomalous experience really exists, especially for those who experience it, although those who never do are unfortunate to not encounter something which, for the defenders, is one of the most amazing experiences for intelligent life on earth.

—There is no lack of people who claim to have encountered anomalous experience in human history.

—For instance, a good illustration concerns those who claims to possess psychic powers: "Early examples of individuals thought by some to have psychic powers include the Oracle of Apollo at Delphi who was thought to provide prophecies from Apollo himself as well as Nostradamus, a French apothecary who is thought by some to have had the ability to predict the future. During the 19th century belief in psychics became more common and many notable individuals gained notoriety including Daniel Dunglas Home. Psychics are also very popular in science fiction today and many works of fiction include individuals with psychic abilities, including *The Dead Zone* by Stephen King as well as Jean Grey from the Marvel and DC comic book universes. Today, belief in psychic phenomena is widespread amongst the general public. A 2005 Gallup poll concluded that 41% of Americans believe in extra-sensory perception." (WK 2007)

—But then, the problem with the anomalous believers is what the skeptics and the agnostics have persistently pointed out, in that there is no conclusive proof of the existence of anomalous experience.

(continued on next page)

Table 6.1. The Theoretical Debate on Anomalous Experience (Part IV)

- **The Unfolding Argument**
  —Lastly, unlike the previous three theoretical approaches is my *unfolding argument*, in the absence of better terms.
  —My unfolding argument goes beyond the previous three approaches so far mentioned and learns from each of them, without, however, favoring one over the others (or even trying to integrate them in a harmonious whole, since they are not very compatible)—and in the process adds something new to the literature. This constitutes my theoretical contribution to the debate.
  —My *unfolding argument* can be more formally called *the unfolding theory of anomalous experience*, in the context of anomalous experience and its relation to the dimension of unconsciousness.
  —Yet, since the most important feature of the theory concerns what I originally call, in the absence of better words, *the unfolding unconsciousness*, the theory can be more precisely called instead as *the theory of unfolding unconsciousness*.
  —This theory of mine contains six major theses, namely, (a) the openness-hiddenness principle, (b) the expansion-contraction principle, (c) the symmetry-asymmetry principle, (d) the progression-regression principle, (e) the explicability-inexplicability principle, and (f) the post-human mastery—to be elaborated in the rest of the book.

Source: From Ch.1 of *FPHU.* See also the table on the six theses in the unfolding theory of anomalous experience.

Table 6.2. Six Theses
in the Unfolding Theory of Anomalous Experience
(Part I)

- **1st Thesis: The Openness-Hiddenness Principle**
  —This principle is in the category of "structure" in existential dialectics, in that reality has its hidden face, just as it is open to outside view in some other ways.
  —In the current context of anomalous experience in relation to unconsciousness and its conscious counterpart, it can be shown in different ways.
  —For instance, certain aspects of reality concerning anomalous experience can be open for examination (e.g., the experiment with SPECT images in *Sec. 2.3.2*, the transmission of telepathemic bit in *Sec. 3.3.3*, the analysis of higher dimensional space-time in *Sec. 3.4*, and the use of metonymies and metaphors in *Sec. 4.5*).
  —Other aspects, however, remain hidden, and examples include the elusive deeper nature of spiritual reality in the intangible realm in *Sec. 2.2.2*, the undetectability of different branched universes in *Sec. 3.3.1*, the underlying mechanisms of signals traveling between different folds of physical space-time in *Sec. 3.4*, and the dependence on language and the bias for science and logic in *Sec. 4.5*.
  —This principle should be used in conjunction with two other principles, also in the category of structure (which were already developed in my previous works), that is, the simpleness-complicatedness principle and the preciseness-vagueness principle.
  —For instance, in relation to the simpleness-complicatedness principle, the analysis of anomalous experience, on the one hand, requires some complication to understand its complexity (as revealed in the various physical theories in Chapter Three), but, on the other hand, runs the risk of violating the scientific quest for simplicity (as required by the Ockham's principle, also known as Occam's razor).
  —And in relation to the preciseness-vagueness principle, the more precise some theories are with the use of quantitative measurement, the more reductionistic they are in ignoring the importance of qualitative analysis (as shown in *Sec. 3.4*).

(continued on next page)

Table 6.2. Six Theses in the Unfolding Theory of Anomalous Experience (Part II)

- **2nd Thesis: The Expansion-Contraction Principle**
  - —This principle is in the category of "process" in existential dialectics, in that entities in the world can both expand in some ways and contract in other ones, as part of their nature. This principle, although not so explicitly called, was already used in my previous works (e.g., the theory of floating consciousness in *FCD* and *FPHC*, the union of the unions in *BWT*, and the cyclical progression of system fragmentation and integration in *FCD*).
  - —In the current context of anomalous experience, one of its most fascinating expressions is none other than the analysis of different causes of the slow but steady expansion (and, furthermore, if put in a different way, unfolding) of unconsciousness in this book. In other words, the brain will undergo a major transformation towards the fuller exploitation of the unconscious domain—in conjunction with floating consciousness, hyper-spatial consciousness, and other forms of the post-human conscious mind in the conscious domain.
  - —This principle should be used in conjunction with three other principles, also in the category of process (which were already introduced in my previous works), namely, the change-constancy principle, the slowness-quickness principle, and the order-chaos principle.
  - —In relation to the change-constancy principle, if the unconscious mind remains constantly potent in shaping intelligent life, it also undergoes changes, be they in terms of being more fully understood and of being more radically transformed later in the process.
  - —In relation to order-chaos principle, if there is order (say, in relation to different patterns of metaphor and metonymy in unconscious fantasies), there is also chaos in the nature of anomalous experience, since, for instance, the use of quantum mechanics in paraphysics also encounters its double, in that randomness at the quantum level defiles any explanation which can be so exact and deterministic.
  - —And in relation to the slowness-quickness principle, while some nature of anomalous experience is known as fast (e.g., subliminal messages), its deepest layer of reality remains extraordinarily slow to be fully unfolded and understood (e.g., the difficult problems confronted by different theories so far introduced).

(continued on next page)

Table 6.2. Six Theses in the Unfolding Theory of Anomalous Experience (Part III)

• **3rd Thesis: The Symmetry-Asymmetry Principle**

—This principle in the category of "agency," is not new, since it was already identified and used in different works of mine. When used in the current context of anomalous experience, four illustrations are shown below.

—Firstly, while all fields of human knowledge have their say on anomalous experience, the research works in the natural sciences (especially physics and chemistry, and also biology and psychology) are often more cited than the comparable ones like political science or economics (as shown in Chs.2-3 and *Sec. 5.4*). To avoid reductionism, however, it should be mentioned that even the use of the natural sciences remains limited, especially when contextualized within the context of reductionism (as shown in *Sec. 3.4*).

—Secondly, if there are numerous individuals who claim to have encountered different forms of paranormal experience, they do not react to them in the same ways (as shown in *Sec. 4.2*, *Sec. 4.3* and *Sec. 4.4*).

—Thirdly, although diferent social organizations can have different research agendas on anomalous experience, they are not necessarily equal in acceptance (as shown in *Sec. 5.2*).

—And fourthly, while there are numerous paranormal research findings, they are not equal in validity, like the plausible work by E.W. Scripture and the questionable one by James Vicary (in *Sec. 5.3*).

—This principle should be used in conjunction with two other principles in the category of "agency" already developed in my past works, namely, the evolution-transformation principle and the softness-hardness principle.

—The evolution-transformation principle is useful in the discussion of natural evolution (as in the context of different worlds) and its non-natural transformation (as in the development of highly advanced technology)—which were especially, though not exclusively, discussed in *Sec. 5.5*).

—And the softness-hardness principle shows that the use of anomalous experience can occur not just in a soft (seductive) way but also in a hard (violent) one. One good illustration here concerns the "soft" use of subliminal seduction in advertising (as analyzed in *Sec. 5.3*) and the "hard" use of psycho- and bio-warfare (as discussed in *Sec. 9.2.5* on "the hi-tech forms of warfare and violence" in *FCD*) and, for that matter, for military training and propaganda (as addressed in *Sec. 5.3*).

(continued on next page)

Table 6.2. Six Theses in the Unfolding Theory of Anomalous Experience (Part IV)

• **4th Thesis: The Progression-Regression Principle**

—This principle in the category of "outcome," is also not new, since it was already used in different works of mine. It refers to the ambivalent reality that, if there is progress, there is likewise regression. In the current context of anomalous experience, it is revealing in different ways.

—For instance, on the one hand, there are some progress in understanding the nature of anomalous experience (e.g., the relationship between moral rectitude and the encounter with anomalous experience in *Sec. 4.2*, the use of sound physics in new paraphysical theories in *Sec. 3.3* and *Sec. 3.4*, since these "newer theories are based upon sound physics rather than the mere inventions of new entities or unmeasurable quantities for the sole purpose of explaining psi"). (J. Beichler 1998) On the other hand, there is likewise regression (e.g., the embarrassing work of James Vicary and the misuse of subliminal advertising and propaganda in *Sec. 5.3*).

—In the end, the virtue of using the numerous case studies in this book is to point out the direction of unfolding consciousness in a way that humans have never known before, although the specific details and arguments have yet to be fully worked out, which constitute a tall task for future humans (and especially in the more distant future, for post-humans).

—In fact, even the American Psychological Association published a report in 2000 which admitted that now is time long overdue to acknowledge the progress made in the study of anomalous experience: "Psychology has achieved enough maturity and breadth it can take a serious look at these unusual but important experiences." (F. MacHovec 2002)

—This principle should be used in conjunction with another principle, also in the category of "outcome," namely, the same-difference principle, in that an entity does not have to change over time only in order to be more different from its opposing alternatives, as it can be more similar. In the current context of anomalous experience (as discussed in *Sec. 5.5*), while unfolding unconsciousness will be more utilized by post-humans for different extraordinary capacities (different from the conscious mind), it is also subject to the influence and guidance of the post-human conscious mind (e.g., the post-human conscious mind in the medium term, and floating consciousness as well as hyper-spatial consciousness in the distant term).

(continued on next page)

Table 6.2. Six Theses in the Unfolding Theory of Anomalous Experience (Part V)

• **5th Thesis: The Explicability-Inexplicability Principle**

—This principle is in the category of "method," which tells us the duality of the research dilemma, in that, if reality can be explained in some ways, it also has its other ways which are not quite explainable, at a given point in time.

—This principle is not very new, since it was already used in my previous works, although it was not so explicitly identified. For instance, in *Sec. 5.1.3* of *FPHC* on "Epistemological and Ontological Inexplicability," I already pointed out some reality (like the one concerning consciousness in that book), which may not be explicable in some fundamental ways, although it can be explained in other ones.

—In the current context of anomalous experience, this principle is useful here. For instance, on the one hand, certain reality in relation to unconsciousness and its conscious counterpart in *Sec. 3.3* and *Sec. 3.4* can be explained, though only to an extent (e.g., the use of different field theories like the curvature of space in Einstein's theory of relativity and the use of some hidden variables). On the other hand, other aspects are not so readily explainable, and good examples concern the works in *Sec. 2.3.3* by Toben, Wolf, and Sarfatti on biogravity, and the mystery surrounding the simultaneous collapse of the wave packet by different people in *Sec. 3.3.1*).

—This principle should be used in conjunction with another principle, also in the category of "method," namely, the predictability-unpredictability principle, in that while some features of reality are readily predictable, others are not, at any given point of time (especially, though not exclusively, in my previous works like *FPHC* and *FC*).

—In the current context of anomalous experience, the work by Michael Persinger on ELF waves (in *Sec. 3.3.3*) is a good example, since "it does have predictive power and some predictions made by Persinger seem to have been validated," and yet other aspects are yet to be predictable, as Persinger did not provide any "plausible mechanisms and does not seriously address real psi expressions." (J. Beichler 1998; H. Edge 1986; J. Mishlove 1994)

(continued on next page)

Table 6.2. Six Theses in the Unfolding Theory of Anomalous Experience (Part VII)

- **6th Thesis: The Post-Human Mastery**
  —The sixth thesis gives a major role to post-humans for their future transformation of the unconscious mind, especially in relation to its unfolding in the context of different anomalous capacities that humans have never had.
  —These extraordinary capacities may involve, just to cite some major examples here for illustration, superior senses (be they through space, as in clair-sentience, clair-voyance, clair-audience, clair-austance, clair-alience, or clair-cognizance—or through time, as in pre-cognition, re-sentiment, retro-cognition, and retro-sentiment), and superior contacts (be they with living minds as in telepathy, with the dead as in midiumship, or with other non-living entities as in telekinesis), as shown in *Table 2.16*.
  —The rise of the unfolding unconscious mind will be played out in conjunction with the post-human conscious mind (especially, though not exclusively, with floating consciousness and hyper-spatial consciousness—together with other post-humans forms like thinking machines, thinking robots, genetically altered superior beings, cyborgs, and the rest), subject to the natural (and non-natural) selection of other worlds in deep space unto multiverses.

Source: A summary of Ch.6 of *FPHU*

Table 6.3. Unconsciousness and the Mind (in the Context of Anomalous Experience)

- **Unconsciousness and Psychology**
  - —Ex: Psychoanalytic theory
  - —Ex: Theory of mind-matter manifestations

- **Unconsciousness and Biology**
  - —Ex: Biochemical theory
  - —Ex: Neurobiological theory
  - —Ex: Biogravitational theory
  - —Ex: Neurophysiological theory

Notes: The examples in the categories are solely illustrative (not exhaustive), and the comparison is relative (not absolute), nor are they necessarily mutually exclusive. And some can be easily re-classified elsewhere. As generalities, they allow exceptions.
Source: A summary of Ch.2 of *FPHU*

Table 6.4. Unconsciousness and Nature (in the Context of Anomalous Experience)

- **Unconsciousness and Chemistry**
  —Ex: Biochemical theory
  —Ex: Physical biochemical theory

- **Unconsciousness and Micro-Physics**
  —Ex: Quantum theory
  —Ex: Electromagnetic theory

- **Unconsciousness and Cosmology (Micro-Physics)**
  —Ex: Hyperspatial theory

Notes: The examples in the categories are solely illustrative (not exhaustive), and the comparison is relative (not absolute), nor are they necessarily mutually exclusive. And some can be easily re-classified elsewhere. As generalities, they allow exceptions.
Source: A summary of Ch.3 of *FPHU*

Table 6.5. Unconsciousness and Culture (in the Context of Anomalous Experience)

- **Unconsciousness and Morality**
  —Ex: Anomalous experience and character discipline

- **Unconsciousness and Religion**
  —Ex: Anomalous experience and religious conviction
  —Ex: Mystical experience, TLE, and religious messages

- **Unconsciousness and Aesthetics**
  —Ex: Anomalous experience and artistic creativity
  —Ex: Anomalous belief and associative creativity

- **Unconsciousness and Epistemology**
  —Ex: Myths and archetypes
  —Ex: Metonymy, metaphor, and the structure of language
  —Ex: Mystical experience and deautomatization

Notes: The examples in the categories are solely illustrative (not exhaustive), and the comparison is relative (not absolute), nor are they necessarily mutually exclusive. And some can be easily re-classified elsewhere. As generalities, they allow exceptions.
Source: A summary of Ch.4 of *FPHU*

Table 6.6. Unconsciousness and Society (in the Context of Anomalous Experience)

- **Unconsciousness and Social Organizations**
  —Ex: Different organizational agendas in anomalous study

- **Unconsciousness and Social Institutions**
  —Ex: Subliminal message for advertising and propaganda
  —Ex: Remote viewing and psychic warfare

- **Unconsciousness and Social Structure**
  —Ex: The scholarly divide on anomalous experience

- **Unconsciousness and Social Systems**
  —Ex: The transformative power of technology
  —Ex: Natural (and non-natural) selection of other worlds
  —Ex: Unfolding unconciousness and the post-human conscious mind

Notes: The examples in the categories are solely illustrative (not exhaustive), and the comparison is relative (not absolute), nor are they necessarily mutually exclusive. And some can be easily re-classified elsewhere. As generalities, they allow exceptions.
Source: A summary of Ch.5 of *FPHU*

Table 6.7. The Concepton of Existential Dialectics (Part I)

- **Sets and Elements**
  - —Sets
    - Ex: the Same
    - Ex: the Others
  - —Elements
    - Ex: whites in 20th century America (in the set of "the Same")
    - Ex: Iraq during the U.S. invasion in 2003 (in the set of "the Others")

- **Relations, Operations, Functions**
  - —Relations (e.g., "belongs," "equals to," "is greater than")
    - Ex: symmetric interactions within the Same (or the Others)
    - Ex: asymmetric interactions between the Same and the Others
  - —Operations (e.g., "and," "or," "not," "if…then")
    - Ex: if the Same oppresses the Others, it will also oppress itself.
    - Ex: the Same is not the Others.
  - —Functions (e.g., goals)
    - Ex: the Same is hegemonic in relation to the Others.

- **Truth Values**
  - —"1" if True (in Symbolic Logic)
    - Ex: the proposition that imperial Japan was hegemonic to China during WWII
  - —"0" if False (in Symbolic Logic)
    - Ex: the proposition that Grenada invaded France in 2003
  - —"1" & "0" if Both True and False (in Dialectic Logic)
    - Ex: the proposition that the rabbit-duck picture refers to a duck
  - —"~1" & "~0" if Neither True Nor False (or N/A)
    - Ex: the proposition that God really exists

(continued on next page)

Table 6.7. The Conception of Existential Dialectics (Part II)

- **Axioms, Postulates, Theorems, Principles**
  - —Axioms
    - Ex: the reflexive axiom—"any quantity is equal to itself"
  - —Postulates
    - Ex: the SSS postulate—"if the three sides of a triangle are congruent to their corresponding parts, then the triangles are congruent"
  - —Theorems (and Principles) in Existential Dialectics
    - <u>In Relation to Method</u>
      - –Ex: the partiality-totality principle
      - –Ex: the predictability-unpredictability principle
      - –Ex: the explicability-inexplicability principle
    - <u>In Relation to Structure</u>
      - –Ex: the preciseness-vagueness principle
      - –Ex: the simpleness-complicatedness principle
      - –Ex: the openness-hiddenness principle
    - <u>In Relation to Process</u>
      - –Ex: the change-constancy principle
      - –Ex: the order-chaos principle
      - –Ex: the slowness-quickness principle
      - –Ex: the expansion-contraction principle
    - <u>In Relation to Agency</u>
      - –Ex: the evolution-transformation principle
      - –Ex: the symmetry-asymmetry principle
      - –Ex: the softness-hardness principle
    - <u>In Relation to Outcome</u>
      - –Ex: the regression-progression principle
      - –Ex: the sameness-difference principle

Notes: The categories and examples in each are solely illustrative (not exhaustive). The comparison is also relative (not absolute), nor are they mutually exclusive. As generalities, they allow exceptions.
Sources: From Ch.6 of *BCPC* and also from other books of mine.

Table 6.8. The Syntax of Existential Dialectics I: The Principles (Part I)

• In Relation to Method

—*The Partiality-Totality Principle*
(On the Relationships between Whole and Parts)

- Any inquiry about a phenomenon in the work is to guard against the varieties of (a) reductionism and (b) reverse-reductionism.
- Reductionism and reverse-reductionism can be (i) conceptual, (ii) theoretical, (iii) methodological, and (iv) ontological.
- Family resemblance: e.g., individualisticness-holisticness
- Sources: Especially from *FC*. See also *FHC*, *FCD*, *FPHC*, *BCPC*, *FPHST*, *BCIV*, *BNN*, *BWT*, *FAE*, *ALD*, and *FPHU*

—*The Predictability-Unpredictability Principle*
(On the Occurrence of Events)

- Both predictability and unpredictability have a major role to play in the occurrence of things, so that neither determinism nor indeterminism wins the centuries-old fight.
- There are events which are predictable, just as there are those which are not. Or what is regarded as unpredictable at one point in time may turn out to be predictable later, and, conversely, what is deemed as predictable may turn out to not be so predictable. Even in predictability, outcomes are subject to uncertainty, the degree of which varies from case to case.
- Family resemblance: e.g., sureness-arbitrariness
- Sources: Especially from *FC*. See also *FHC*, *FCD*, *FPHC*, *BCPC*, *FPHST*, *BCIV*, *BNN*, *BWT*, *FAE*, *ALD*, and *FPHU*

(continued on next page)

Table 6.8. The Syntax of Existential Dialectics I: The Principles (Part II)

- **In Relation to Method (cont'd)**

—*The Explicability-Inexplicability Principle*
(On the Underlying Mechanisms of Things)

- Both explicability and inexplicability are part of the understanding of things.
- This principle tells us the duality of the research dilemma, in that, if reality can be explained in some ways, it also has its other ways which are not quite explainable, at a given point in time.
- Family resemblance: e.g., underlyingness-regularness
- Sources: Especially from *FPHU*—and also *FPHC*. See also *FHC*, *FCD*, *BCPC*, *FPHST*, *BCIV*, *BNN*, *BWT*, *FAE*, and *ALD*.

- **In Relation to Structure**

—*The Simpleness-Complicatedness Principle*
(On the Interconnection among Things)

- Both simpleness and complicatedness are vital, without favoring one over the other, in that each is utilized, depending on the basis of the perspectives of nature, the mind, culture, and society. And even when a combination of them is preferred, the dilemma is only shifted to a combinational degree of concern.
- In relation to taxonomy, simpleness has its heuristic usefulness, just as complicatedness has its realistic representation, for instance. And in relation to network, simpleness has its economical attractiveness, just as complicatedness has its practical reliability, for instance.
- Family resemblance: e.g., inflexibility-flexibility, standardization-specialization
- Sources: Especially from *FIA*. See also *FPHU*.

(continued on next page)

Table 6.8. The Syntax of Existential Dialectics I: The Principles (Part III)

- **In Relation to Structure (cont'd)**

—The Preciseness-Vagueness Principle
(On the Refinement of Things)

- Both preciseness and vagueness are important, not that one is better than the other, but that both are used, in different degrees of preference, in accordance to the contextual application from the perspectives of nature, the mind, culture, and society. Even when both are used in a combination, the dilemma is shifted instead to one of combinational concern.
- In relation to taxonomy, preciseness has its taxonomic clarity, just as vagueness has its classificatory flexibility, for instance. And in relation to network, vagueness has its explorative liberty, just as preciseness has its conceptual definitiveness, for instance.
- Family resemblance: e.g., clarity-ambiguity, directness-indirectness
- Sources: Especially from *FIA*. See also *FPHU.*

—The Openness-Hiddenness Principle
(On the Detection of things)

- This principle suggests that reality has its hidden face, just as it is open to outside view in some other ways.
- For instance, in the current context of anomalous experience, certain aspects of reality concerning anomalous experience can be open for examination (e.g., the experiment with SPECT images, the transmission of telepathemic bit, and the use of metonymies and metaphors). Other aspects, however, remain hidden, and examples include the elusive deeper nature of spiritual reality in the intangible realm, the undetectability of different branched universes, the underlying mechanisms of signals traveling between different folds of physical space-time, and the dependence on language and the bias for science and logic).
- Family resemblance: e.g., overtness-covertness
- Sources: Especially from *FPHU.*

(continued on next page)

Table 6.8. The Syntax of Existential Dialectics I: The Principles (Part IV)

• In Relation to Process

—*The Slowness-Quickness Principle*
(On the Speed of Change)

- Both slowness and quickness co-exist, with their own internal tension, to the extent that each fights for its own relevance with the other, in accordance to the perspectives of nature, the mind, culture, and society, without one being the victor and the other being the vanquished in the long haul. Even when both are chosen in other cases, this dilemma is only transferred into something else with a combinational character.
- In relation to taxonomy, quickness has its efficient usability, just as slowness has its aesthetic appeal, for instance. And in relation to network, quickness has its adventurous readiness, just as slowness has its risk-adverse convenience, for instance.
- So, in the end, the dilemma still remains, and the dialectic continues its relevance, with the two co-existing in ever new ways, but the window of transcending into something else of interest is opened.
- Family resemblance: e.g., inconvenience-convenience
- Sources: Especially from *FIA*. See also *FPHU.*

—*The Expansion-Contraction Principle*
(On the Growth of Things)

- Entities in the world can both expand in some ways and contract in other ones, as part of their nature
- For instance, in the context of anomalous experience, one of its most fascinating expressions is none other than the analysis of different causes of the slow but steady expansion (and, furthermore, if put in a different way, unfolding) of unconsciousness.
- Family resemblance: e.g., conquest-autarky
- Sources: Especially from *FPHU*. See also *FCD*, *FPHC*, and *BWT*.

(continued on next page)

Table 6.8. The Syntax of Existential Dialectics I: The Principles (Part V)

• In Relation to Process (cont'd)

—*The Change-Constancy Principle*
(On the Alteration of Things)

- Change occurs over time, although constancy is also allowed.
- Asymmetry undergoes changes over time, so does symmetry.
- Old players fade away, and new ones emerges, with ever new causes and ever new forms.
- Family resemblance: e.g., dynamicness-staticness, instability-stability
- Sources: First named in *BCPC*. Especially from *FHC*, *FCD*, and *FPHC*. See also *BDPD*, *FPHST*, *BCIV*, *BNN*, *BWT*, *FC*, *FAE*, *ALD*, and *FPHU*.

—*The Order-Chaos Principle*
(On the Pattern of Things)

- Both order and chaos are vital in the process of change in the world. The preference for order is biased, since it does not give sufficient attention to the vital role of chaos in the transformation of the world (without somehow reducing it for the understanding of order).
- The scientific search for order in the world is often a hidden bias in its ontological obsession with order, since chaos is often treated as the "bad" guy, with order as the "good" guy (for the end goal of science).
- Neither order nor chaos is the final end of the world, and one is not to be treated as the means for the other in the transformation of things. Both are fundamental in their recurrent dialectical interactions with each other over time, without reducing one for the other.
- Family resemblance: e.g., lawfulness-disorder
- Sources: Especially from *FC*. See also *FHC*, *FCD*, *FPHC*, *BCPC*, *FPHST*, *BCIV*, *BNN*, *BWT*, *FAE*, *ALD*, and *FPHU*.

(continued on next page)

Table 6.8. The Syntax of Existential Dialectics I: The Principles (Part VI)

• **In Relation to Agency**

—*The Evolution-Transformation Principle*
(On the Multiple Kinds of Agency)

- This principle (and the symmetry-asymmetry principle) are both about *the agency of change*. The word "agency," in a formal definition, refers to "a person or thing through which power is exerted or an end is achieved." (MWD 2007b) It therefore does not have to necessarily involve an intelligent lifeform.
- Because of this dual meaning in agency, the evolution-transformation principle is more concerned with *the multiple kinds of agency*, that is, both about the *evolution* in the state of nature (e.g., an object of natural beauty) and the *transformation* in the world of intelligent lifeforms (e.g., a work of art).
- And the transformative part of the principle precisely refers to the other dimension in the dual meaning of agency, in giving technology a major role to play in the change of the world, which is something that I extensively analyzed in *FHC* in the context of the technophilic lifeworld, espeically though not exclusively since modern times.
- Family resemblance: e.g., inorganicness-volition
- Sources: Especially from *FAE*. See also *FHC*, *FCD*, *FPHC*, *BDPD*, *BCPC*, *FPHST*, *BCIV*, *BNN*, *BWT*, *FC*, *FAE*, *ALD*, and *FPHU*.

—*The Softness-Hardness Principle*
(On the Force of Change)

- This has to do with *the force of change* under the category about agency in existential dialectics, in that any change by an agent, be it organic (like humans) or non-organic (like natural objects), can occur in a forceful (aggressive) or gentle (pacific) way, which can come in all shapes and sizes, of course.
- Family resemblance: e.g., peacefulness-violence, cooperation-competition
- Sources: Especially from *ALD*. See also *FHC*, *FCD*, *FPHC*, *BCPC*, *FPHST*, *BCIV*, *BNN*, *BWT*, *FAE*, and *FPHU*.

(continued on next page)

Table 6.8. The Syntax of Existential Dialectics I: The Principles (Part VII)

• **In Relation to Agency (cont'd)**

—*The Symmetry-Asymmetry Principle*
(On the Relationships among Existents)

• The relationships are relatively asymmetric between the Same and the Others but relatively symmetric within the Same (or the Others). There is no asymmetry without symmetry. This is true, even when the Same can be relatively asymmetric towards itself in self-oppression, just as the Others can be likewise towards themselves.
• The subsequent oppressiveness is dualistic, as much by the Same against the Others and itself, as by the Others against the Same and themselves.
• Both oppression and self-oppression can be achieved by way of downgrading differences between the Same and the Others and of accentuating them.
• Family resemblance: e.g., strength-weakness
• Sources: From all my books, starting with *FHC*. First named in *BCPC*.

• **In Relation to Outcome**

—*The Regression-Progression Principle*
(On the Direction of History)

• Neither the cyclical nor the linearviews are adequate for explaining many phenomena at all levels.
• History progresses to more advanced forms, but with a regressive touch. Examples include no freedom without unfreedom, no equality without inequality, and no civilization without barbarity.
• This is not an inevitable law, but merely a highly likely empirical trend.
• Family resemblance: e.g., decline-growth
• Sources: From all my books, starting with *FHC*. First named in *BCPC*.

(continued on next page)

Table 6.8. The Syntax of Existential Dialectics I: The Principles (Part VIII)

• **In Relation to Outcome (cont'd)**

—*The Same-Difference Principle*
(On the Metamorphosis of Change)

- This has to do with *the metamorphosis of change* under the category about outcome in existential dialectics, in that an entity, as it evolves over time, can be both different from and similar to its opposing alternatives and does not have to be solely more different from them over time.
- Opposites are not absolute in a black-or-white fashion; so, an entity can become relatively more similar to (or more different from) its opposite over time.
- Family resemblance: e.g., homogeneity-heterogeneity
- Sources: Especially from *ALD*. See also *FHC*, *FCD*, *FPHC*, *BCPC*, *BDPD*, *FPHST*, *BCIV*, *BNN*, *BWT*, *FC*, *FAE*, and *FPHU*.

Notes: The features in each principle are solely illustrative (not exhaustive). The comparison is also relative (not absolute), nor are they mutually exclusive. As generalities, they allow exceptions.

Table 6.9. The Syntax of Existential Dialectics II: The Dialectic Constraints Imposed by the Principles (Part I)

• **Co-Existent and Asymmetric**

—The principles, as they constitute the syntax of existential dialectics, are dialectic in character, such that, when they are applied, they impose dialectic constraints on how reality is to be understood. Consider, say, the symmetry-asymmetry principle as an illustration here, in order to summarize two main characters of the dialectic constraints in question.

—Firstly, to be dialectic here is to go beyond the narrow dichotomies (and, for that matter, any rigid multi-dimensional classificatory scheme), be they about "self" vs. "world," "freedom" vs. "unfreedom," "barbarity" vs. "civilization," "individuality" vs. "communality," and so on.

—One way to do so (to go beyond) is to consider them all in terms of co-existence (without favoring one over the rest). For instance, my theory of "post-civilization" (to be summarized later in the section on the pragmatics of existential dialectics) is to go beyond barbarity and civilization in terms of understanding barbarity and civilization as being co-existent. And the same logic can be said in relation to my theories of "post-democracy," "post-capitalsm," and others (also to be introduced later in the section on the pragmatics of existential dialectics), in regard to freedom vs. unfreedom, equality vs. inequality, communality vs. individuality, spirituality vs. materiality, and so on.

—But to consider them all (in the dichotomies—and, for that matter, in any rigid multi-dimensional classifactory schme) as co-existent is not the same as to imply that the opposites in any classificatory scheme are all equal, since, in accordance to the symmetry-asymmetry principle (as an illustration here), if they are equal in terms of being considered as co-existent, they are asymmetric in terms of being unequal in dialectic interaction (e.g., X can be more dominant than Y in case A, or Y is more dominant than X in case B).

—For this reason, there are different versions of "post-democracy" and "post-capitalism" in my theories. As an illustration, in version I of the theory of post-democracy, freedom is more dominant than equality, whereas in version II of the theory of post-democracy, equality is more so than freedom.

(continued on next page)

Table 6.9. The Syntax of Existential Dialectics II: The Dialectic Constraints Imposed by the Principles (Part II)

—But this "X more than Y" has to be understood in the context of dialectic logic (not in conventional logic), in that both "X" and "Y" are important in post-democracy (in the context of dialectic logic), but in an asymmetry way. By contrast, in conventional logic, it often favors one over the other—be it in regard to privileging freedom over equality in Fascism, favoring freedom relatively more than equality in Liberal Democracy, or favoring equality relatively more than freedom in Socialist Democracy. In the latter two cases (about Liberal Democracy and Socialist Democracy), the difference between dialectic logic and conventional logic can be one in degree, not in kind—in this sense, albeit not in other senses.

—The same logic can be said about the relatonships between individuality and communality, between spirituality and materiality, and between formal legalism and informal legalism in the different versions of my theory of post-capitalism.

• **Transcendent**

—Secondly, to be dialectic is to go beyond the narrow dichotomies (and, for that matter, any rigid multi-dimensional classificatory scheme) in another way, this time, in a transcendent way, that is, in exploring other possibilities or even other issues not considered within the narrow confines of narrow dichotomies (and, for that matter, any rigid multi-dimensional classificatory scheme).

—As an analogy, to go beyond the narrow color dichotomy of "black" and "white" is not just to choose both "black" and "white" (as in the first meaning) but also to explore other color options (e.g., "green," "purple," "blue," etc.—and, alternatively, "shade," "line," "curve," etc.). By the same logic, to go beyond "democracy" is to transcend democracy (as in version III of the theory of "post-democracy") and to explore other possibilties of lifeforms (e.g., floating consciousness, hyper-spatial consciousness, etc., to live beyond the narrow obsession with freedom and equality).

—This dialectic character of the principles in existential dialectics has important implications for the pragmatics of existential dialectics (as will be clear shortly, in the section on the pragmatics of existential dialectics).

(continued on next page)

Table 6.9. The Syntax of Existential Dialectics II: The Dialectic Constraints Imposed by the Principles (Part III)

Notes: The examples here are solely illustrative (not exhaustive). The comparison is also relative (not absolute), nor are they mutually exclusive. As generalities, they allow exceptions.
Sources: From my previous books like *FHC*, *FCD*, *FPHC*, *BDPD*, *BCPC*, *BNN*, *FC*, *FAE*, etc.

Table 6.10. The Semantics of Existential Dialectics

- **Abstract Structure vs. Specific Meanings**
  —The syntax of existential dialectics so understood in terms of ontological principles only gives us the structure of ontology in the world, in an abstract (general) sense. These principles by themselves do not tell us the specific meanings in a given context.
  —In order to grasp the specific meanings of the principles in a given context, it is necessary to study the semantics of existential dialectics. For this reason, I have often gone in great lengths in my previous books on different subjects to explain the specific meanings of the principles when applied in different contexts.

- **Specific Meanings in Specific Fields**
  —For instance, in *FPHST*, I used the first three principles (i.e., the change-constancy principle, the regression-progression principle, and the symmetry-asymmetry principle) to propose "the perspectival theory of space-time," for a better way to understand space and time—especially, though not exclusively, in relation to future post-human history (as summarized in *Table 3.6*, *Table 3.7*, *Table 3.8*, and *Table 3.9*). In so doing, I had to introduce concepts and theories specific to the field of physics and other related fields (e.g., "absolute space" and "absolute time" in "classical mechanics" and "relative space-time" in "the theory of relativity").
  —In *BNN*, I also exploited the three principles to propose the "transcendent" approach to the study of genes and memes as a new way to understand the interaction between nature and nurture. In so doing, I had to explore concepts and theories in the world of evolutionary theory (e.g., "mutation," "variation," "adaptation," "selection," and "inheritance" in Darwinian evolutionary theory) and neural biology (e.g., "chromosome," "gene," "DNA," "RNA," "protein," "neuron," "neural network," and "behavior").

Notes: The categories and examples in each are solely illustrative (not exhaustive). The comparison is also relative (not absolute), nor are they mutually exclusive. As generalities, they allow exceptions.
Sources: From all of my previous books

Table 6.11. The Pragmatics of Existential Dialectics (Part I)

• **The Two-Way Street Connecting Theory and Meta-Theory**

—The pragmatics of existential dialectics is not a one-way street (that is, using the ontological principles for theoretical insights in praxis) but a two-way one, that is, (a) from meta-theory to theory, and (b) from theory to meta-theory.

—(a) On one side of the street, the ontological principles can inspire some theoretical insights in praxis, that is, in relation to some specific fields.

—(b) On the other (opposing) side of the street, however, the study of a subject matter in the specific fields in turn reveals some more hitherto unknown ontological principles to be discovered and identified. For this reason, three new principles were added in *FC*, one in *FAE*, and two in *ALD*, on top of the original three in *BCPC*—after some research on the specific subject matters.

• **Direct and Indirect Applications**

—*Direct*

- The logic of existential dialectics can shed some theoretical insights on diverse phenomena in the world, and good instances are the pertinent use of the principles of existential dialectics for the theoretical insights on the freedom/unfreedom dialectics, the equality/inequality dialectics, and the wealth/poverty dialectics in my previous works.
- My latest books like *FPHST* and *BNN* also use the principles to reveal some theoretical insights on the perspectives of space and time (as in *FPHST*) and of nature and nurture (as in *BNN*).

—*Indirect*

- The theoretical insights can further be used to reveal other phenomena directly from them (viz., the theoretical insights) and therefore indirectly from the principles themselves. A good instance is the use of the theoretical insights on the freedom/unfreedom and equality/inequality dialectics for the understanding of the civilization/barbarity dialectics.
- Even in indirect applications, however, a phenomenon under study can still be directly related back to the principles themselves. In the example as cited above, the civilization/barbarity dialectics can be directly related to the principles of existential dialectics without the intermediate role of the freedom/unfreedom and equality/inequality dialectics.

(continued on next page)

Table 6.11. The Pragmatics of Existential Dialectics (Part II)

- **Multiple Levels of Application**
  —The theoretical insights can be applied to different levels of analysis, even though in a given example, it may refer to one level only. For instance, in the example concerning the freedom/unfreedom dialectics, it can be used at the structural level (e.g., in relation to the theory of cyclical progression of hegemony), but it can be exploited as well for other levels (e.g., the theory of post-capitalism at the institutional level).

Notes: The categories and examples in each are solely illustrative (not exhaustive). The comparison is also relative (not absolute), nor are they mutually exclusive. As generalities, they allow exceptions.
Sources: From Ch.6 of *BCPC* and also from *FHC*, *FCD*, *FPHC*, *BDPD*, *BNN*, *FC*, *FAE*, and *ALD*

Table 6.12. The Freedom-Unfreedom Dialectics (Part I)

- **On Having**
  - —*In Relation to the Technological*
    - (1) if freer from submission to Nature, then less free from ecological degradation (Deep and Social Ecology), even if in a hi-tech form
    - (2) if freer from technological inconvenience / backwardness, then less free from technological control and the loss of privacy
    - (3) if freer from technological (material) backwardness, then less free from the abusive (barbaric) maltreatment of the primitive Others
  - —*In Relation to the Everyday*
    - (1) if freer from abject poverty, then less free from artificial needs/discontents (Frankfurt School)
    - (2) if freer from sensual suppression, then less free from violent sublimation (Freud)
    - (3) if freer from the snobbishness of high culture, then less free from the shabbiness (leveling-off effect) of mass culture (Tocqueville)
    - (4) if freer from the inefficiency of traditional "compassionate economy," then less free from the bondage of a "ruthless [competitive] economy" (Keynes)
    - (5) if freer from anarchy in the state of nature (system fragmentation), then less free from government regulations and controls in system integration

- **On Belonging**
  - —*In Relation to the Good and the Just*
    - (1) if freer from disciplinary society, then less free from society of control (Foucault)
    - (2) if freer from the tyranny of one or a few, then less free from the tyranny of the majority (or sometimes, minority veto)
    - (3) if freer from elitist decision making, then less free from political gridlock/cleavage
    - (4) if freer from arbitrary (discretionary) administration, then less free from bureaucratic irrationality (Weber) and legal trickery (loopholes)

(continued on next page)

Table 6.12. The Freedom-Unfreedom Dialectics (Part II)

- **On Being**
  - —*In Relation to the True*
    - (1) if freer from unscientific dogmas, then less free from instrumental abyss (nihilism). Or conversely, if freer from meaninglessness, then less free from dogmas.
    - (2) if freer from the bondage of partiality/partisanship (e.g., prejudice, discrimination), then less free from the danger of impartiality and neutrality (e.g., opportunism, unrealisticness, lack of compassion, inaction)
    - (3) if freer from making generalizations, then less free from being unable to understand much of anything
  - —*In Relation to the Holy*
    - (1) if freer from collective conscience, then less free from social loneliness
    - (2) if freer from religious absoluteness, then less free from spiritual emptiness
  - —*In Relation to the Beautiful/Sublime*
    - (1) if freer from artistic non-autonomy, then less free from aesthetic disillusion (deconstruction)

Notes: The examples in each category are solely illustrative (not exhaustive), and the comparison is relative (not absolute), nor are they necessarily mutually exclusive. And some can be easily re-classified elsewhere. As generalities, they allow exceptions.
Sources: A reconstruction from Ch.10 of *FCD*, based on *FHC*

Table 6.13. The Equality-Inequality Dialectics (Part I)

- **On Having**
  - —*In Relation to the Technological*
    - (1) if more equal in treating Nature with spiritual unity, then less equal in suppressing the dominant drive to transcend it altogether
  - —*In Relation to the Everyday*
    - (1) if more equal in building social plurality, then less equal in leveling-off effects (e.g., the subsequent relative intolerance of high/intellectual ethos in mass culture industry)
    - (2) if more equal in socioeconomic distribution beyond a certain point, then less equal in efficiency (e.g. resentment, the erosion of work ethics)
    - (3) if more equal in urging an affirmative action program, then less equal in creating victim mentality (in oneself), stigma (from others), reverse discrimination (against the once privileged), and mediocracy (against the more able)

- **On Belonging**
  - —*In Relation to the Good and the Just*
    - (1) if more equal in banning monarchic/oligarchic exclusion, then less equal in producing "the tyranny of the majority" or of "minority veto"
    - (2) if more equal in encouraging participatory decision making, then less equal in inducing political divisiveness (gridlock/cleavage in power blocs) and organizational oligarchy
    - (3) if more equal in institutionalizing a decentralized bureaucracy, then less equal in falling into more territorial/turf politics (intrigues)

(continued on next page)

Table 6.13. The Equality-Inequality Dialectics (Part II)

- **On Being**
  - —In Relation to the Beautiful / Sublime
    - (1) if more equal in accepting diverse styles ("anything goes" mentality), then less equal in artistic good quality (in leveling-off effects against the best)
  - —In Relation to the True
    - (1) if more equal in tolerating multiple viewpoints (no matter how extreme), then less equal in epistemic standards
  - —In Relation to the Holy
    - (1) if more equal in celebrating any cults and sects (no matter how questionable), then less equal in spiritual depth and authenticity

Notes: The examples in each category are solely illustrative (not exhaustive), and the comparison is relative (not absolute), nor are they mutually exclusive. And some can be easily reclassified elsewhere. As generalities, they allow exceptions.

Sources: A reconstruction from Ch.10 of *FCD*, based on *FHC*

Table 6.14. The Duality of Oppression in Existential Dialectics: Oppression and Self-Oppression (Part I)

- **From the Same to the Others and Itself**
  - —The Oppression by the Same against the Others
    - *By way of downgrading differences*
      - –Ex: on judiciary caprice for corporate crimes (*Sec.2.2.1.2.1*)
      - –Ex: on the deceptive politics of liberation (*Sec.3.5*)
      - –Ex: on the humanitarian mystique (*Sec.4.4*)
      - –Ex: on the fad of emotional intelligence (*Sec.5.3*)
    - *By way of accentuating differences*
      - –Ex: on the legal sophistry of self-defense (*Sec.2.3*)
      - –Ex: on the legal semantics of proportionality (*Sec.2.4*)
      - –Ex: on the tricky politics of external threat (*Sec.3.4*)
      - –Ex: on the appeal of the Far Right for democracy (*Sec.5.4*)
      - –Ex: on the democratic axis of evil (*Sec.5.5*)
      - –Ex: on the democratic way of brutality and revenge (*Sec.5.6*)
      - –Ex: on democratic autocracy (*Sec.6.4*)
  - —The Oppression by the Same against Itself
    - *By way of downgrading differences*
      - –Ex: on the politics of fear (*Sec.2.2*)
      - –Ex: on the trickery of compassionate conservatism (*Sec.3.2*)
      - –Ex: on the deceptive politics of patriotism (*Sec.3.3*)
    - *By way of accentuating differences*
      - –Ex: on the caprice of due process on domestic suspects (*Sec.2.2*)
      - –Ex: on the false security/freedom dilemma (*Sec.6.5.2*)

(continued on next page)

Table 6.14. The Duality of Oppression in Existential Dialectics: Oppression and Self-Oppression (Part II)

- **From the Others to the Same and Themselves**
  —The Oppression by the Others against the Same
  - *By way of downgrading differences*
    - –Ex: on judiciary caprice in the reverse direction (*Sec.2.2.1.2.2*)
    - –Ex: on equal pay (*Sec.6.2.1.1*)
    - –Ex: on equal representation (*Sec.6.2.1.2*)
    - –Ex: on affirmative action program (*Sec.6.3.1.1*)
    - –Ex: on same-sex marriage (*Sec.6.3.1.2*)
  - *By way of accentuating differences*
    - –Ex: on sexual harassment (*Sec.6.2.2.1*)
    - –Ex: on physical violence (*Sec.6.2.2.2*)
    - –Ex: on sexual exploitation (*Sec.6.2.2.3*)

  —The Oppression by the Others against Themselves
  - *By way of downgrading differences*
    - –Ex: on the reverse-class mystique (*Sec.4.2*)
    - –Ex: on the reverse-black mystique (*Sec.4.3*)
    - –Ex: on self-discrimination by downgrading (*Sec.6.3.2.2*)
  - *By way of accentuating differences*
    - –Ex: on self-discrimination by accentuating (*Sec.6.3.2.1*)

Notes: The examples are solely illustrative (not exhaustive), nor are they mutually exclusive. As generalities, they allow exceptions. Also, both forms of oppression co-exist in all of the examples, so the listing of them are only meant in a relative, not absolute, sense.
Source: A summary of the sections (as cited) in Chs.2-6 of *BDPD*. See text for more info and references.

Table 6.15. The Structure of Existential Dialectics I: The Freedom/Unfreedom and Equality/Inequality Dialectics

• Each freedom and equality produces its own unfreedom and inequality, regardless of whether the pair occurs in political society (with the nation-state), in civil society (with some autonomy from the state), or elsewhere (e.g., in the private sphere of individual homes)—and regardless of whether freedom and equality are understood as "negative" or "positive."

• Oppression is dualistic, as much by the Same against the Others and itself, as by the Others against the Same and themselves.

• Both forms of oppression and self-oppression can be achieved by way of downgrading differences (between the Same and the Others) and of accentuating them.

• The relationships are relatively asymmetric between the Same and the Others and relatively symmetric within them. This is true, even when the Same can be relatively asymmetric towards itself in self-oppression, just as the Others can be likewise towards themselves.

• Symmetry and asymmetry change over time, with ever new players, new causes, and new forms.

Notes: The examples in each category are solely illustrative (not exhaustive) nor necessarily mutually exclusive, and the comparison is relative (not absolute). As generalities, they allow exceptions. "Negative" freedom is freedom "from" (e.g., freedom from poverty), whereas "positive" freedom is freedom "to" (e.g., freedom to the state of enlightenment). "Negative" equality is "procedural" equality (e.g., equality of opportunity), while "positive" equality is "substantive" equality (e.g., equality of outcome). Existential dialectics impose constraints on freedom and equality in democracy, non-democracy, and post-democracy. There is no utopia, in the end; even should there be one, dystopia would exist within it.
Sources: From *Table 1.5* of *BDPD*—and also from *FHC*, *FCD*, and *FPHC*

Table 6.16. The Structure of Existential Dialectics II: The Wealth/Poverty Dialectics

- There is no wealth without poverty, just as there is no poverty without wealth.

- The wealth/poverty dialectics occurs in the realms of having, belonging, and being, in relation to the material, relational, and spiritual.

- The wealth/poverty dialectics also expresses itself at the multiple levels of analysis in accordance to methodological holism, be they about the micro-physical, the chemical, the biological, the psychological, the organizational, the institutional, the structural, the systemic, the cultural, and the cosmological.

- The wealth/poverty dialectics is a different manifestation of existential dialectics in general, subject to the principles in its logic of ontology—just as the freedom/unfreedom and equality/inequality dialectics are likewise.

- There is no economic utopia, in the end; even should there be one, dystopia would exist within it.

Notes: The main points here are solely illustrative (not exhaustive) nor necessarily mutually exclusive, and the comparison is relative (not absolute). As generalities, they allow exceptions.
Sources: From *BCPC*. See also *FCD* and *FHC*.

Table 6.17. The Structure of Existential Dialectics III: The Civilization/Barbarity Dialectics

• There is no civilization without barbarity.

• The civilization/barbarity dialectics applies in the four civilizing processes (e.g., the rationalizing process, the pacifying process, the stewardizing process, and the subliming process).

• The civilization/barbarity dialectics is another (different) manifestation of existential dialectics in general, subject to the principles in its logic of ontology—just as the freedom/unfreedom and equality/inequality dialectics and the wealth/poverty dialectics are likewise.

• There is no utopia, in the end; even should there be one, dystopia would exist within it.

Notes: The main points here are solely illustrative (not exhaustive) nor necessarily mutually exclusive, and the comparison is relative (not absolute). As generalities, they allow exceptions.
Sources: From *BCIV*. See also *FCD*, *FHC*, and *BDPD*.

BIBLIOGRAPHY

Alexander, John; Richard Groller & Janet Morris. 1990. *The Warrior's Edge*. New York: Morrow.

Alexander, Thea. 1976. *2150 A.D.* New York: Warner Books.

Baofu, Peter. 2008. *The Future of Information Architecture: Conceiving a New Way to Understand Taxonomy, Network, and Intelligence*. Oxford, United Kingdom: Chandos Publishing (Oxford) Ltd.

_____.2007. *The Rise of Authoritarian Liberal Democracy: A Preface to a New Theory of Comparative Political Systems*. Cambridge, England: Cambridge Scholars Publishing.

_____.2007a. *The Future of Aesthetic Experience: Conceiving a Better Way to Beauty, Ugliness, and the Rest*. Cambridge, England: Cambridge Scholars Publishing.

_____.2007b. *The Future of Complexity: Conceiving a Better Way to Understand Order and Chaos*. London, United Kingdom: World Scientific Publishing Co.

_____.2007c. *Beyond the World of Titans, and the Remaking of World Order: A Preface to a New Logic of Empire-Building*. Cambridge, England: Cambridge Scholars Publishing.

_____.2006. *Beyond Nature and Nurture: Conceiving a Better Way to Understand Genes and Memes*. Cambridge, England: Cambridge Scholars Publishing.

_____.2006a. *The Future of Post-Human Space-Time: Conceiving a Better Way to Understand Space and Time*. New York: Peter Lang Publishing, Inc.

_____.2006b. *Beyond Civilization to Post-Civilization: Conceiving a Better Model of Life Settlement to Supersede Civilization*. New York: Peter Lang Publishing, Inc.

_____.2005. *Beyond Capitalism to Post-Capitalism: Conceiving a Better Model of Wealth Acquisition to Supersede Capitalism*. New York: The Edwin Mellen Press.

_____.2004. *The Future of Post-Human Consciousness*. New York: The Edwin Mellen Press.

_____.2004a. *Beyond Democracy to Post-Democracy: Conceiving a Better Model of Governance to Supersede Democracy* (2 volumes). New York: The Edwin Mellen Press.

_____.2002. *The Future of Capitalism and Democracy*. Maryland: The University Press of America.

_____.2000. *The Future of Human Civilization* (2 volumes). New York: The Edwin Mellen Press.

Begley, Sharon. 2001. "Religion and The Brain" (May 07). *Newsweek*. <http://www.geocities.com/islampencereleri3/religion_and_the_brain.htm>.

Beichler, Jim, ed. 1998. "The Emergence of Paraphysics during the Scientific Era: 1970 to Present." *YGGDRASIL: The Journal of Paraphysics*. <http://members.aol.com/jebco1st/Paraphysics/search3.htm>.

Bem, Daryl & Charles Honorton. 1994. "Does Psi Exist? Replicable Evidence for an Anomalous Process of Information Transfer." *Psychological Bulletin.*

Biletzki, Anat & Anat Matar. 2006. "Ludwig Wittgenstein" (Nov. 17). *Stanford Encyclopedia of Philosophy*. <http://plato.stanford.edu/entries/wittgenstein/http://plato.stanford.edu/entries/wittgenstein/>.

Boese, Alex. 2002. *The Museum of Hoaxes: A Collection of Pranks, Stunts, Deceptions, and Other Wonderful Stories Contrived for the Public from the Middle Ages to the New Millennium*. New York, NY: Dutton.

Borch-Jacobsen, Mikkel. 2000. "How Fabrications Differ from a Lie" (April 13). *London Review of Books*. <http://www.lrb.co.uk/v22/n08/borc01_.html>.

Chari, C. T. K., 1977. "Some Generalized Theories and Models of Psi: A Critical Evaluation." In *Handbook of Parapsychology*. Benjamin B. Wolman, ed. New York: Reinhold.

Crowley, Candy. 2000. "Bush Says 'RATS' Ad Not Meant as Subliminal Message" *CNN.com* (Sept. 12). <http://archives.cnn.com/2000/ALLPOLITICS/stories/09/12/bush.ad/>.

Davis, G. A.; J. M. Peterson & F. H. Farley. 1973. "Attitudes, Motivation, Sensations Seeking, and Belief in ESP as Predictors of Real Creative Behavior." *Journal of Creative Behavior*, 8: 31-39.

Deikman, Arthur. 2007. "Mystic Experience and Two Modes of Consciousness." *Meta-Religion*. <http://www.meta-religion.com/Psychiatry/Mysticism/mystic_experience.htm>.

Dowling, Jonathan. 1995. "Stapp's PK Theory" (July). *Physics Today*. <www.hia.com/hia/pcr/pktheory.html>.

Dubrov, Alexander. 1977. "Biogravitation and Psychotronics." In *Future Science: Life Energies and the Physics of Paranormal Phenomena*. John White and Stanley Krippner, editors. Gardern City, New York: Anchor Doubleday.

Edge, Hoyd; Robert Morris; Joseph H. Rush & John Palmer. 1986. *Foundations of Parapsychology: Exploring the Boundaries of Human Capability*. Boston: Routledge and Kegan Paul.

Encarta (EC). 2007. "The Mind as an Iceberg." <http://encarta.msn.com/media_461543697/The_Mind_as_an_Iceberg.html>.

Eysenck, Hans. 1986. *Decline and Fall of the Freudian Empire*. Harmondsworth: Pelican.

Feinberg, Gerald. 1974. "Foreword." *Psychic Exploration: A Challenge for Science*. Edgar Mitchell, ed. New York: Putnam's.

Firehammer, Reginald. 2005. "Basic Principles of Ontology" (January 05). <http://usabig.com/autonomist/philosophy/ontology2.html>.

Freud, Sigmund. 1913. *The interpretation of Dreams*. A. A. Brill, tr. New York, Macmillan.

Gianotti, Lorena; Christine Mohr; Diego Pizzagalli; Dietrich Lehmann; and Peter Brugger. 2001. "Associative Processing and Paranormal Belief." *Psychiatry and Clinical Neurosciences*, 55: 595–603. <www.wjh.harvard.edu/~daplab/pubs/pdf/Giannotti_PCN01.pdf>.

Good, I. J., ed. 1965. "Speculations Concerning Precognition." *The Scientist Speculates: An Anthology of Partly-Baked Ideas*. New York: Capricorn Books.

Highfield, Roger. 2006. "Light at End of the Tunnel over Near Death Experiences" (Nov. 04). *Telegraph.co.uk*. <http://www.telegraph.co.uk/news/main.jhtml?xml=/news/2006/04/11/wdeath11.xml&sSheet=/news/2006/04/11/ixworld.html>.

Holt, Nicola. 2007. "Creativity and Anomalous Experiences" (August). Presented at the 2007 Parapsychological Association Convention in Halifax, Canada. <http://nicola.j.holt.googlepages.com/recentlycompletedresearchprojects>.

_____.2006. "Developing Experience-Sampling Methodology to Explore Psi in 'Everyday Life.'" Parapsychological Association Convention in Stockholm.

Jahn, Robert. 2001. "The Challenge of Consciousness." *Journal of Scientific Exploration*, Vol.15, No.4: 443-57.

_____.& Brenda J. Dunne. 1987. *Margins of Reality: The Role of Consciousness in the Physical World*. San Diego: Harcourt Brace Jovanovich.

Josephson, Brian & Jessica Utts. 1996. "The Paranormal: The Evidence and Its Implications for Consciousness." *Physics Today*. <www.tcm.phy.cam.uk/~bdj10/psi/tucson.psi>.

_____. & Fotini Pallikari-Viras. 1991. "Biological Utilisation of Quantum NonLocality." *Foundations of Physics*, 21 (1991): 197-207; <www.phy.cam.uk/www/research/mm/articles/Bell.psi>.

Kennedy, J. E. & H. Kanthamanil. 1995. "Association Between Anomalous Experiences and Artistic Creativity and Spirituality." *The Journal of the American Society for Psychical Research*, Vol. 89: 333-343.

_____. 1995a. "An Exploratory Study of the Effects of Paranormal and Spiritual Experiences on Peoples' Lives and Well-Being." *The Journal of the American Society for Psychical Research*, Vol. 89: 249-265.

_____. 1994. "Psychic and Spiritual Experiences, Health, Well-Being, and Meaning in Life." *Journal of Parapsychology*, 58: 353-383.

Key, Wilson Bryan, 1973. *Subliminal Seduction: Ad Media's Manipulation of a Not So*

Innocent America. New York: New American Library.

Kihlstrom, J. F. 2002. "The unconscious." *Encyclopedia of the Human Brain*, 4: 635-646. V.S. Ramachandran, ed. San Diego, CA: Academic.

_____. J.S. Beer & S. B. Klein. 2002a. "Self and Identity as Memory." *Handbook of Self and Identity*. M. R. Leary & J. Tangney, eds. New York: Guilford Press.

Kinseher, Richard. 2006. *Geborgen in Liebe und Licht - Gemeinsame Ursache von Intuition, Déjà-vu-, Schutzengel- und Nahtod-Erlebnissen.* (*A New Theory: During a Near-Death-Experience, a Person Can Observe the Scan of the Own Episodic Memory*.)

Knapp, George. 2003. "Psychic Warfare" (Thursday, April 03). *Las Vegas Mercury: Nevada's Largest Alternative Newsweekly*. <http://www.lasvegasmercury.com/2003/MERC-Apr-03-Thu-2003/21007160.html>.

LaPlante, E. 1993. *Seized*. New York: HarperCollins.

Lindzey, G. & C. S.Hall. 1985. *Introduction to Theories of Personality*. New York: John Wiley & Sons.

Loftus, E. F. & M. R. Klinger, M. R. 1992. *Is the Unconscious Smart or Dumb? American Psychologist*, 47(6): 761-765.

MacHovec, Frank. 2002. The review of *Varieties of Anomalous Experiences: Examining Scientific Evidence*. Etzel Cardena, Steven Jay Lynn, and Stanley Krippner, eds. Washington, D.C.: American Psychological Association.

Management Consulting News (MCN). 2007. "Meet the MasterMinds: Daniel Pink on a Whole New Mind." <http://www.managementconsultingnews.com/interviews/pink_interview.php>.

Mattuck, Richard. 1977. "Random Fluctuation Theory of Psychokinesis: Thermal Noise Model." *Research in Parapsychology*. J. D. Morris, W. G. Roll and R. L. Morris. London: Scarecrow Press.

McConnell, R.A. & T.K. Clark. 1991. "National Academy of Sciences' Opinion on Parapsychology." *Journal of the American Society for Psychical Research*, 85: 333-365.

Merriam-Webster's Collegiate Dictionary Online (MWD). 2007. "Telepahty." (December 07). <http://www.m-w.com/dictionary/telekinesis>.

_____.2007a. "Reincarnation." (December 07). <http://www.m-w.com/dictionary/reincarnation>.

_____.2007b. "Haunting." (December 07). <http://www.m-w.com/dictionary/haunting>.

Mishlove, Jeffrey. 1994. *The Roots of Consciousness: The Classic Encyclopedia of Consciousness Studies, Revised and Expanded*. Tulsa: Council Oaks Books.

Moon, M.L. 1975. "Artists Contrasted with Non-Artists Concerning Belief in ESP: A Poll." *Journal of the American Society for Psychical Research*, 69: 161-166.

Newberg, Andrew; Eugene d'Aquili & Vince Rause. 2001.*Why God Won't Go Away: Brain Science and the Biology of Belief.* New York: Ballantine Books.

Packard, Vance Oakley, 1957. *The Hidden Persuaders*. New York: D. McKay Co.

Pickover, Clifford. 1999. "Transcendent Experience and Temporal Lobe Epilepsy."

<http://www.science-spirit.org/articles/Articledetail.cfm?article_ID=130>.

Pink, Daniel. 2005. *A Whole New Mind: Moving from the Information Age to the* Conceptual Age. New York: Riverhead Books.

Porush, David. 1985. *The Soft Machine: Cybernetic Fiction.* NY: Methuen, Inc.

Pratkanis, Anthony. 1992. "The Cargo-Cult Science of Subliminal Persuasion." *Skeptical Inquirer*. Committee for the Scientific Investigation of Claims of the Paranormal, Spring: 260-272.

Regis, Ed. 1990. *Great Mambo Chicken and the Transhuman Condition: Science Lightly Over the Edge.* NY: Addison-Wesley Publishing Co.

Sarfatti, Jack. 1998. "Quantum Back Action." <www.hia.com/hia/pcr/qmotion.html>. Listed in <http://members.aol.com/jebco1st/Paraphysics/search3.htm>.

Schlitz, M. & C. Honorton. 1992. "Ganzfeld Psi Performance within an Artistically Gifted Population." *Journal of the American Society for Psychical Research*, 86: 83-98.

Schmeidler, Gertrude. 1972. "Respice, adspice, and prospice." *Proceedings of the Parapsychology Association*, 8: 117-145.

Scripture, E. W. 1898. *The New Psychology*. London: The W. Scott publishing co., ltd.

Sirag, Saul-Paul. 1994. "Consciousness: A Hyperspace View." *The Roots of Consciousness: The Classic Encyclopedia of Consciousness Studies, Revised and Expanded.* Jeffrey Mishlove, ed. Tulsa: Council Oaks Books.

Smith, Angela. 1998. *Remote Perceptions: Out-of-Body Experiences, Remote Viewings, and Other Normal Abilities*. Charlottesville, VA: Hampton Roads Pub.

Stafford, Tom & Matt Webb. 2004. *Mind Hacks*. CA: O'Reilly Media.

Stapp, Henry. 1995. "Stapp's PK Theory." <www.hiua.com/hia/pcr/pktheory.html>. Originally from Stapp's letter to *Physics Today* (July).

Strassman, Rick. 2001. *DMT: The Spirit Molecule: A Doctor's Revolutionary Research into the Biology of Near-Death and Mystical Experiences*. Rochester, Vt.: Park Street Press.

Strieber, W. 1987. *Communion*. New York: Avon.

Toben, Bob & Fred Wolf. 1975. *Space-Time and Beyond*. New York: E.P. Dutton.

Wagner, M. W. & M. Monnet. 1979. "Attitudes of College Professors toward Extra-Sensory Perception." *Zetetic Scholar* (5): 7–17.

Walker, E. H. 1974. "Consciousness and Quantum Theory." *Psychic Exploration: A Challenge for Science*. Edgar Mitchell, ed. New York: Putnam's.

Wikipedia (WK). 2007. "Psychic" (November 24). <http://en.wikipedia.org/wiki/Psychic>.

_____.2007a. "Unconsciousness" (November 24). <http://en.wikipedia.org/wiki/Unconsciousness>.

_____.2007b. "Sigmund Freud" (November 24). <http://en.wikipedia.org/wiki/Freud>.

_____.2007c. "Unconscious Mind" (November 24). <http://en.wikipedia.org/wiki/Unconscious_mind>.

_____.2007d. "Near-Death Experience." (November 25). <http://en.wikipedia.org/wiki/

Near-death_experience>.

_____.2007e. "Unconscious Mind." (December 01). <http://en.wikipedia.org/wiki/Unconscious_mind>.

_____.2007f. "Collective Unconscious." (December 01). <http://en.wikipedia.org/wiki/Collective_unconscious>.

_____.2007g. "Carl Jung." (December 01). <http://en.wikipedia.org/wiki/Collective_unconscious>.

_____.2007h. "Mythology." (December 01). <http://en.wikipedia.org/wiki/Mythology>.

_____.2007i. "Sulbiminal Message." (December 02). <http://en.wikipedia.org/wiki/Subliminal_message>.

_____.2007j. "Clairvoyance." (December 02). <http://en.wikipedia.org/wiki/Clairvoyance>.

_____.2007k. "Extrasensory Perception." (December 02). <http://en.wikipedia.org/wiki/Extrasensory_perception>.

_____.2007l. "Parapsychology." (December 02). <http://en.wikipedia.org/wiki/Parapsychology>.

_____.2007m. "Telepathy." (December 03). <http://en.wikipedia.org/wiki/ Telepathy>.

_____.2007n. "Precognition." (December 07). <http://en.wikipedia.org/wiki/Precognition>.

Wilson, T. D. 2002. *Strangers to Ourselves: Discovering the Adaptive Unconscious*. Cambridge, MA: Belknap Press of Harvard University Press.

Wittgenstein, Ludwig. 1953. *Philosophical Investigations*. G. E. M. Anscombe and R. Rhees, eds. G.E.M. Anscombe, tr. Oxford: Blackwell.

Yahoo.com (YH). 2007. "Alternative Science/Skeptics/Organizations." <http://ca.dir.yahoo.com/Science/Alternative_Science/Skeptics/Organizations/>.

_____.2007a. "Paranormal Phenomena/Organizations." <http://ca.dir.yahoo.com/Science/Alternative/Paranormal_Phenomena/Organizations?sort=lf>.

Zaman, Aparthib. 2003. "Science, Miracles, & the Paranormal" (July 19). <http://groups.yahoo.com/group/mukto-mona/message/12044>.

Zinchenko, W.P.; A.N. Leontiev; B.M. Lomov & A.R. Luria. 1978. "Parapsychology in the Soviet Union." In *The Signet Handbook of Parapsychology*. Martin Ebon, ed. New York: Signet.

Zipern, Karen. 2004. "Fleeting Images of Fearful Faces Reveal Neurocircuitry of Unconscious Anxiety" (December 18). *Medical News Today*. <http://www.medicalnewstoday.com/articles/18022.php>.

INDEX

•A•

•B•

•C•

•D•

•F•

•G•

•J•

•K•

•L•

•M•

•P•

•Q•

•R•

•T•

•U•

•V•

•W•

•X•

•Z•